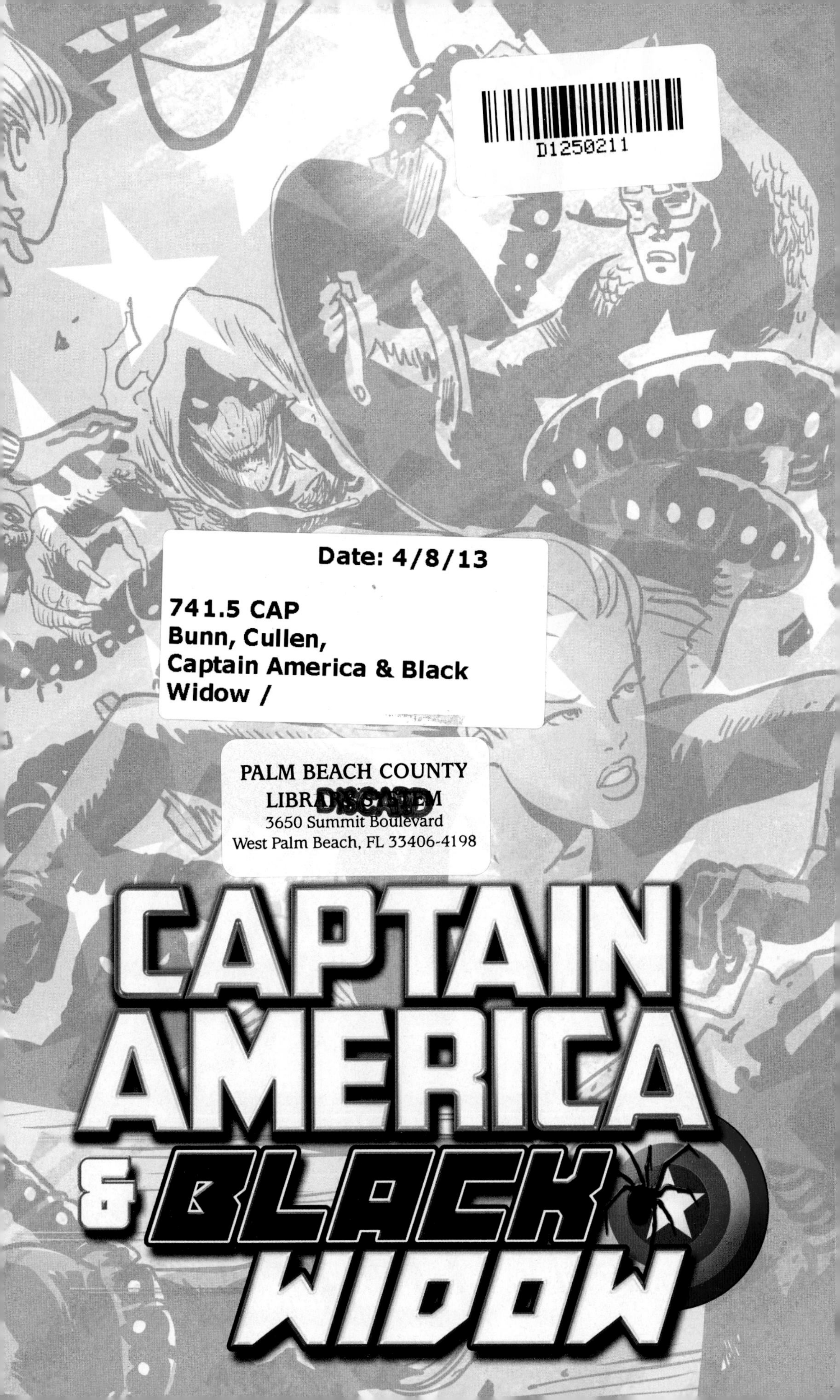
CAPTAIN AMERICA
& BLACK WIDOW

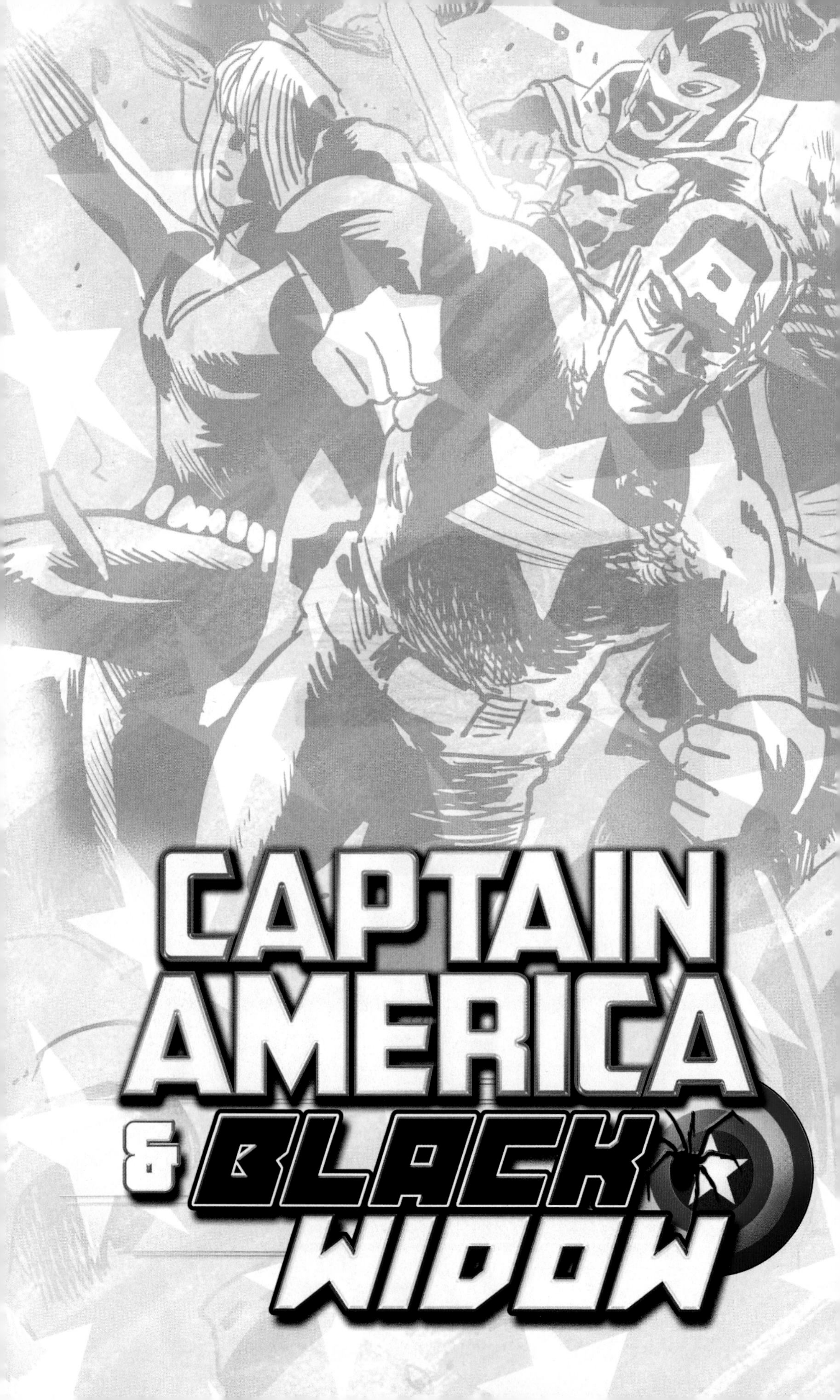
CAPTAIN AMERICA
& BLACK WIDOW

WRITER
CULLEN BUNN
ARTIST & COVERS
FRANCESCO FRANCAVILLA
LETTERER
VC'S JOE CARAMAGNA
WITH **CORY PETIT**
ASSISTANT EDITOR
JAKE THOMAS
EDITOR
LAUREN SANKOVITCH
CAPTAIN AMERICA CREATED BY
JOE SIMON & JACK KIRBY

COLLECTION EDITOR
CORY LEVINE
ASSISTANT EDITORS
ALEX STARBUCK & NELSON RIBEIRO
EDITORS, SPECIAL PROJECTS
JENNIFER GRÜNWALD & MARK D. BEAZLEY
SENIOR EDITOR, SPECIAL PROJECTS
JEFF YOUNGQUIST
SVP OF PRINT & DIGITAL PUBLISHING SALES
DAVID GABRIEL
BOOK DESIGN
JEFF POWELL

EDITOR IN CHIEF
AXEL ALONSO
CHIEF CREATIVE OFFICER
JOE QUESADA
PUBLISHER
DAN BUCKLEY
EXECUTIVE PRODUCER
ALAN FINE

CAPTAIN AMERICA AND BLACK WIDOW. Contains material originally published in magazine form as CAPTAIN AMERICA AND BLACK WIDOW #636-640. First printing 2013. ISBN# 978-0-7851-6528-6. Published by MARVEL WORLDWIDE, INC., a subsidiary of MARVEL ENTERTAINMENT, LLC. OFFICE OF PUBLICATION: 135 West 50th Street, New York, NY 10020. Copyright © 2012 and 2013 Marvel Characters, Inc. All rights reserved. All characters featured in this issue and the distinctive names and likenesses thereof, and all related indicia are trademarks of Marvel Characters, Inc. No similarity between any of the names, characters, persons, and/or institutions in this magazine with those of any living or dead person or institution is intended, and any such similarity which may exist is purely coincidental. **Printed in the U.S.A.** ALAN FINE, EVP - Office of the President, Marvel Worldwide, Inc. and EVP & CMO Marvel Characters B.V.; DAN BUCKLEY, Publisher & President - Print, Animation & Digital Divisions; JOE QUESADA, Chief Creative Officer; TOM BREVOORT, SVP of Publishing; DAVID BOGART, SVP of Operations & Procurement, Publishing; RUWAN JAYATILLEKE, SVP & Associate Publisher, Publishing; C.B. CEBULSKI, SVP of Creator & Content Development; DAVID GABRIEL, SVP of Print & Digital Publishing Sales; JIM O'KEEFE, VP of Operations & Logistics; DAN CARR, Executive Director of Publishing Technology; SUSAN CRESPI, Editorial Operations Manager; ALEX MORALES, Publishing Operations Manager; STAN LEE, Chairman Emeritus. For information regarding advertising in Marvel Comics or on Marvel.com, please contact Niza Disla, Director of Marvel Partnerships, at ndisla@marvel.com. For Marvel subscription inquiries, please call 800-217-9158. **Manufactured between 12/27/2012 and 1/29/2013 by QUAD/GRAPHICS, DUBUQUE, IA, USA.**

10 9 8 7 6 5 4 3 2 1

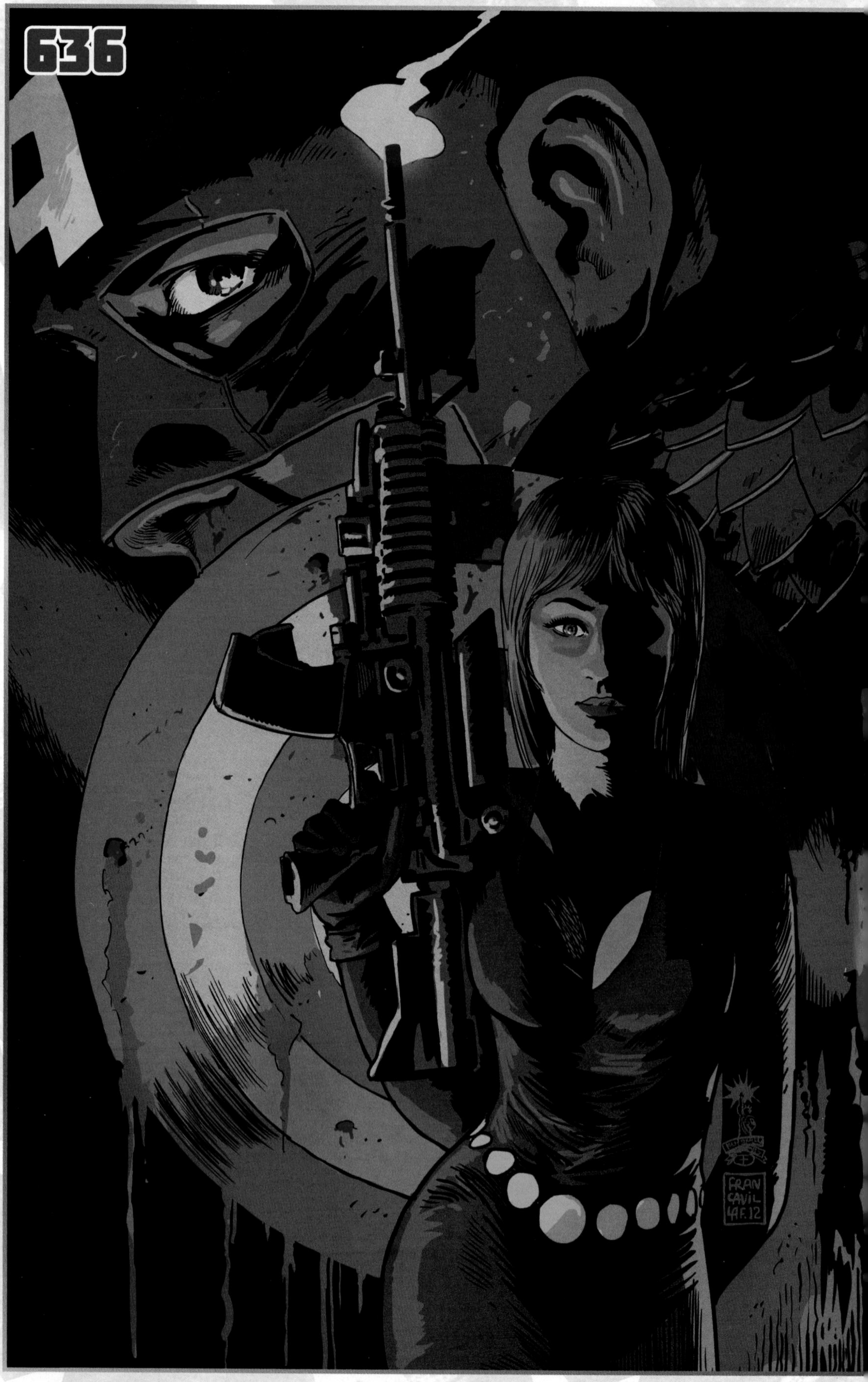
636
FRAN
CAVIL
LA F.12

CAPTAIN AMERICA
STEVE ROGERS
PEAK STRENGTH, REFLEXES AND ENDURANCE.
TACTICAL GENIUS. THE SUPER-SOLDIER OF WORLD WAR II.
LEADER OF THE AVENGERS.

BLACK WIDOW
NATASHA ROMANOFF.
FORMER RUSSIAN SUPER-SPY. CURRENT S.H.I.E.L.D. AGENT. AVENGER.
MASTER OF STEALTH, COMBAT AND STRATEGY.

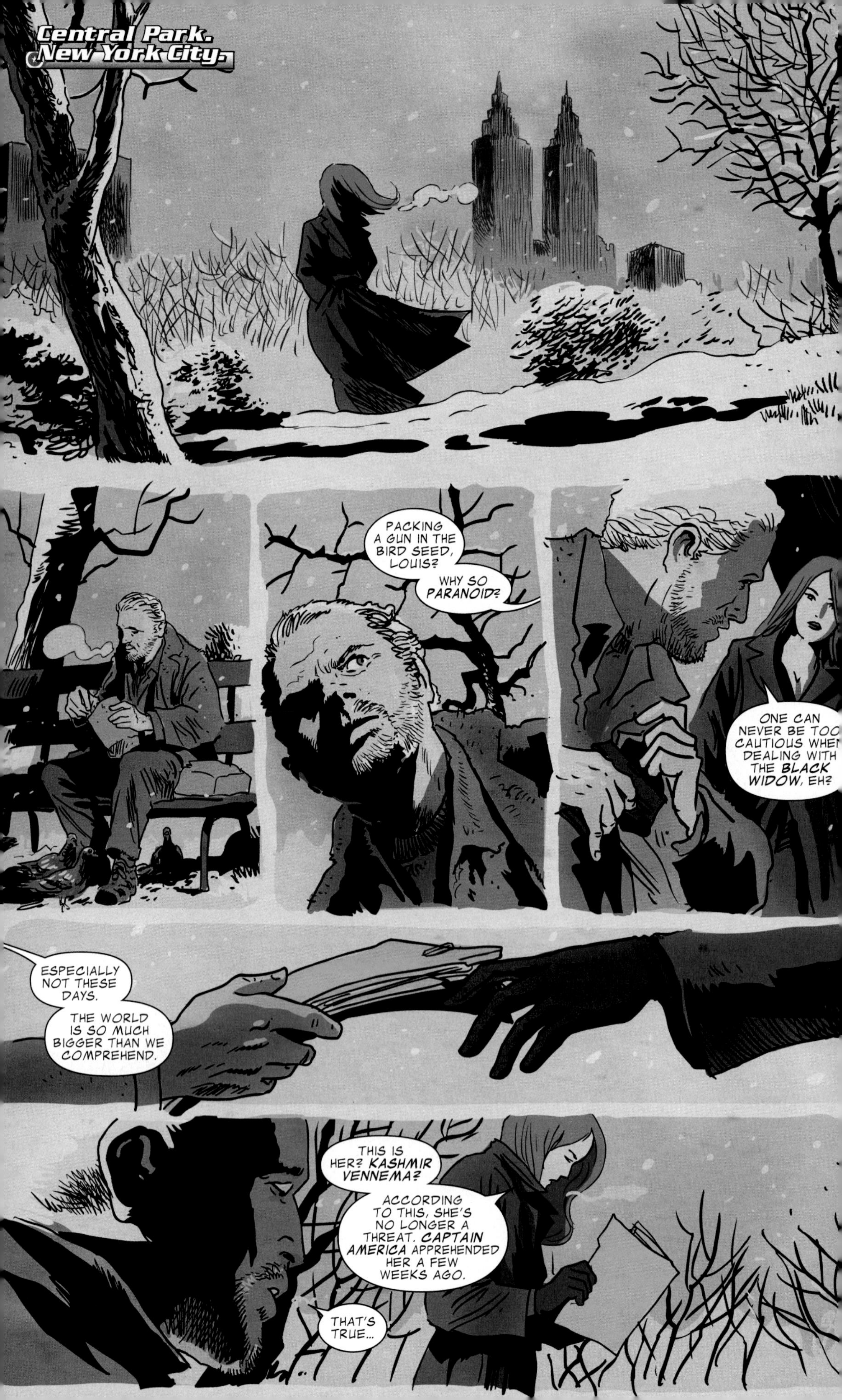
Central Park.
New York City.
PACKING A GUN IN THE BIRD SEED, LOUIS?
WHY SO PARANOID?
ONE CAN NEVER BE TOO CAUTIOUS WHEN DEALING WITH THE BLACK WIDOW, EH?
ESPECIALLY NOT THESE DAYS.
THE WORLD IS SO MUCH BIGGER THAN WE COMPREHEND.
THIS IS HER? KASHMIR VENNEMA?
ACCORDING TO THIS, SHE'S NO LONGER A THREAT. CAPTAIN AMERICA APPREHENDED HER A FEW WEEKS AGO.
THAT'S TRUE...

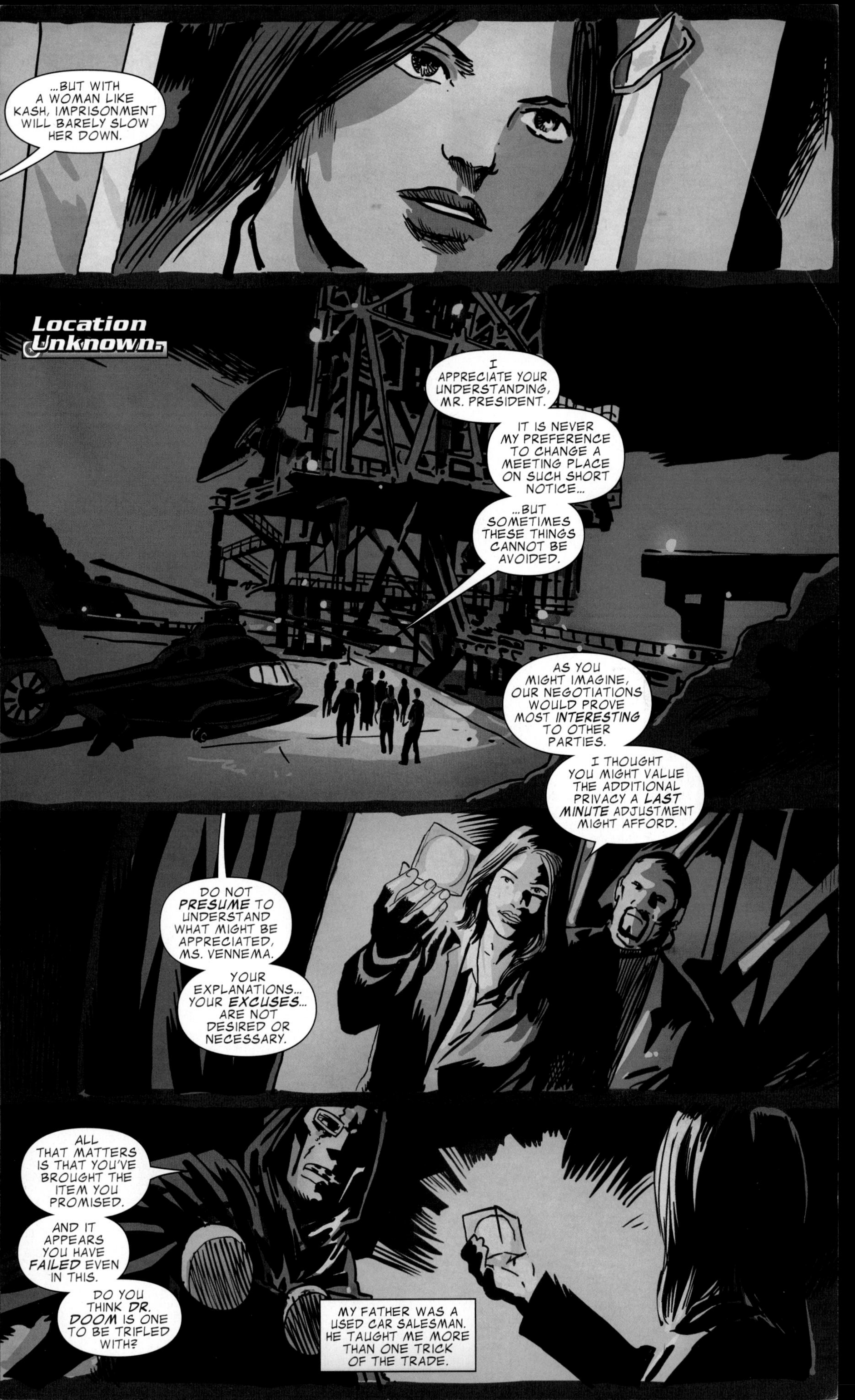
...BUT WITH A WOMAN LIKE KASH, IMPRISONMENT WILL BARELY SLOW HER DOWN.
Location Unknown
I APPRECIATE YOUR UNDERSTANDING, MR. PRESIDENT.
IT IS NEVER MY PREFERENCE TO CHANGE A MEETING PLACE ON SUCH SHORT NOTICE...
...BUT SOMETIMES THESE THINGS CANNOT BE AVOIDED.
AS YOU MIGHT IMAGINE, OUR NEGOTIATIONS WOULD PROVE MOST INTERESTING TO OTHER PARTIES.
I THOUGHT YOU MIGHT VALUE THE ADDITIONAL PRIVACY A LAST MINUTE ADJUSTMENT MIGHT AFFORD.
DO NOT PRESUME TO UNDERSTAND WHAT MIGHT BE APPRECIATED, MS. VENNEMA.
YOUR EXPLANATIONS... YOUR EXCUSES... ARE NOT DESIRED OR NECESSARY.
ALL THAT MATTERS IS THAT YOU'VE BROUGHT THE ITEM YOU PROMISED.
AND IT APPEARS YOU HAVE FAILED EVEN IN THIS.
DO YOU THINK DR. DOOM IS ONE TO BE TRIFLED WITH?
MY FATHER WAS A USED CAR SALESMAN. HE TAUGHT ME MORE THAN ONE TRICK OF THE TRADE.

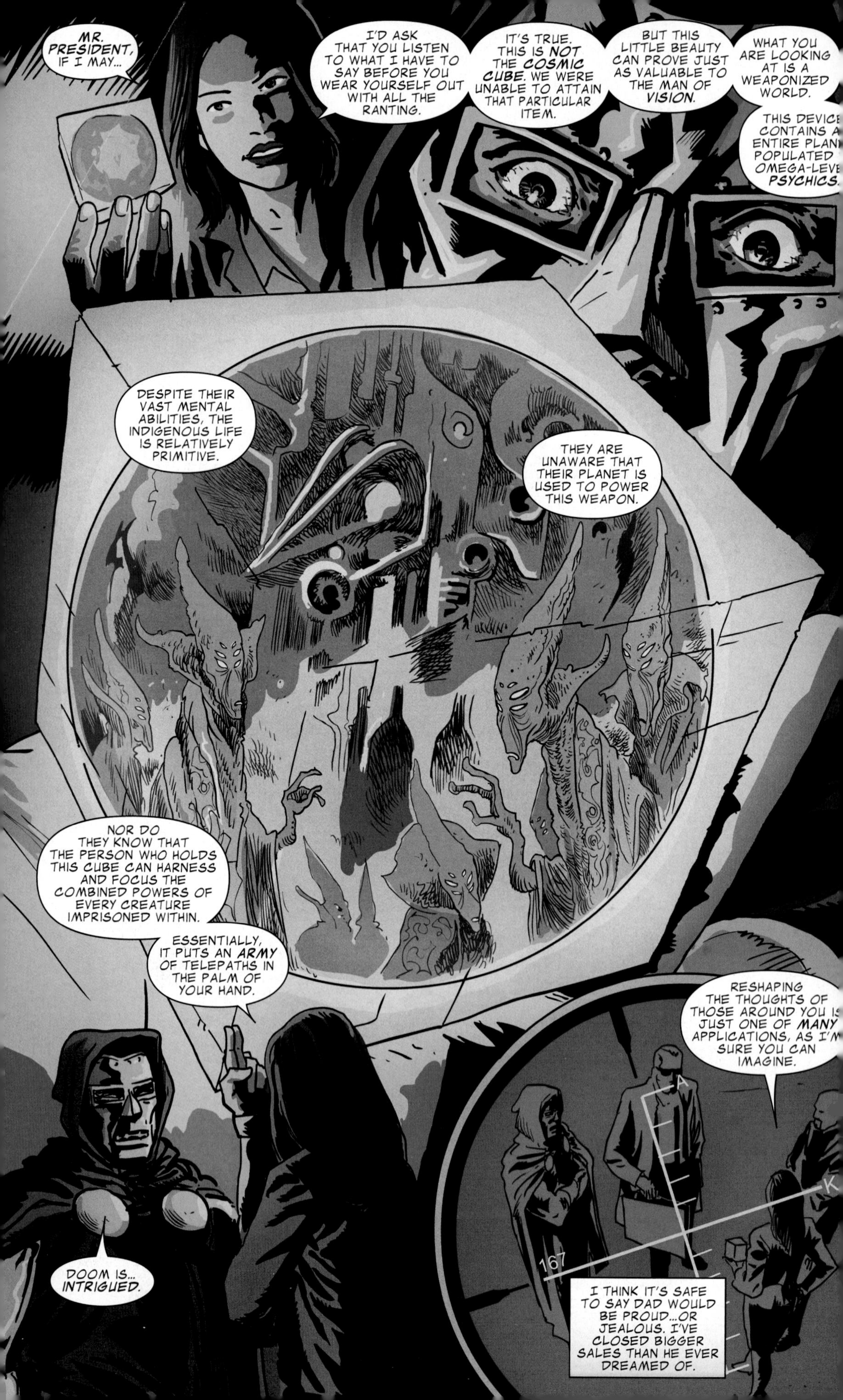

MR. PRESIDENT, IF I MAY...
I'D ASK THAT YOU LISTEN TO WHAT I HAVE TO SAY BEFORE YOU WEAR YOURSELF OUT WITH ALL THE RANTING.
IT'S TRUE. THIS IS NOT THE COSMIC CUBE. WE WERE UNABLE TO ATTAIN THAT PARTICULAR ITEM.
BUT THIS LITTLE BEAUTY CAN PROVE JUST AS VALUABLE TO THE MAN OF VISION.
WHAT YOU ARE LOOKING AT IS A WEAPONIZED WORLD.
THIS DEVICE CONTAINS A ENTIRE PLAN POPULATED OMEGA-LEVE PSYCHICS.
DESPITE THEIR VAST MENTAL ABILITIES, THE INDIGENOUS LIFE IS RELATIVELY PRIMITIVE.
THEY ARE UNAWARE THAT THEIR PLANET IS USED TO POWER THIS WEAPON.
NOR DO THEY KNOW THAT THE PERSON WHO HOLDS THIS CUBE CAN HARNESS AND FOCUS THE COMBINED POWERS OF EVERY CREATURE IMPRISONED WITHIN.
ESSENTIALLY, IT PUTS AN ARMY OF TELEPATHS IN THE PALM OF YOUR HAND.
DOOM IS... INTRIGUED.
RESHAPING THE THOUGHTS OF THOSE AROUND YOU IS JUST ONE OF MANY APPLICATIONS, AS I'M SURE YOU CAN IMAGINE.
A
K
167
I THINK IT'S SAFE TO SAY DAD WOULD BE PROUD...OR JEALOUS. I'VE CLOSED BIGGER SALES THAN HE EVER DREAMED OF.

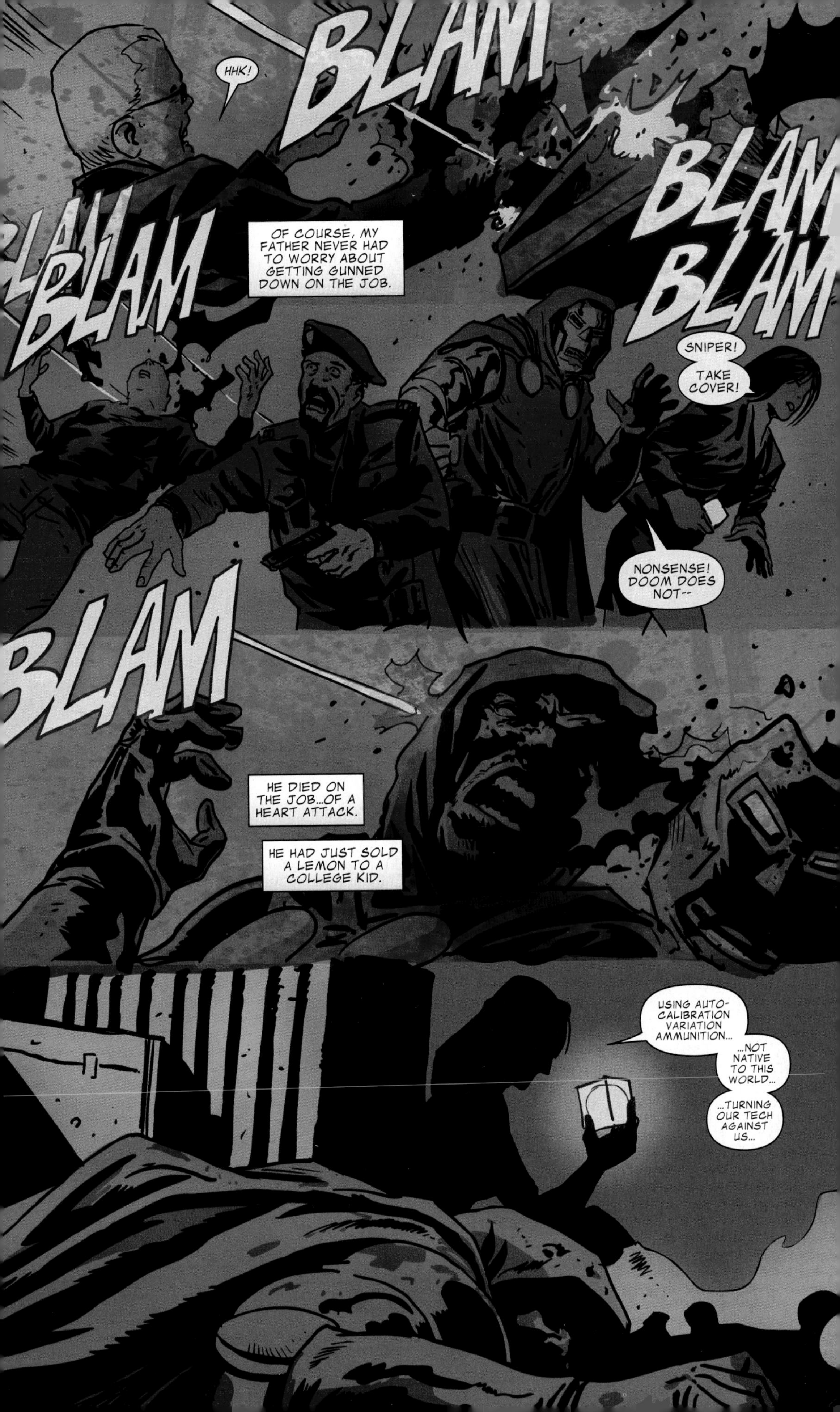
HHK!
BLAM
BLAM
BLAM
OF COURSE, MY FATHER NEVER HAD TO WORRY ABOUT GETTING GUNNED DOWN ON THE JOB.
BLAM
BLAM
SNIPER!
TAKE COVER!
NONSENSE! DOOM DOES NOT--
BLAM
HE DIED ON THE JOB...OF A HEART ATTACK.
HE HAD JUST SOLD A LEMON TO A COLLEGE KID.
USING AUTO-CALIBRATION VARIATION AMMUNITION...
...NOT NATIVE TO THIS WORLD...
...TURNING OUR TECH AGAINST US...

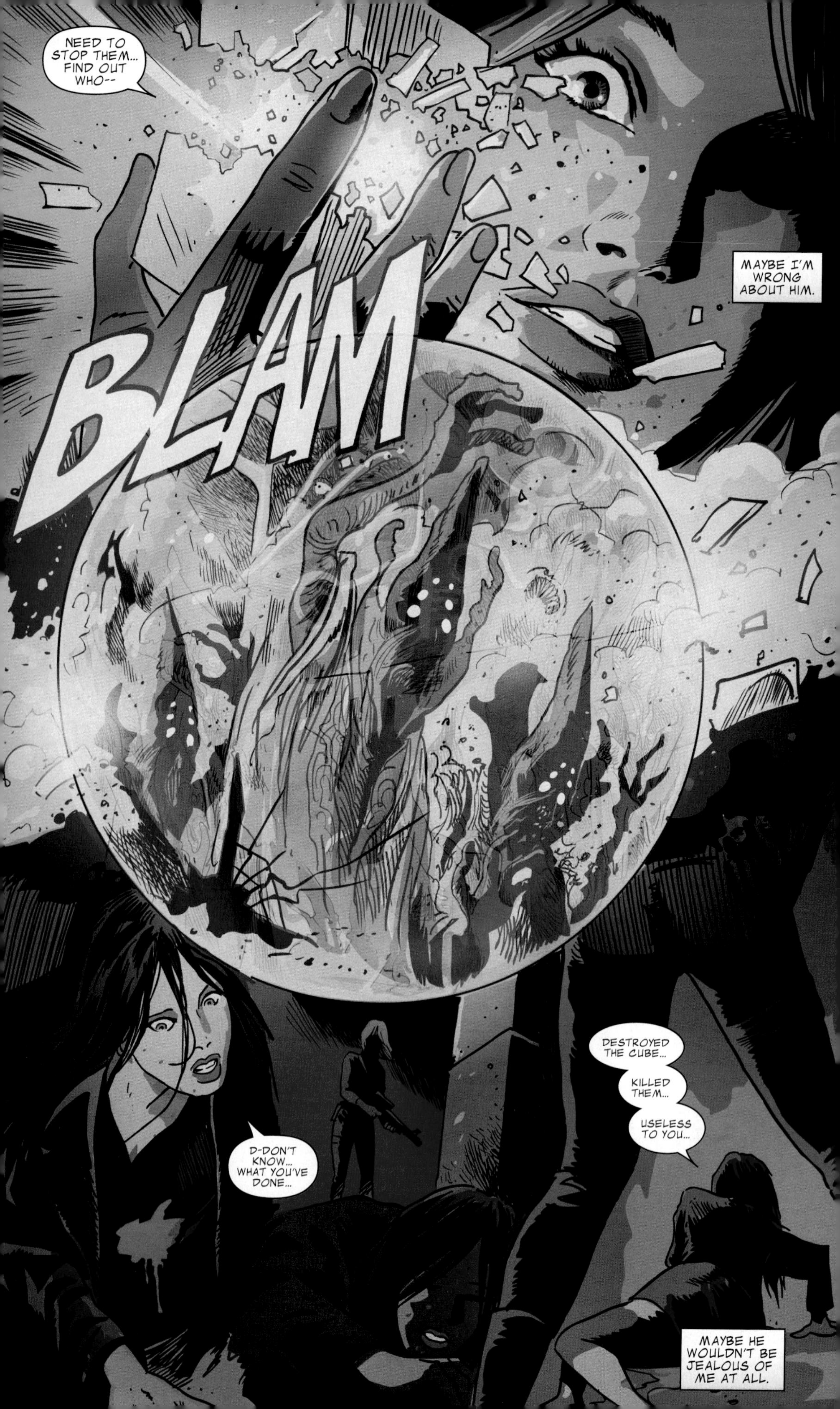
NEED TO STOP THEM... FIND OUT WHO--
BLAM
MAYBE I'M WRONG ABOUT HIM.
DESTROYED THE CUBE...
KILLED THEM...
USELESS TO YOU...
D-DON'T KNOW... WHAT YOU'VE DONE...
MAYBE HE WOULDN'T BE JEALOUS OF ME AT ALL.

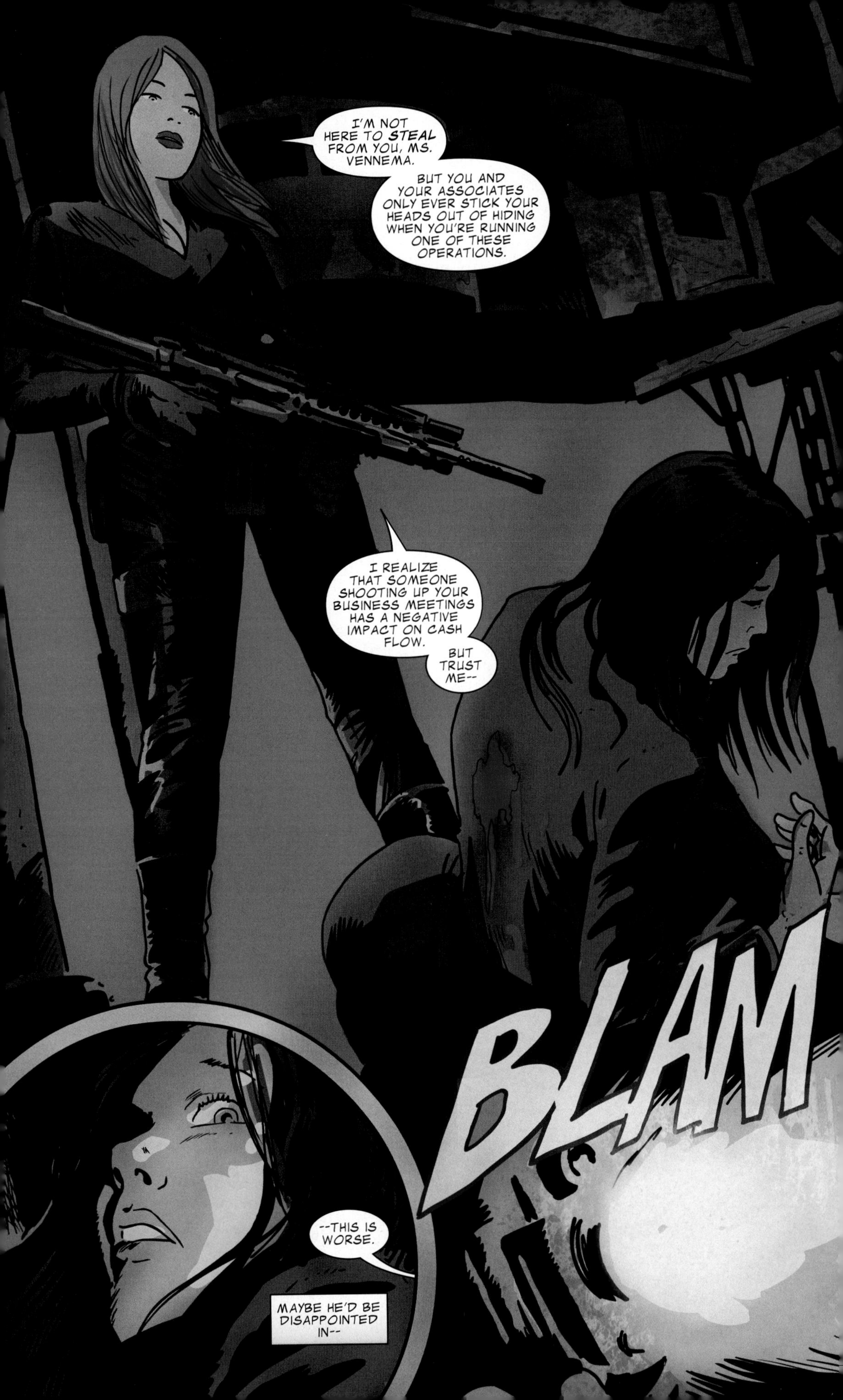
I'M NOT HERE TO STEAL FROM YOU, MS. VENNEMA.
BUT YOU AND YOUR ASSOCIATES ONLY EVER STICK YOUR HEADS OUT OF HIDING WHEN YOU'RE RUNNING ONE OF THESE OPERATIONS.
I REALIZE THAT SOMEONE SHOOTING UP YOUR BUSINESS MEETINGS HAS A NEGATIVE IMPACT ON CASH FLOW.
BUT TRUST ME--
BLAM
--THIS IS WORSE.
MAYBE HE'D BE DISAPPOINTED IN--

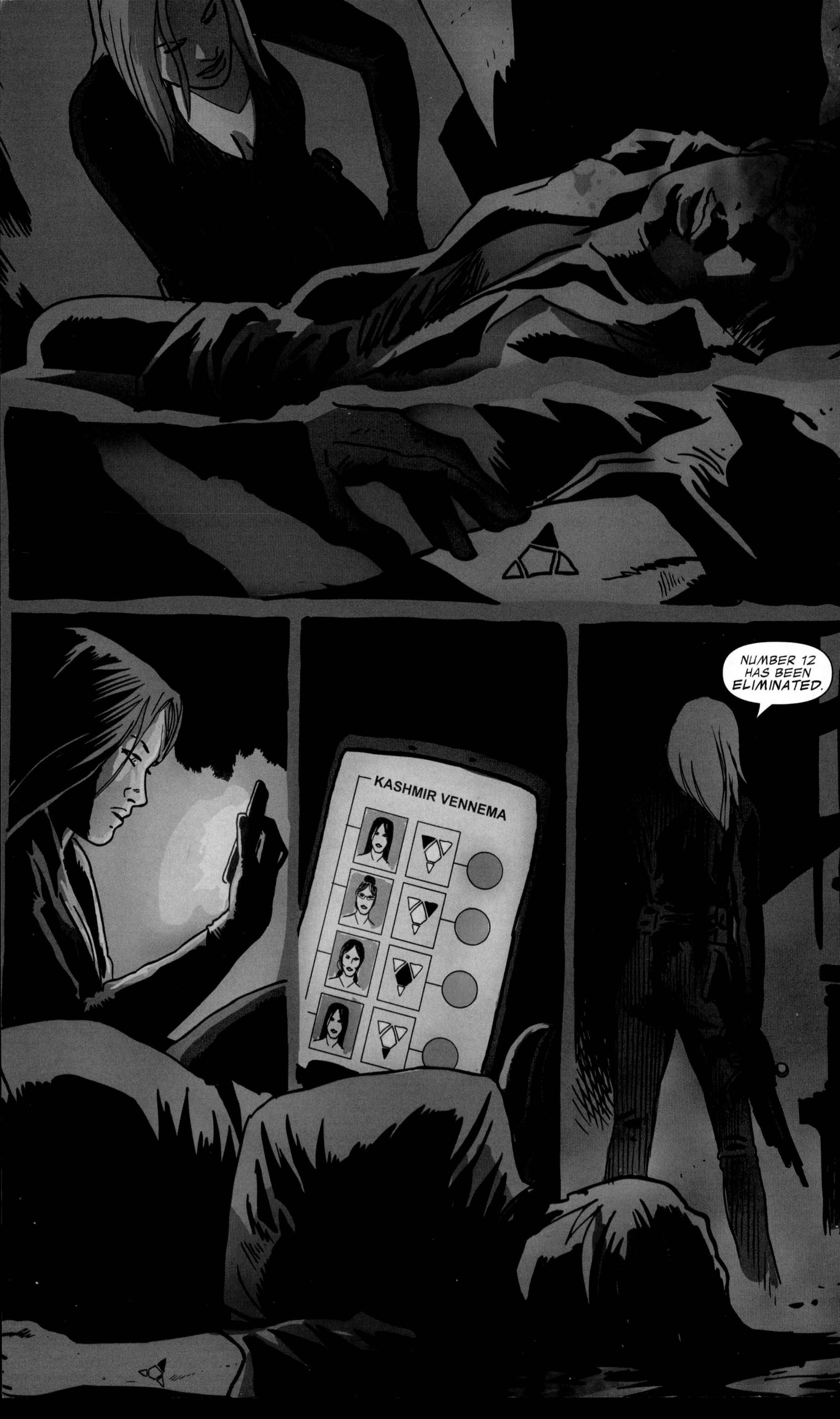
KASHMIR VENNEMA
NUMBER 12 HAS BEEN ELIMINATED.

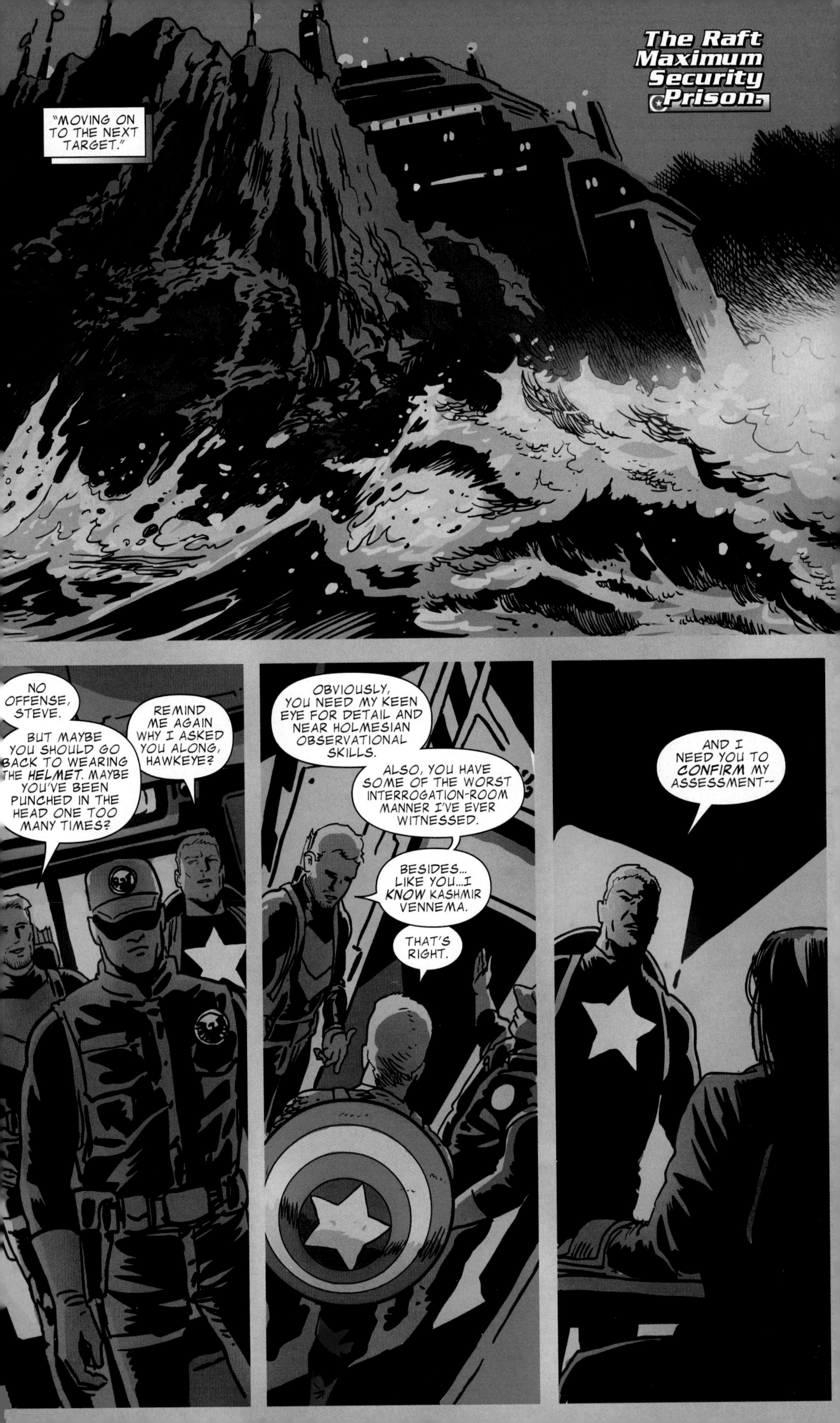
The Raft Maximum Security Prison.
"MOVING ON TO THE NEXT TARGET."
NO OFFENSE, STEVE.
BUT MAYBE YOU SHOULD GO BACK TO WEARING THE HELMET. MAYBE YOU'VE BEEN PUNCHED IN THE HEAD ONE TOO MANY TIMES?
REMIND ME AGAIN WHY I ASKED YOU ALONG, HAWKEYE?
OBVIOUSLY, YOU NEED MY KEEN EYE FOR DETAIL AND NEAR HOLMESIAN OBSERVATIONAL SKILLS.
ALSO, YOU HAVE SOME OF THE WORST INTERROGATION-ROOM MANNER I'VE EVER WITNESSED.
BESIDES... LIKE YOU...I KNOW KASHMIR VENNEMA.
THAT'S RIGHT.
AND I NEED YOU TO CONFIRM MY ASSESSMENT--

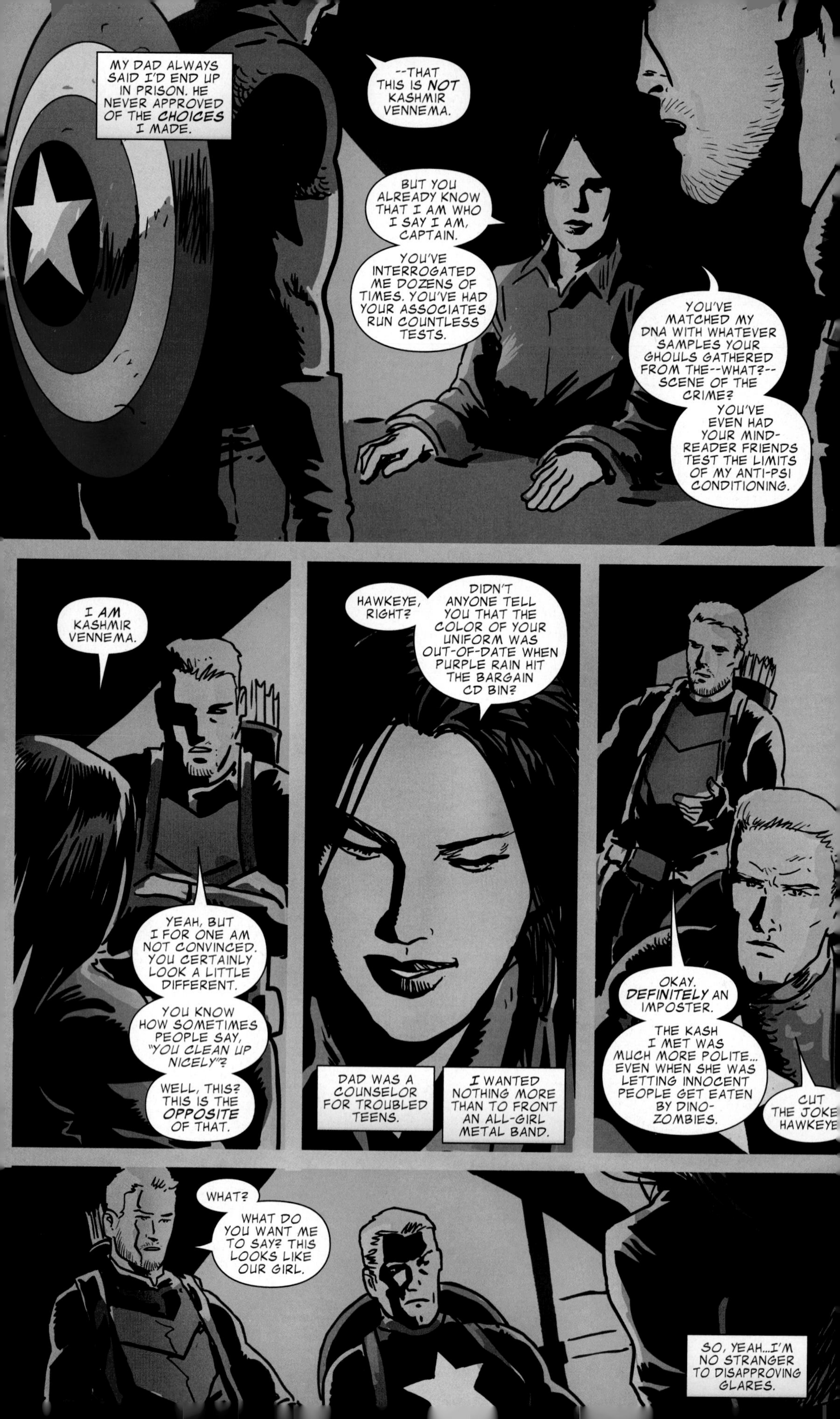
MY DAD ALWAYS SAID I'D END UP IN PRISON. HE NEVER APPROVED OF THE CHOICES I MADE.
--THAT THIS IS NOT KASHMIR VENNEMA.
BUT YOU ALREADY KNOW THAT I AM WHO I SAY I AM, CAPTAIN.
YOU'VE INTERROGATED ME DOZENS OF TIMES. YOU'VE HAD YOUR ASSOCIATES RUN COUNTLESS TESTS.
YOU'VE MATCHED MY DNA WITH WHATEVER SAMPLES YOUR GHOULS GATHERED FROM THE--WHAT?--SCENE OF THE CRIME?
YOU'VE EVEN HAD YOUR MIND-READER FRIENDS TEST THE LIMITS OF MY ANTI-PSI CONDITIONING.
I AM KASHMIR VENNEMA.
YEAH, BUT I FOR ONE AM NOT CONVINCED. YOU CERTAINLY LOOK A LITTLE DIFFERENT.
YOU KNOW HOW SOMETIMES PEOPLE SAY, "YOU CLEAN UP NICELY"?
WELL, THIS? THIS IS THE OPPOSITE OF THAT.
HAWKEYE, RIGHT?
DIDN'T ANYONE TELL YOU THAT THE COLOR OF YOUR UNIFORM WAS OUT-OF-DATE WHEN PURPLE RAIN HIT THE BARGAIN CD BIN?
DAD WAS A COUNSELOR FOR TROUBLED TEENS.
I WANTED NOTHING MORE THAN TO FRONT AN ALL-GIRL METAL BAND.
OKAY. DEFINITELY AN IMPOSTER.
THE KASH I MET WAS MUCH MORE POLITE... EVEN WHEN SHE WAS LETTING INNOCENT PEOPLE GET EATEN BY DINO-ZOMBIES.
CUT THE JOKE HAWKEYE
WHAT?
WHAT DO YOU WANT ME TO SAY? THIS LOOKS LIKE OUR GIRL.
SO, YEAH...I'M NO STRANGER TO DISAPPROVING GLARES.

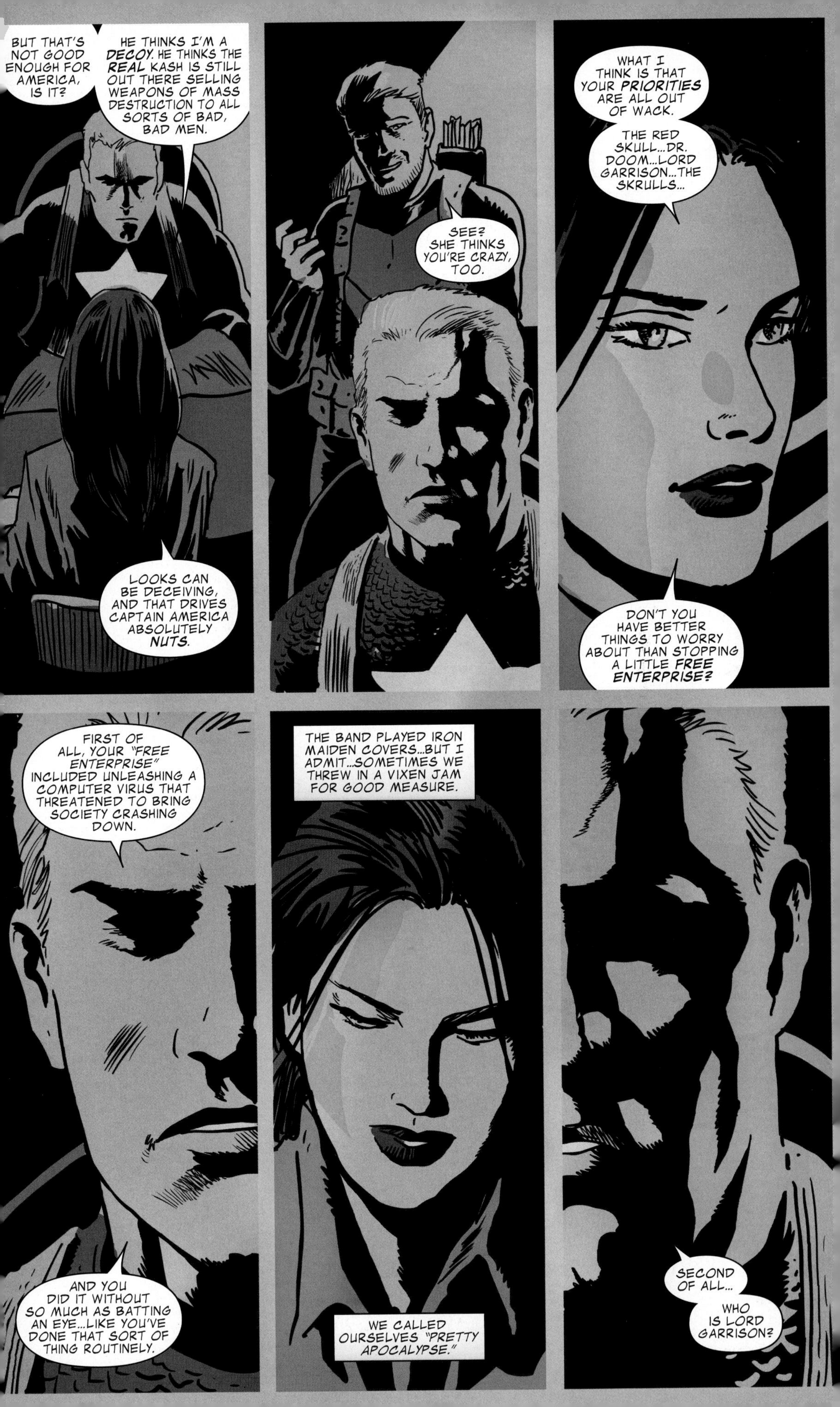
BUT THAT'S NOT GOOD ENOUGH FOR AMERICA, IS IT?
HE THINKS I'M A DECOY. HE THINKS THE REAL KASH IS STILL OUT THERE SELLING WEAPONS OF MASS DESTRUCTION TO ALL SORTS OF BAD, BAD MEN.
LOOKS CAN BE DECEIVING, AND THAT DRIVES CAPTAIN AMERICA ABSOLUTELY NUTS.
SEE? SHE THINKS YOU'RE CRAZY, TOO.
WHAT I THINK IS THAT YOUR PRIORITIES ARE ALL OUT OF WACK.
THE RED SKULL...DR. DOOM...LORD GARRISON...THE SKRULLS...
DON'T YOU HAVE BETTER THINGS TO WORRY ABOUT THAN STOPPING A LITTLE FREE ENTERPRISE?
FIRST OF ALL, YOUR "FREE ENTERPRISE" INCLUDED UNLEASHING A COMPUTER VIRUS THAT THREATENED TO BRING SOCIETY CRASHING DOWN.
AND YOU DID IT WITHOUT SO MUCH AS BATTING AN EYE...LIKE YOU'VE DONE THAT SORT OF THING ROUTINELY.
THE BAND PLAYED IRON MAIDEN COVERS...BUT I ADMIT...SOMETIMES WE THREW IN A VIXEN JAM FOR GOOD MEASURE.
WE CALLED OURSELVES "PRETTY APOCALYPSE."
SECOND OF ALL...
WHO IS LORD GARRISON?

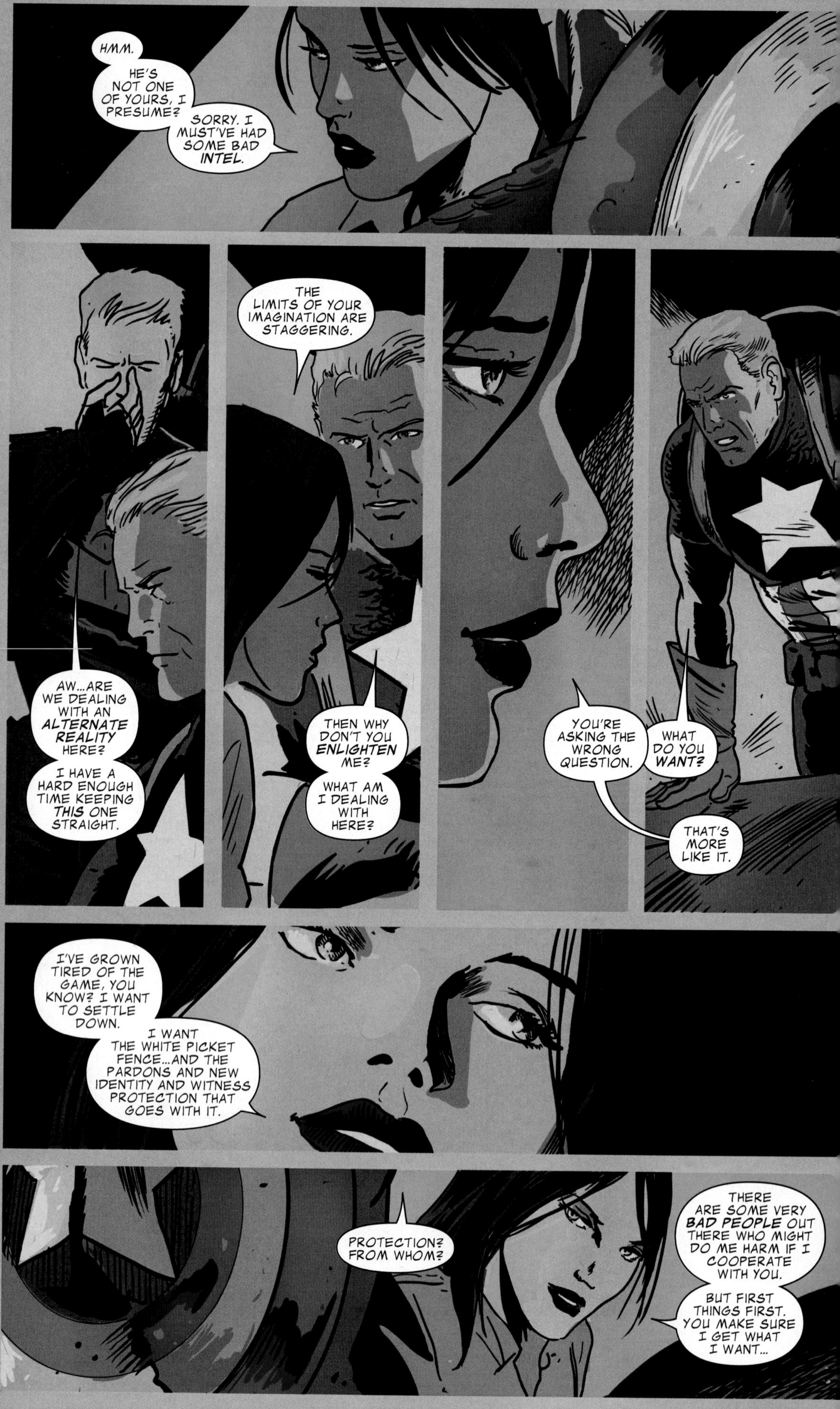
HMM.
HE'S NOT ONE OF YOURS, I PRESUME?
SORRY. I MUST'VE HAD SOME BAD INTEL.
AW...ARE WE DEALING WITH AN ALTERNATE REALITY HERE?
I HAVE A HARD ENOUGH TIME KEEPING THIS ONE STRAIGHT.
THE LIMITS OF YOUR IMAGINATION ARE STAGGERING.
THEN WHY DON'T YOU ENLIGHTEN ME?
WHAT AM I DEALING WITH HERE?
YOU'RE ASKING THE WRONG QUESTION.
WHAT DO YOU WANT?
THAT'S MORE LIKE IT.
I'VE GROWN TIRED OF THE GAME, YOU KNOW? I WANT TO SETTLE DOWN.
I WANT THE WHITE PICKET FENCE...AND THE PARDONS AND NEW IDENTITY AND WITNESS PROTECTION THAT GOES WITH IT.
PROTECTION? FROM WHOM?
THERE ARE SOME VERY BAD PEOPLE OUT THERE WHO MIGHT DO ME HARM IF I COOPERATE WITH YOU.
BUT FIRST THINGS FIRST. YOU MAKE SURE I GET WHAT I WANT...

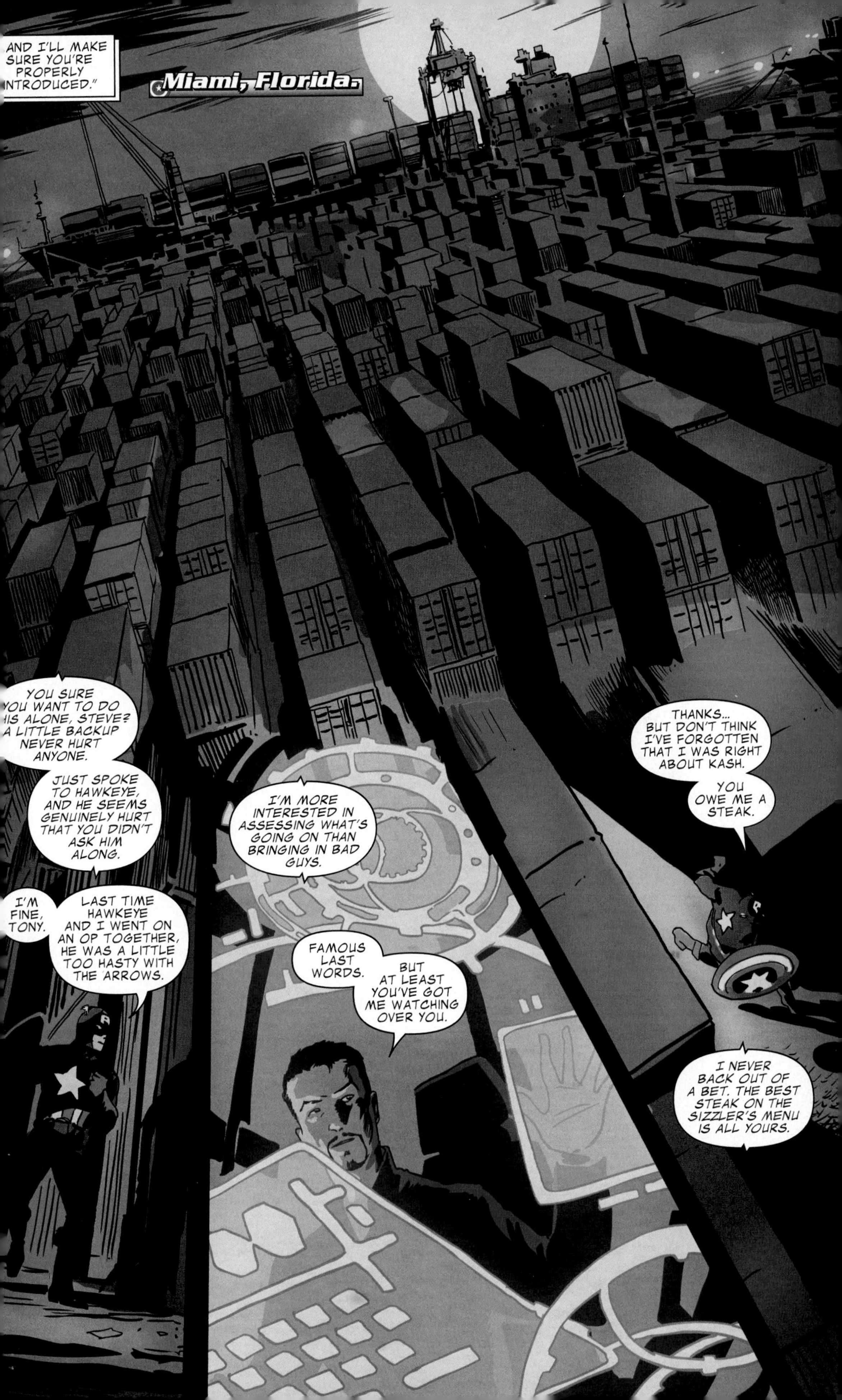

AND I'LL MAKE SURE YOU'RE PROPERLY INTRODUCED."
Miami, Florida.
YOU SURE YOU WANT TO DO THIS ALONE, STEVE? A LITTLE BACKUP NEVER HURT ANYONE.
JUST SPOKE TO HAWKEYE, AND HE SEEMS GENUINELY HURT THAT YOU DIDN'T ASK HIM ALONG.
I'M FINE, TONY.
LAST TIME HAWKEYE AND I WENT ON AN OP TOGETHER, HE WAS A LITTLE TOO HASTY WITH THE ARROWS.
I'M MORE INTERESTED IN ASSESSING WHAT'S GOING ON THAN BRINGING IN BAD GUYS.
FAMOUS LAST WORDS.
BUT AT LEAST YOU'VE GOT ME WATCHING OVER YOU.
THANKS... BUT DON'T THINK I'VE FORGOTTEN THAT I WAS RIGHT ABOUT KASH.
YOU OWE ME A STEAK.
I NEVER BACK OUT OF A BET. THE BEST STEAK ON THE SIZZLER'S MENU IS ALL YOURS.

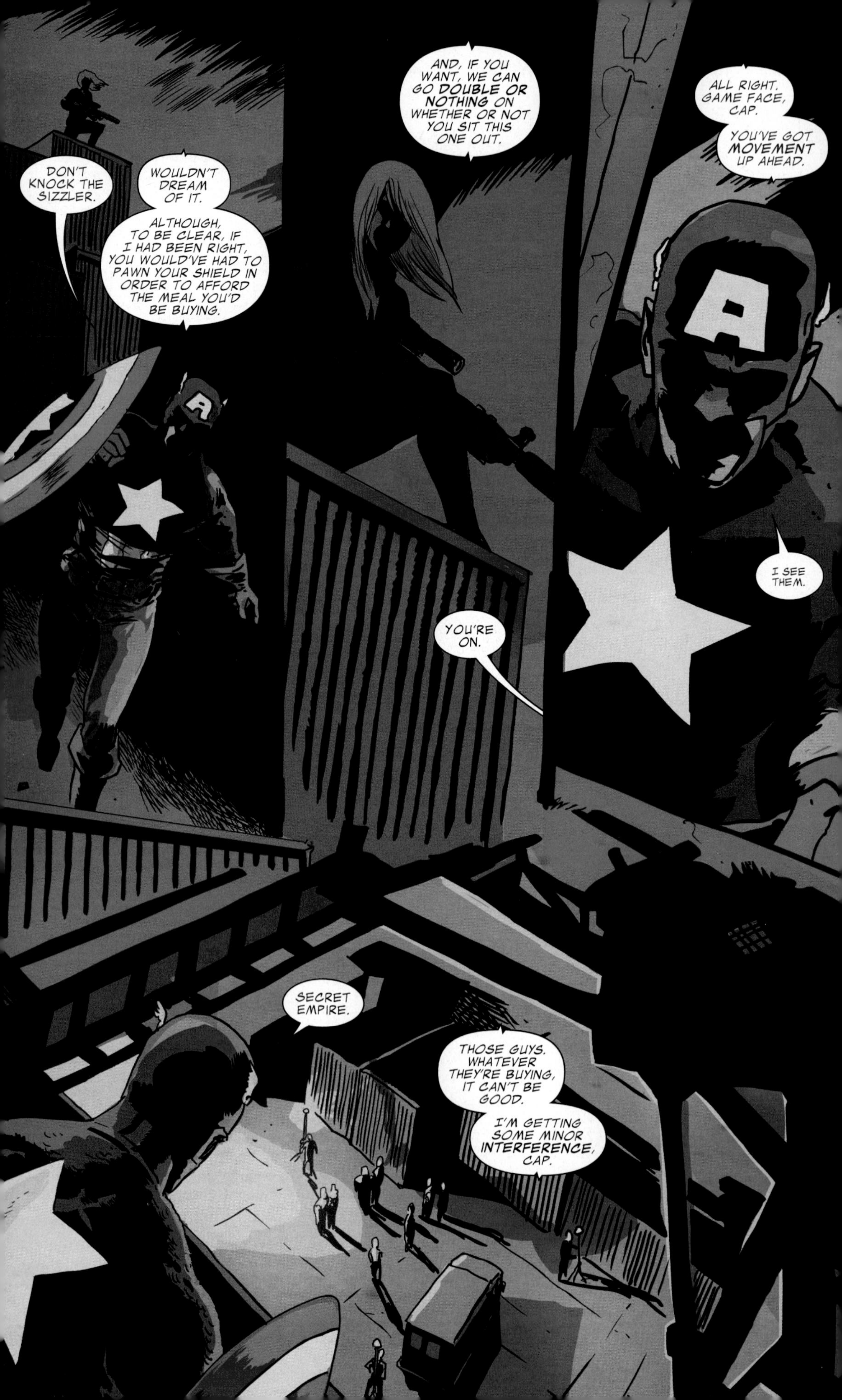
DON'T KNOCK THE SIZZLER.
WOULDN'T DREAM OF IT.
ALTHOUGH, TO BE CLEAR, IF I HAD BEEN RIGHT, YOU WOULD'VE HAD TO PAWN YOUR SHIELD IN ORDER TO AFFORD THE MEAL YOU'D BE BUYING.
AND, IF YOU WANT, WE CAN GO **DOUBLE OR NOTHING** ON WHETHER OR NOT YOU SIT THIS ONE OUT.
YOU'RE ON.
ALL RIGHT. GAME FACE, CAP.
YOU'VE GOT **MOVEMENT** UP AHEAD.
I SEE THEM.
SECRET EMPIRE.
THOSE GUYS. WHATEVER THEY'RE BUYING, IT CAN'T BE GOOD.
I'M GETTING SOME MINOR **INTERFERENCE**, CAP.

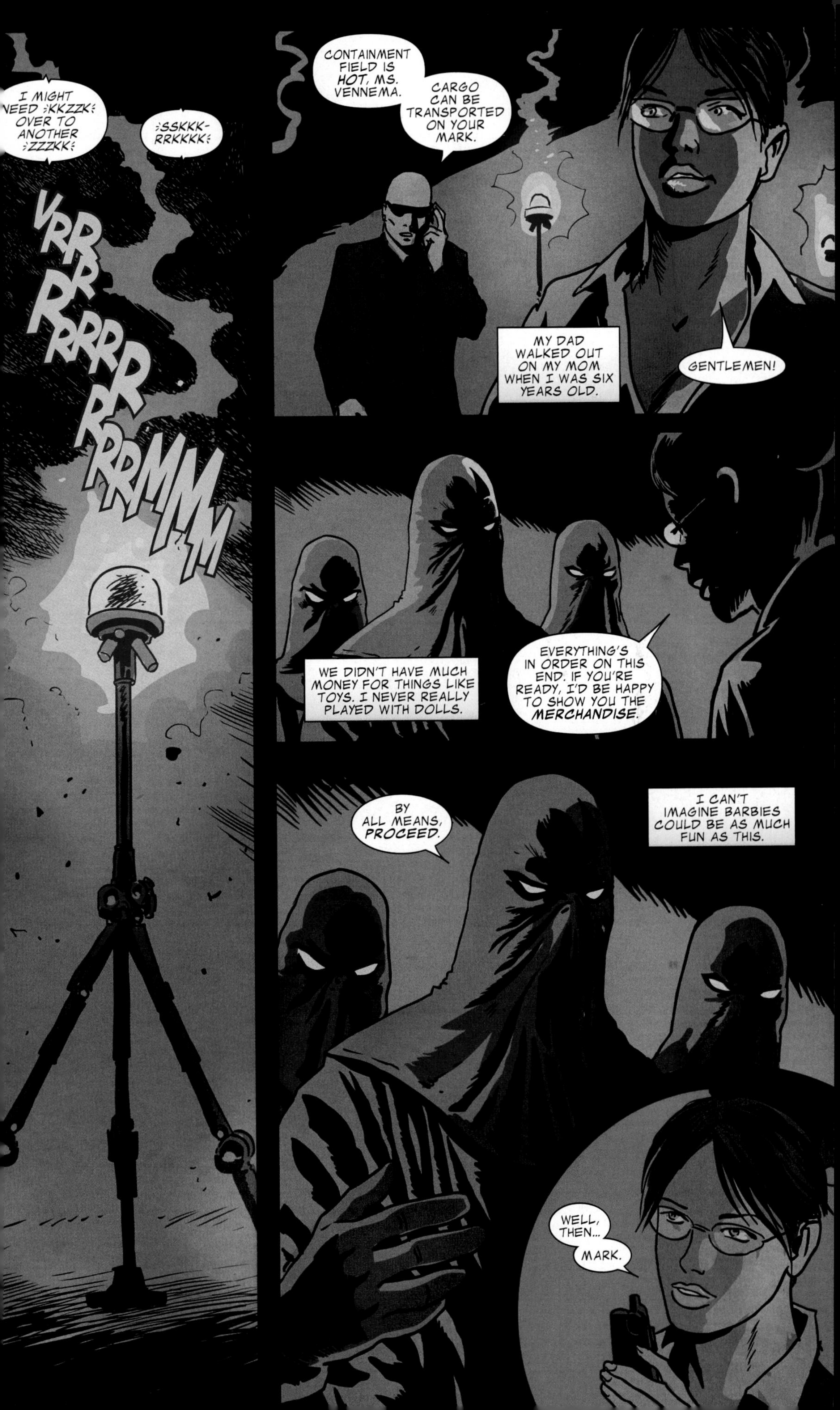
I MIGHT NEED ⁝KKZZK⁝ OVER TO ANOTHER ⁝ZZZKK⁝
⁝SSKKK-RRKKKK⁝
VRRRRRRRRRRRMMMM
CONTAINMENT FIELD IS HOT, MS. VENNEMA.
CARGO CAN BE TRANSPORTED ON YOUR MARK.
MY DAD WALKED OUT ON MY MOM WHEN I WAS SIX YEARS OLD.
GENTLEMEN!
WE DIDN'T HAVE MUCH MONEY FOR THINGS LIKE TOYS. I NEVER REALLY PLAYED WITH DOLLS.
EVERYTHING'S IN ORDER ON THIS END. IF YOU'RE READY, I'D BE HAPPY TO SHOW YOU THE MERCHANDISE.
BY ALL MEANS, PROCEED.
I CAN'T IMAGINE BARBIES COULD BE AS MUCH FUN AS THIS.
WELL, THEN...
MARK.

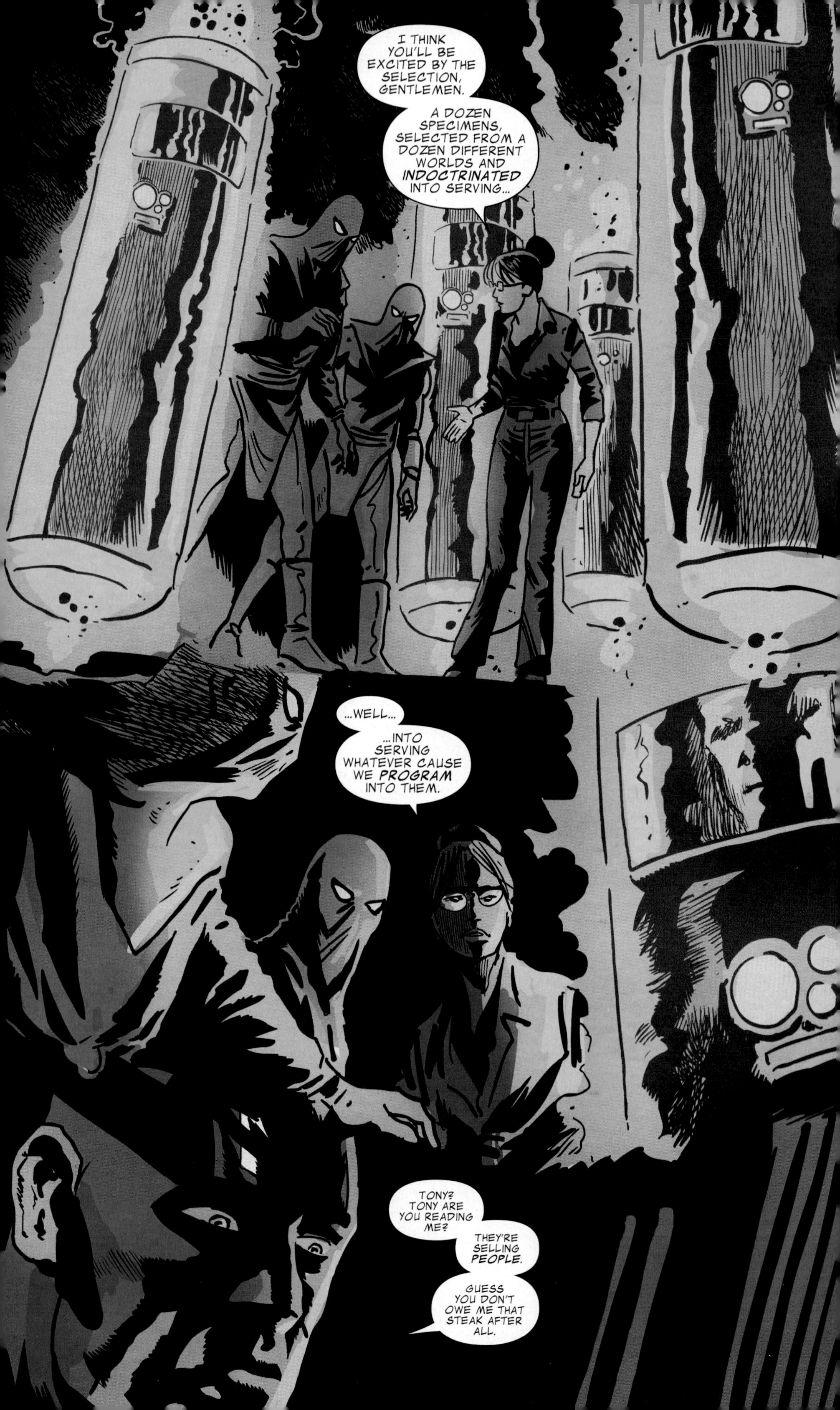
I THINK YOU'LL BE EXCITED BY THE SELECTION, GENTLEMEN.
A DOZEN SPECIMENS, SELECTED FROM A DOZEN DIFFERENT WORLDS AND ***INDOCTRINATED*** INTO SERVING...
...WELL...
...INTO SERVING WHATEVER CAUSE WE ***PROGRAM*** INTO THEM.
TONY? TONY ARE YOU READING ME?
THEY'RE SELLING ***PEOPLE***.
GUESS YOU DON'T OWE ME THAT STEAK AFTER ALL.

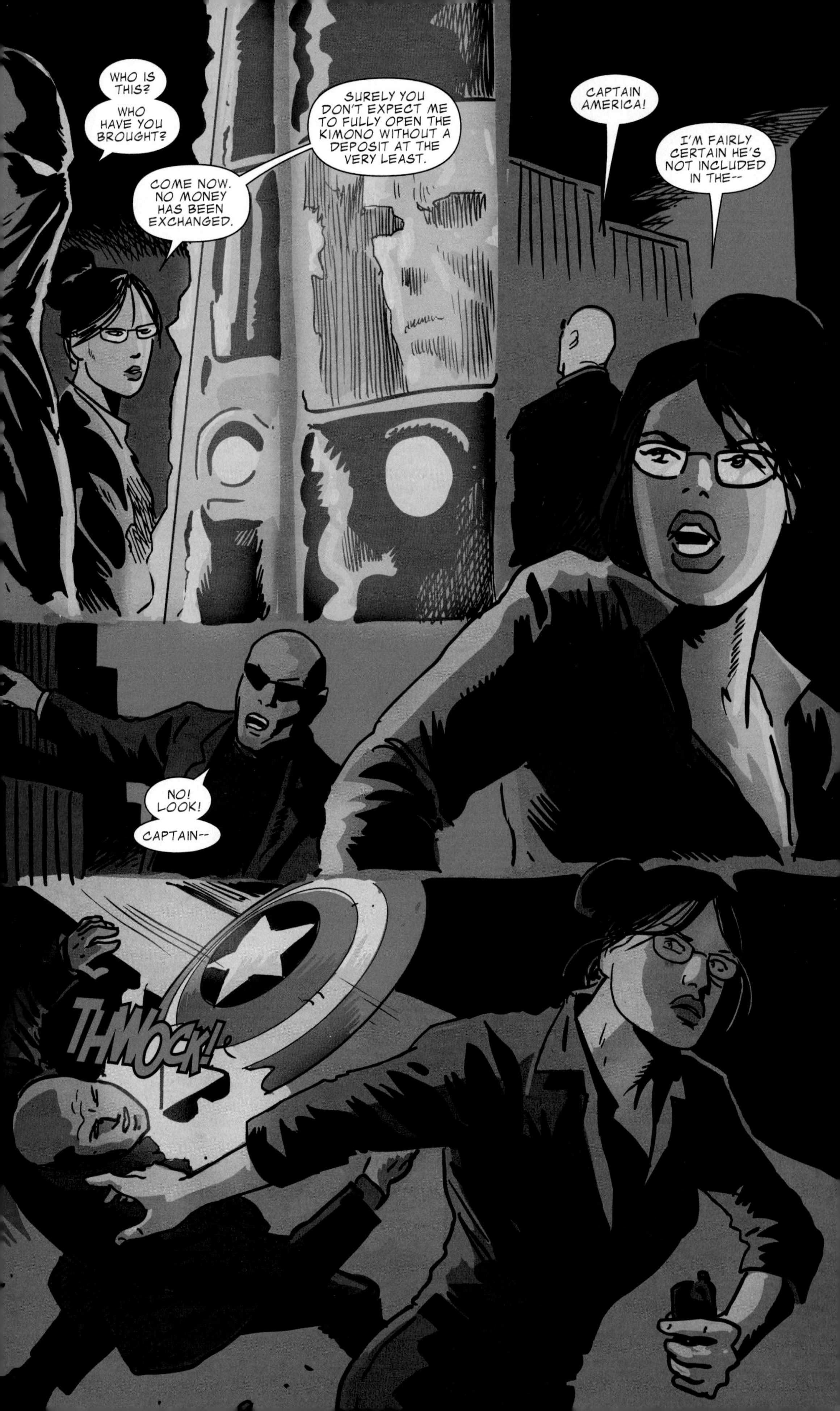
WHO IS THIS?
WHO HAVE YOU BROUGHT?
COME NOW. NO MONEY HAS BEEN EXCHANGED.
SURELY YOU DON'T EXPECT ME TO FULLY OPEN THE KIMONO WITHOUT A DEPOSIT AT THE VERY LEAST.
CAPTAIN AMERICA!
I'M FAIRLY CERTAIN HE'S NOT INCLUDED IN THE--
NO! LOOK!
CAPTAIN--
THWOCK!

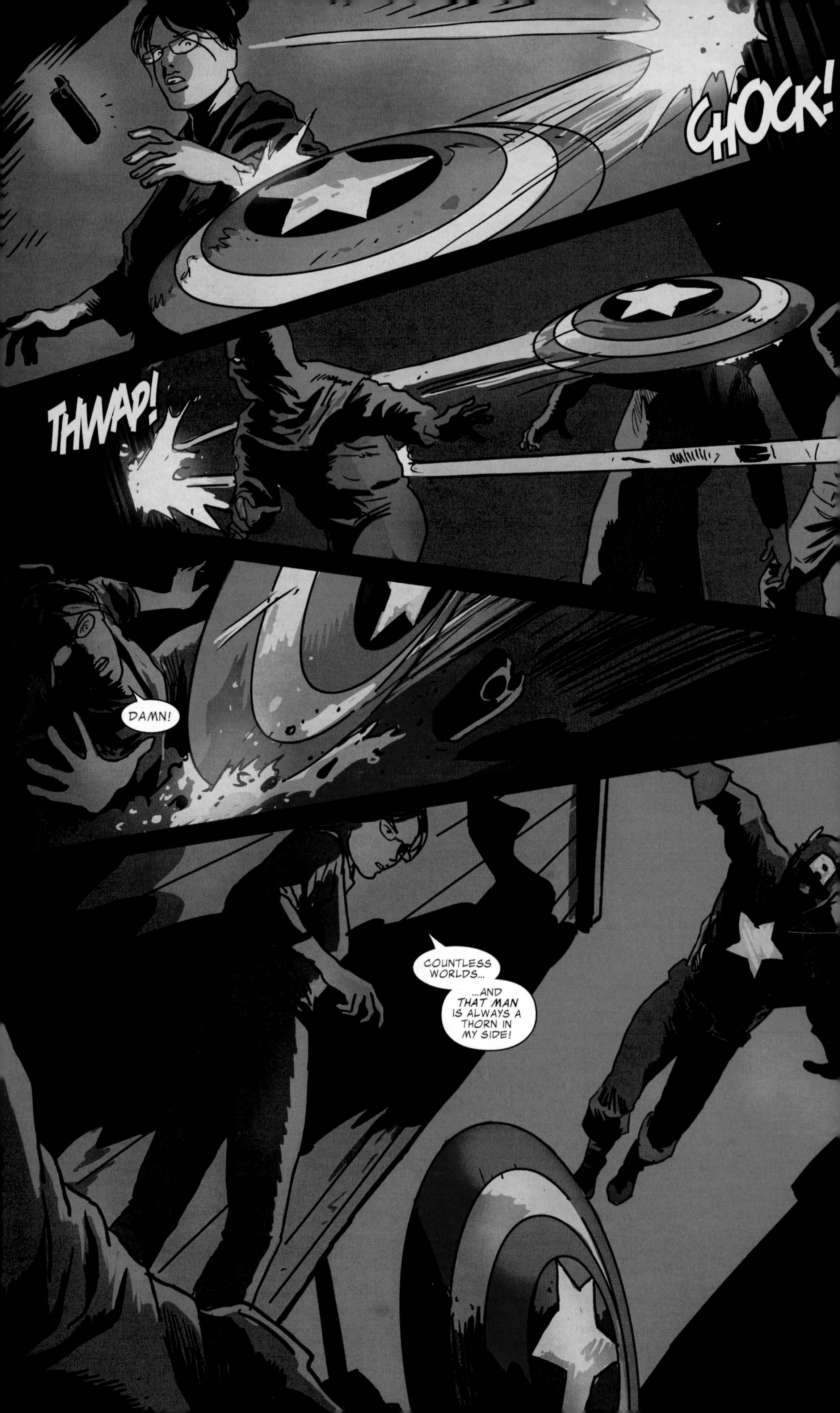
CHOCK!
THWAP!
DAMN!
COUNTLESS WORLDS...
...AND THAT MAN IS ALWAYS A THORN IN MY SIDE!

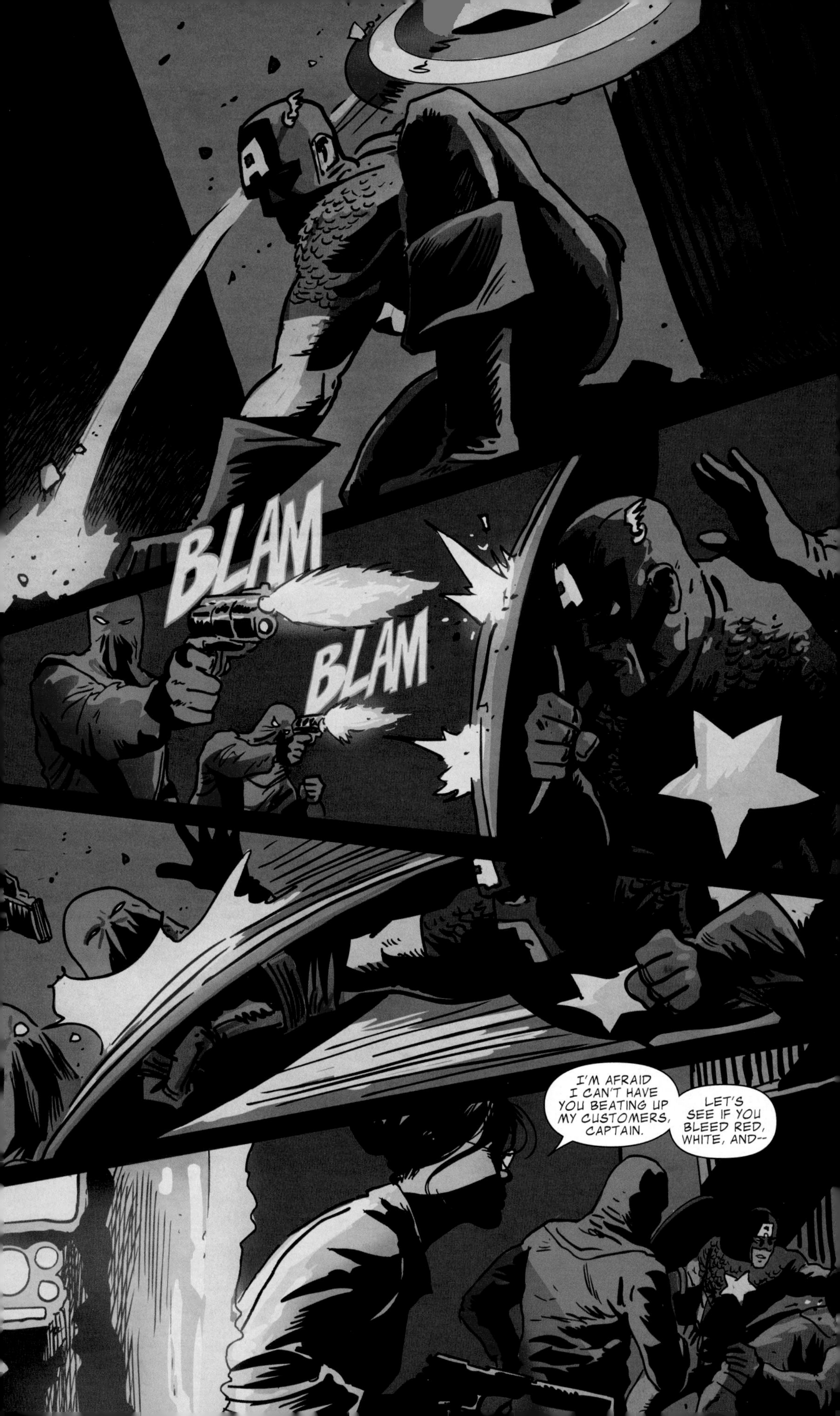
BLAM
BLAM
I'M AFRAID I CAN'T HAVE YOU BEATING UP MY CUSTOMERS, CAPTAIN.
LET'S SEE IF YOU BLEED RED, WHITE, AND--

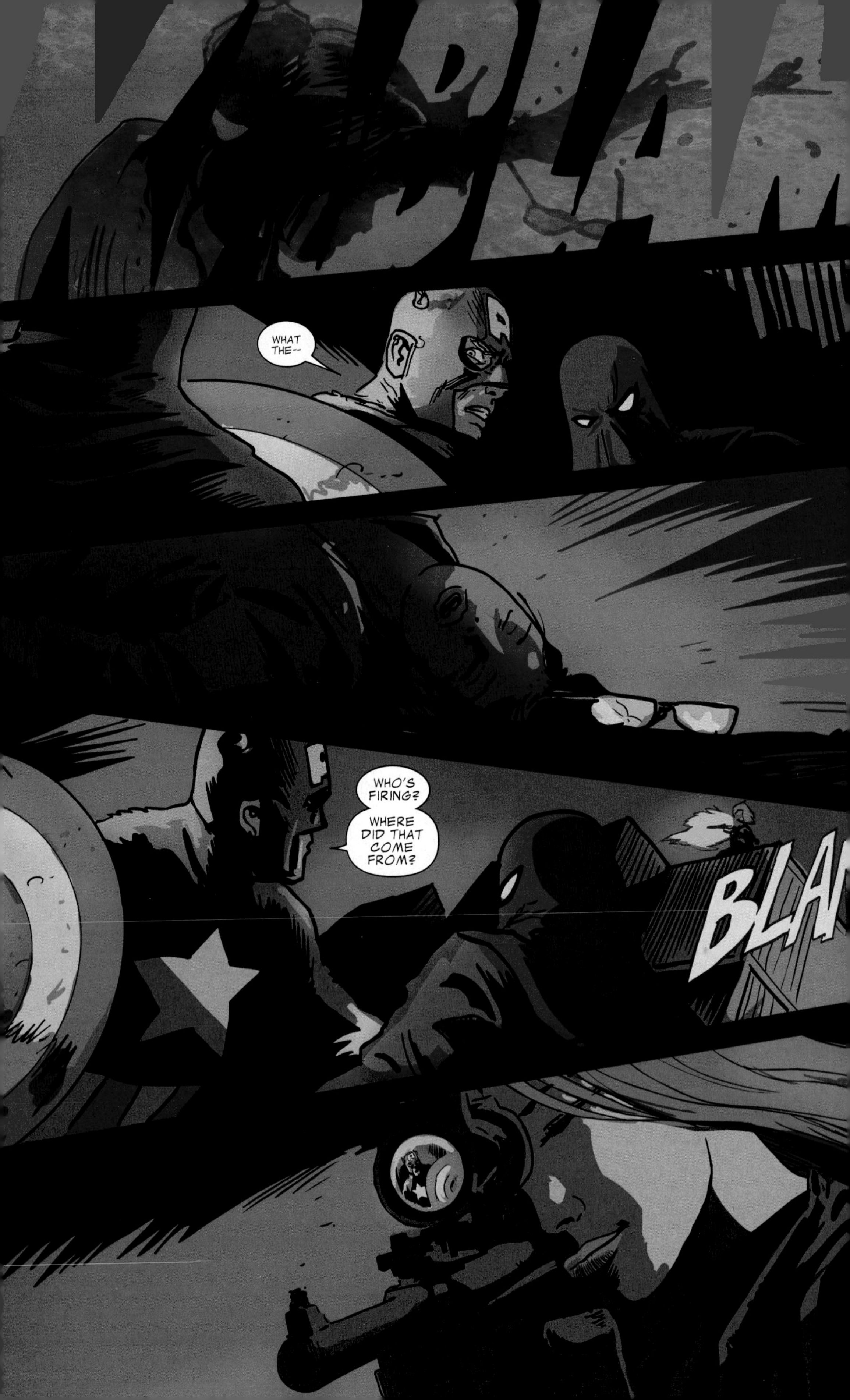
WHAT THE--
WHO'S FIRING?
WHERE DID THAT COME FROM?
BLA

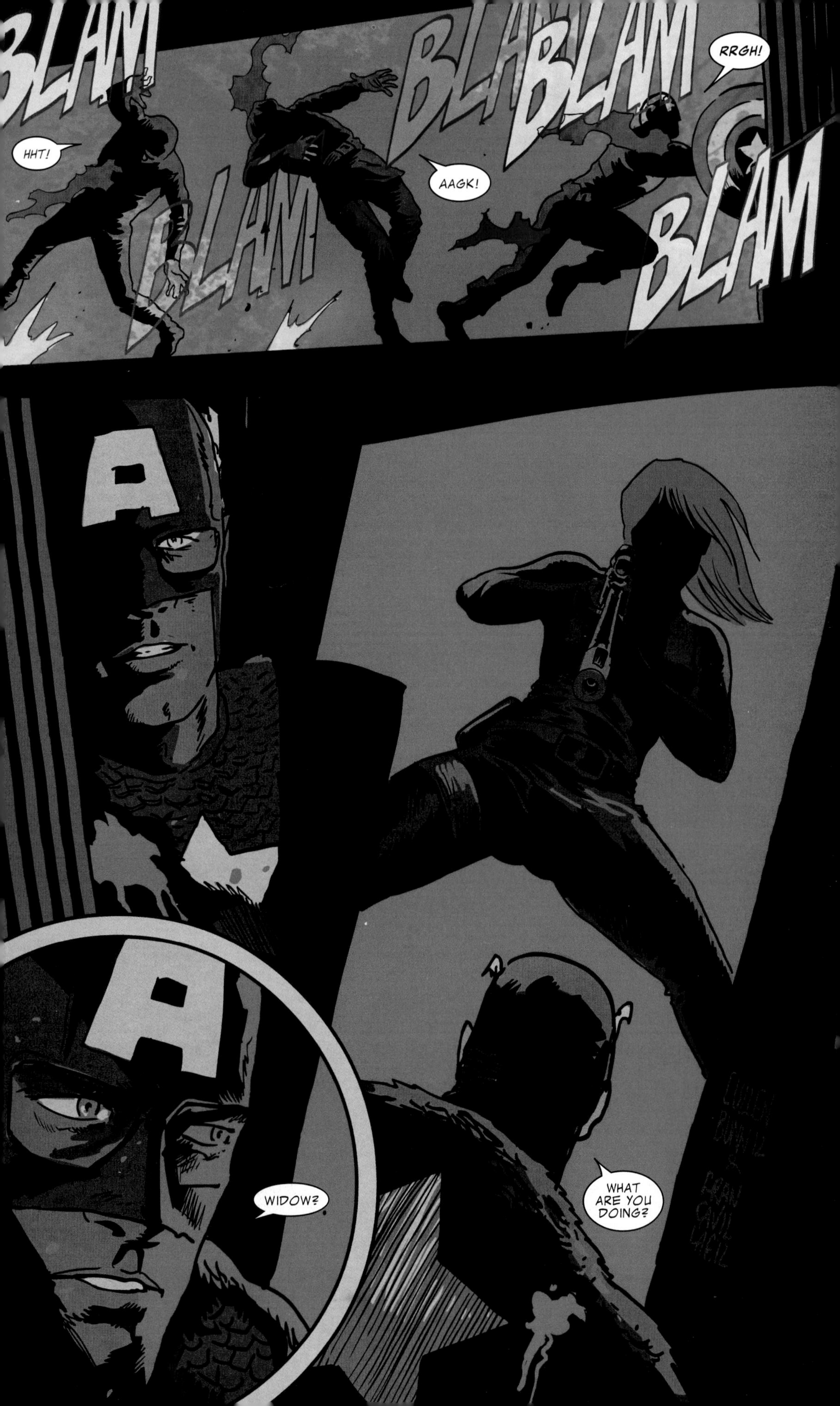
BLAM
HHT!
BLAM
BLABLAM
AAGK!
RRGH!
BLAM
WIDOW?
WHAT ARE YOU DOING?

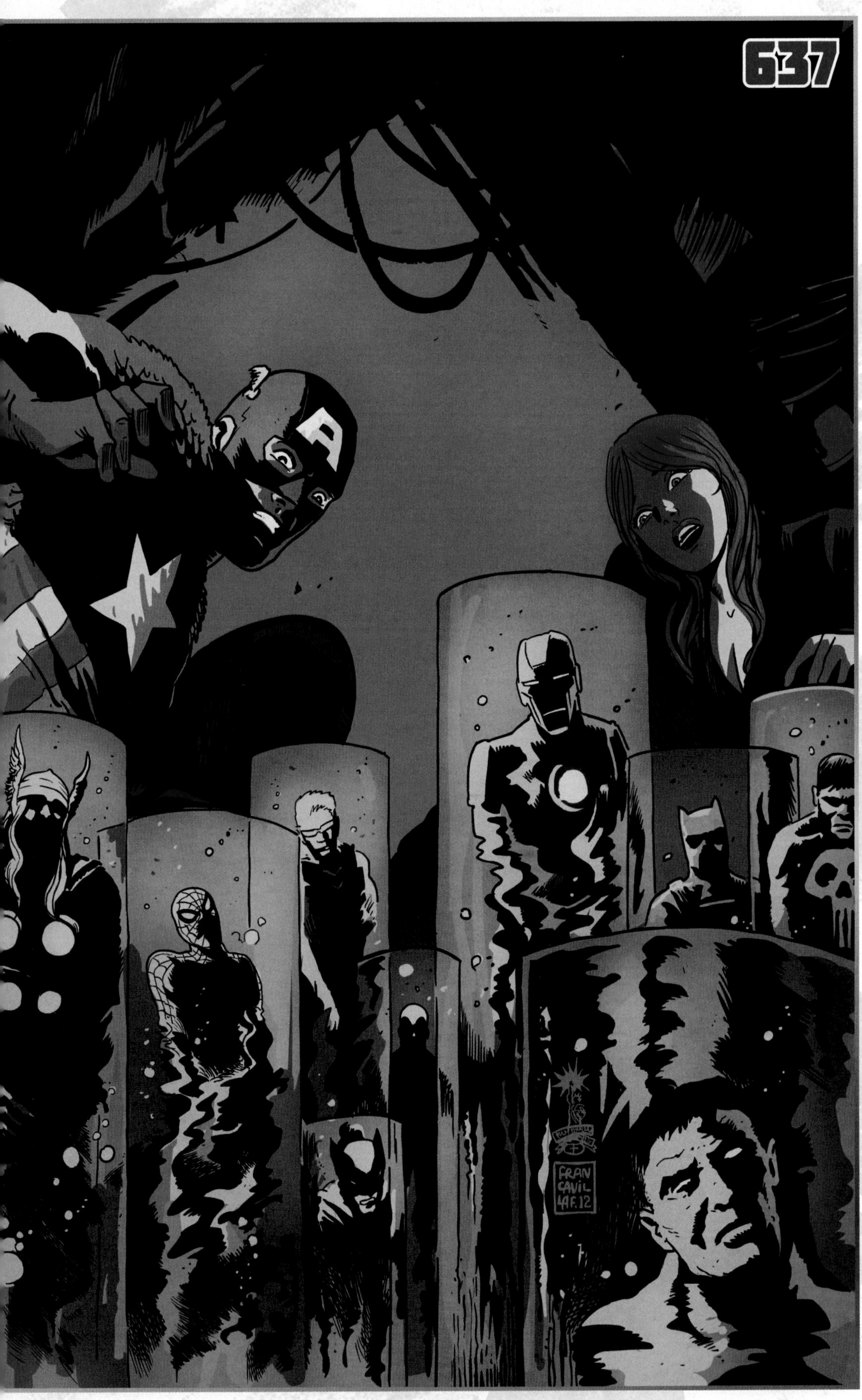
637

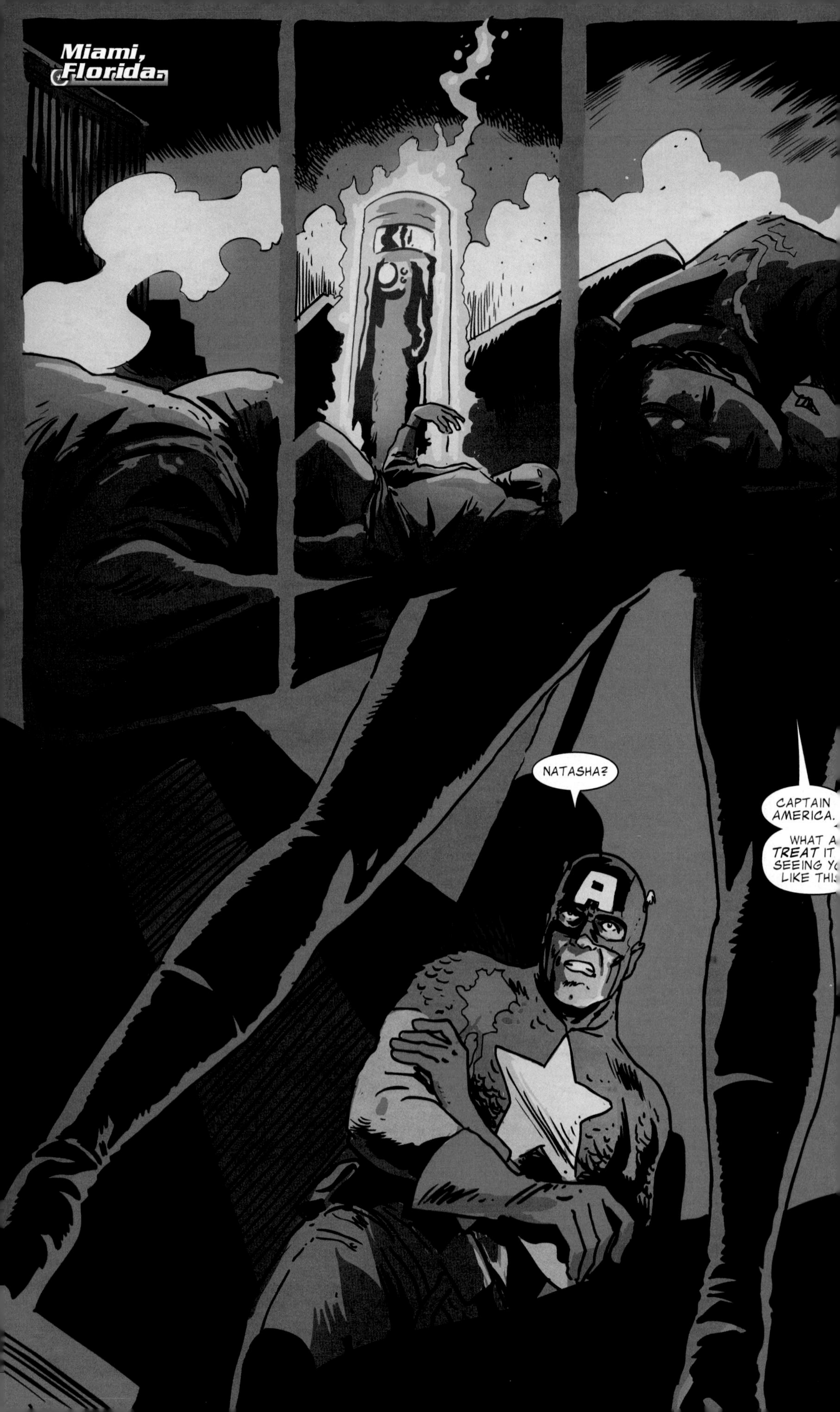
Miami, Florida.
NATASHA?
CAPTAIN AMERICA.
WHAT A TREAT IT SEEING Y LIKE THIS

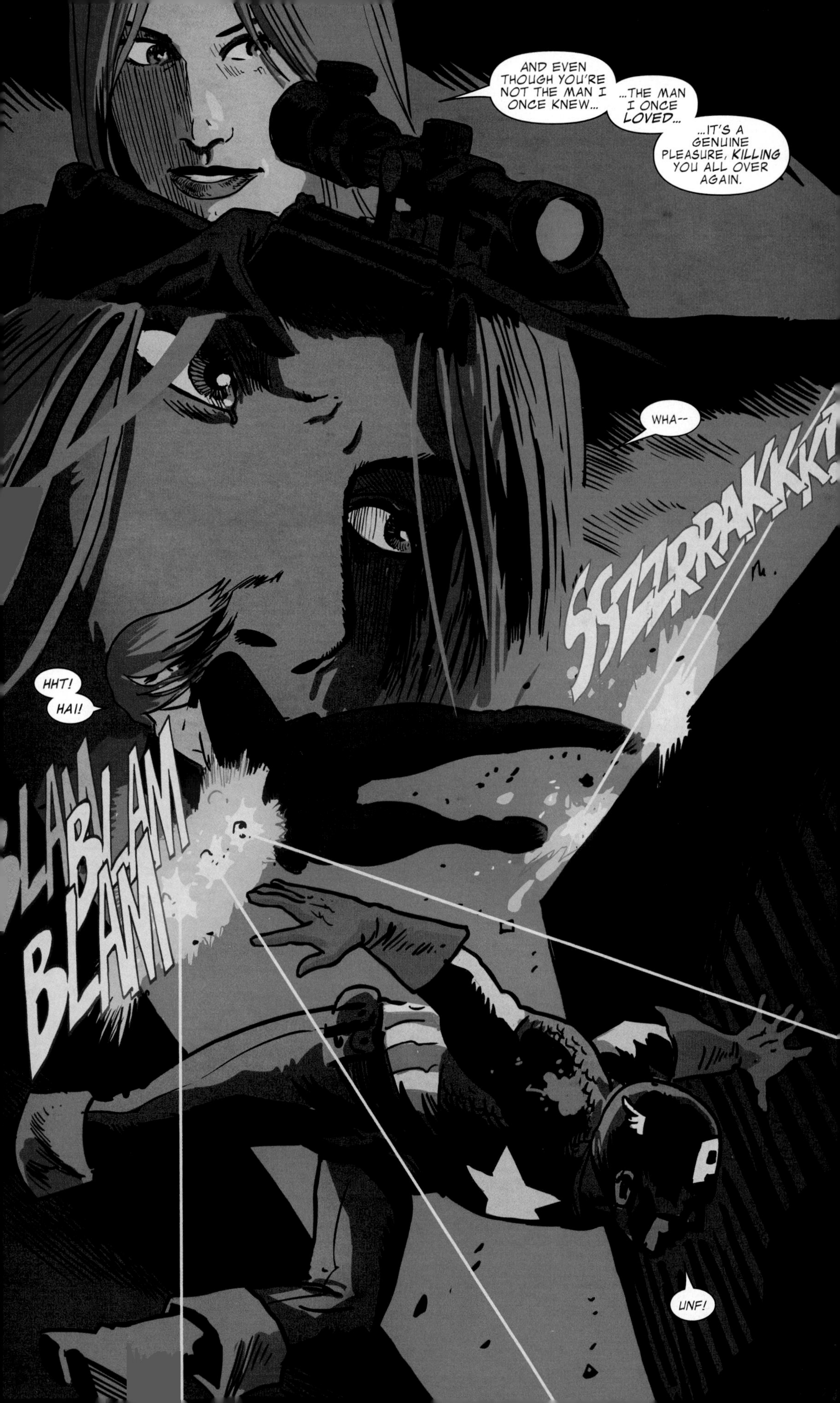
AND EVEN THOUGH YOU'RE NOT THE MAN I ONCE KNEW...
...THE MAN I ONCE LOVED...
...IT'S A GENUINE PLEASURE, KILLING YOU ALL OVER AGAIN.
WHA--
SSZZZRRAKKK!
HHT! HAI!
BLAM BLAM BLAM
UNF!

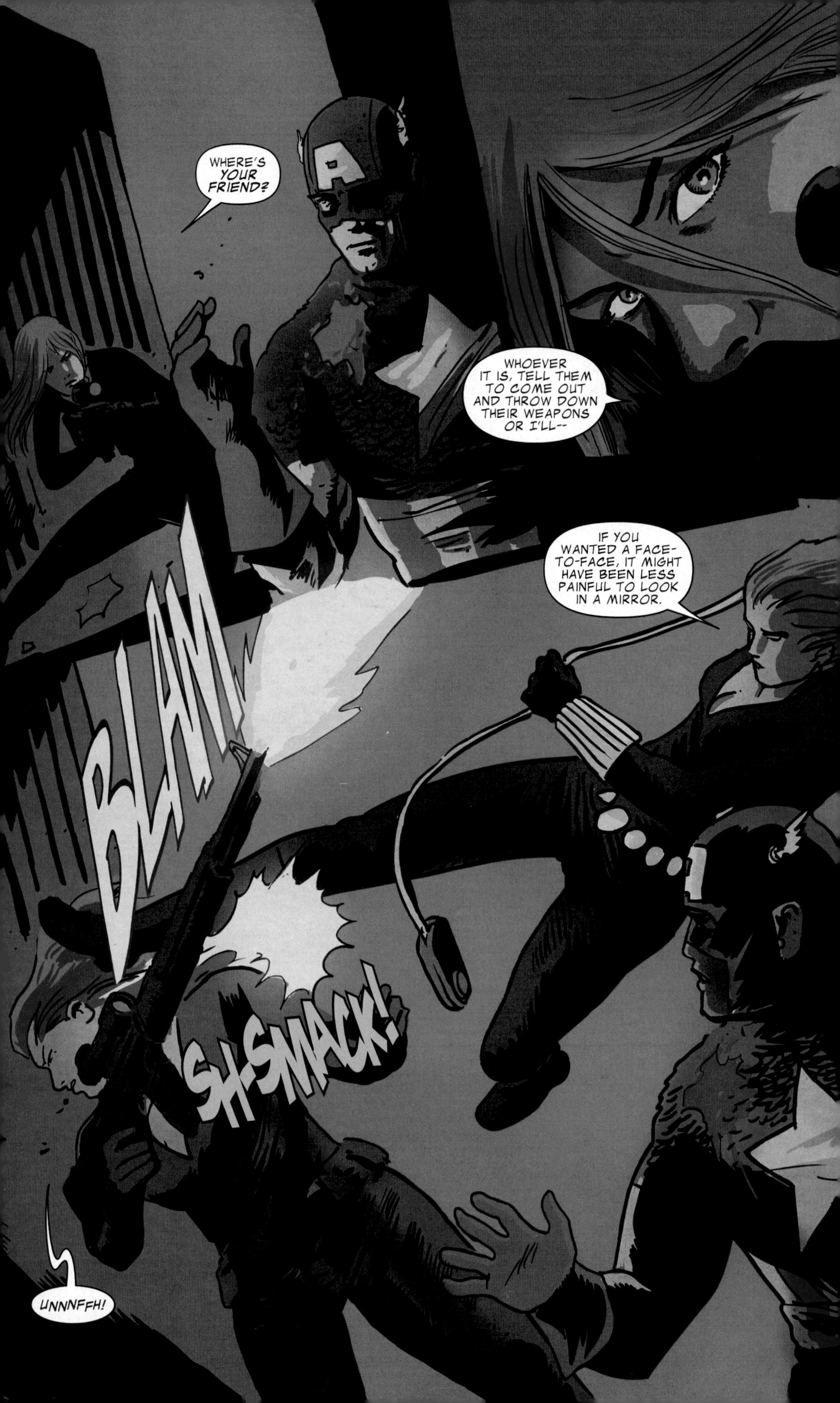

WHERE'S YOUR FRIEND?
WHOEVER IT IS, TELL THEM TO COME OUT AND THROW DOWN THEIR WEAPONS OR I'LL--
IF YOU WANTED A FACE-TO-FACE, IT MIGHT HAVE BEEN LESS PAINFUL TO LOOK IN A MIRROR.
BLAM!
SH-SMACK!
UNNNFFH!

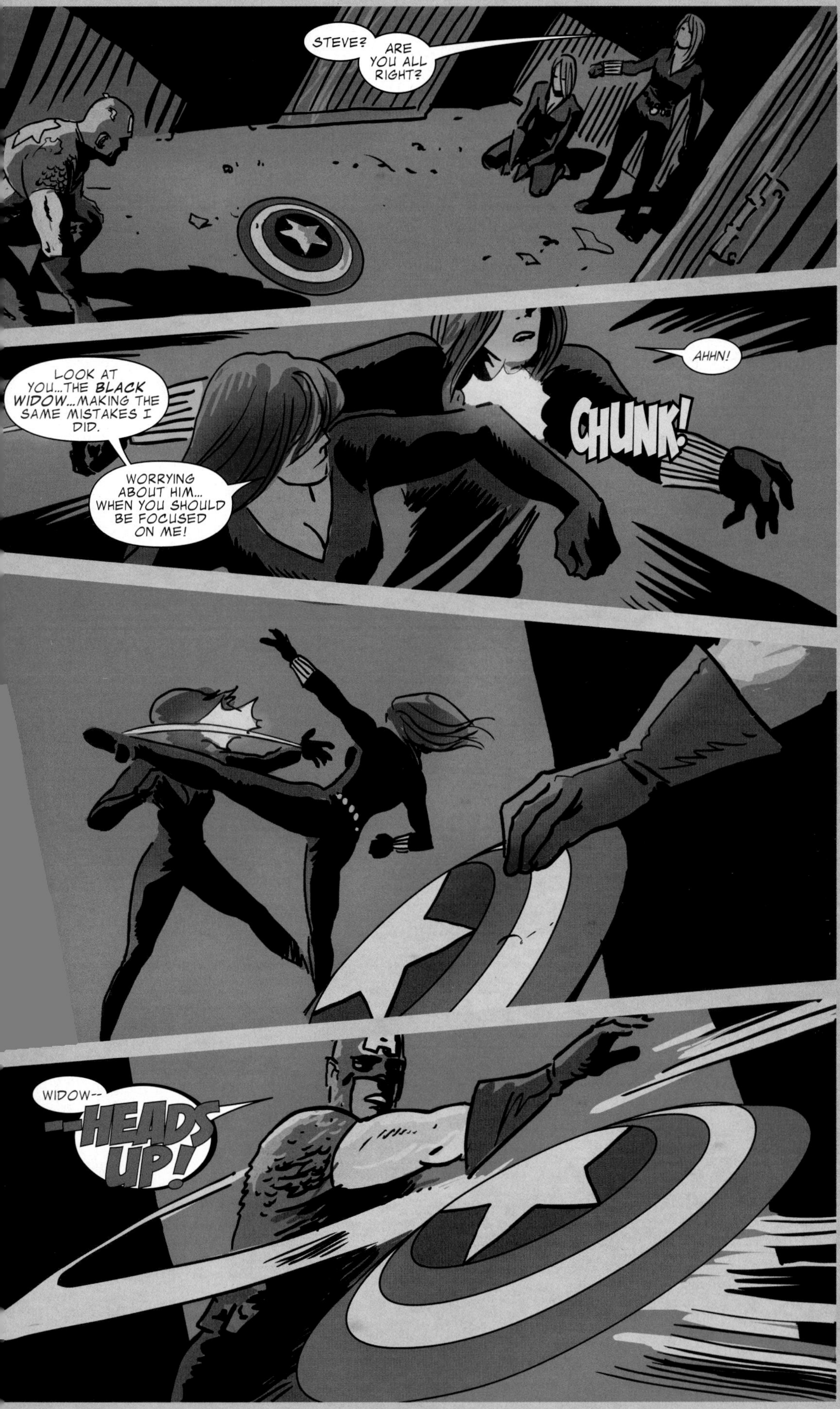
STEVE?
ARE YOU ALL RIGHT?
AHHN!
LOOK AT YOU...THE BLACK WIDOW...MAKING THE SAME MISTAKES I DID.
WORRYING ABOUT HIM... WHEN YOU SHOULD BE FOCUSED ON ME!
CHUNK!
WIDOW--
--HEADS UP!

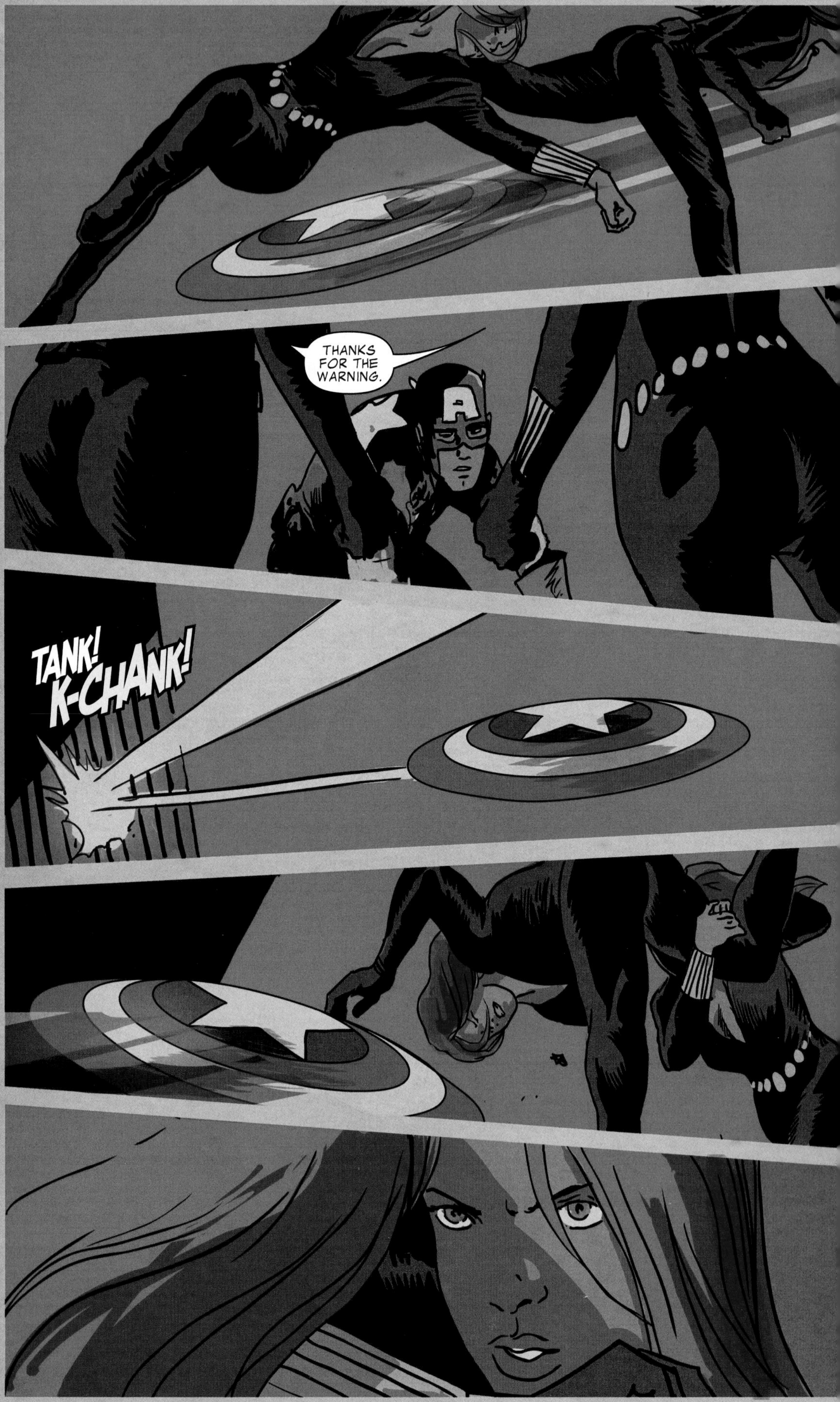

THANKS FOR THE WARNING.
TANK! K-CHANK!

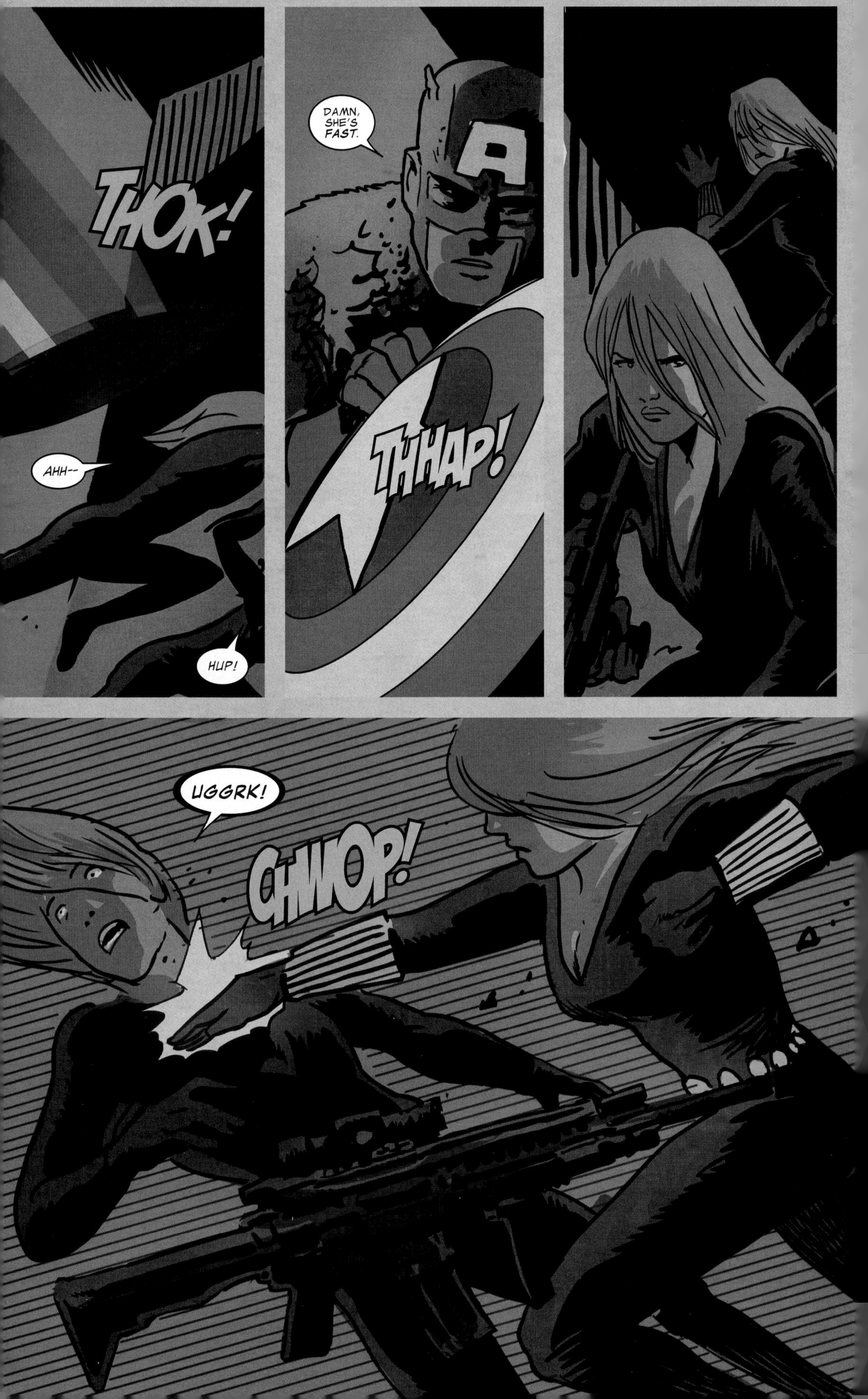
THOK!
AHH--
HUP!
DAMN, SHE'S FAST.
THHAP!
UGGRK!
CHWOP!

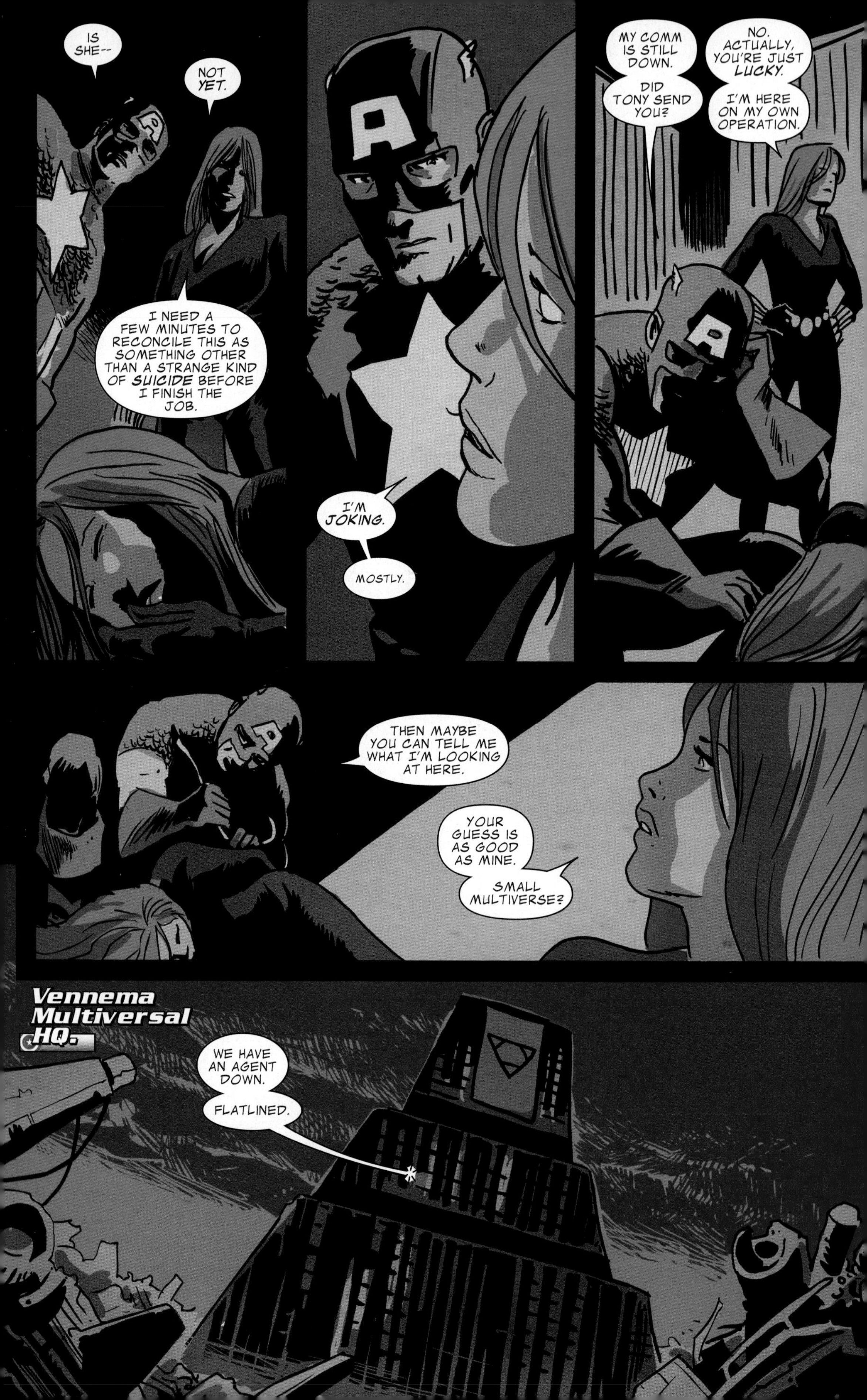
IS SHE--
NOT YET.
I NEED A FEW MINUTES TO RECONCILE THIS AS SOMETHING OTHER THAN A STRANGE KIND OF SUICIDE BEFORE I FINISH THE JOB.
I'M JOKING.
MOSTLY.
MY COMM IS STILL DOWN.
DID TONY SEND YOU?
NO. ACTUALLY, YOU'RE JUST LUCKY.
I'M HERE ON MY OWN OPERATION.
THEN MAYBE YOU CAN TELL ME WHAT I'M LOOKING AT HERE.
YOUR GUESS IS AS GOOD AS MINE.
SMALL MULTIVERSE?
Vennema Multiversal HQ.
WE HAVE AN AGENT DOWN.
FLATLINED.

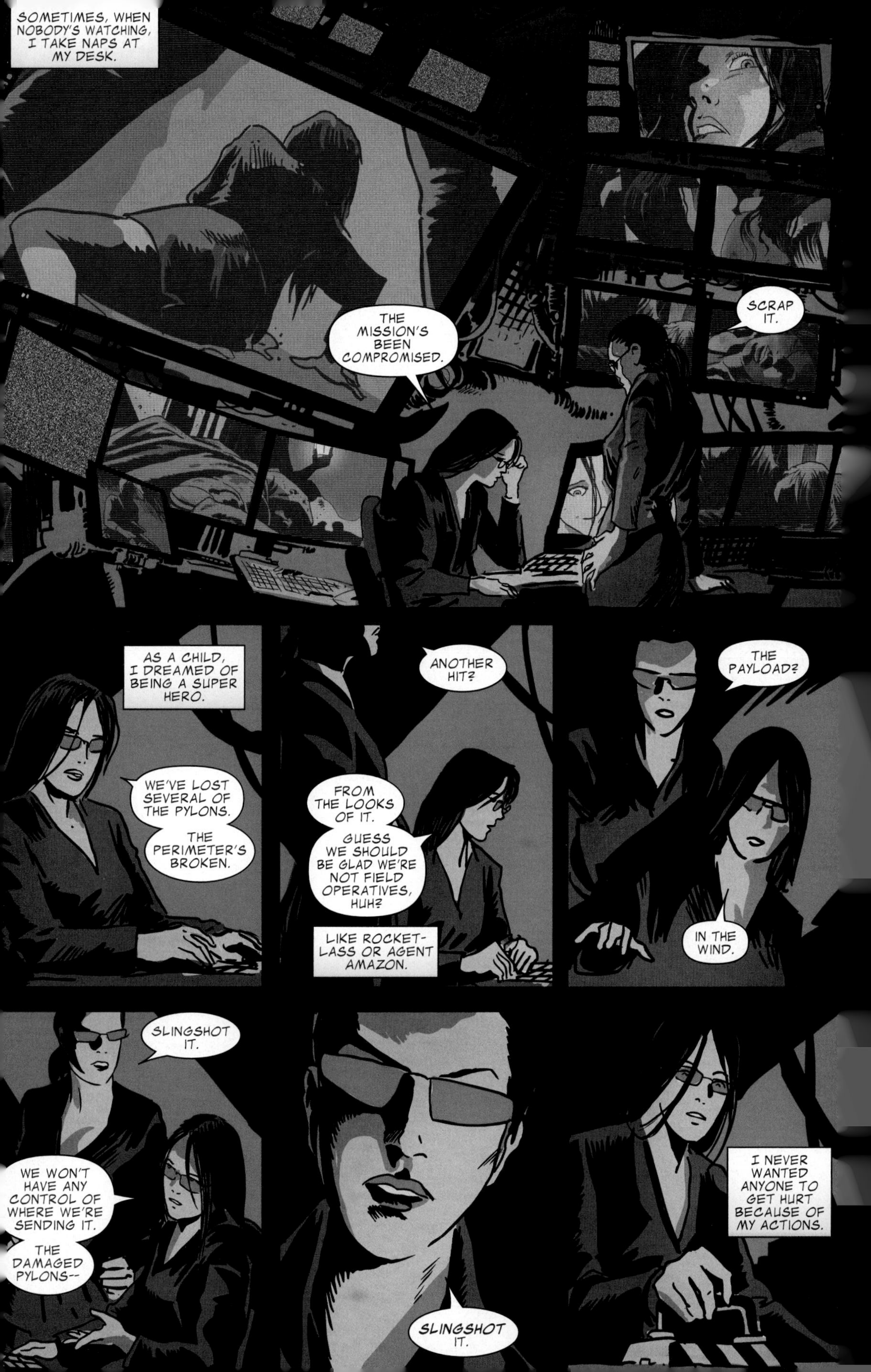

SOMETIMES, WHEN NOBODY'S WATCHING, I TAKE NAPS AT MY DESK.
THE MISSION'S BEEN COMPROMISED.
SCRAP IT.
AS A CHILD, I DREAMED OF BEING A SUPER HERO.
WE'VE LOST SEVERAL OF THE PYLONS.
THE PERIMETER'S BROKEN.
ANOTHER HIT?
FROM THE LOOKS OF IT.
GUESS WE SHOULD BE GLAD WE'RE NOT FIELD OPERATIVES, HUH?
LIKE ROCKET-LASS OR AGENT AMAZON.
THE PAYLOAD?
IN THE WIND.
SLINGSHOT IT.
WE WON'T HAVE ANY CONTROL OF WHERE WE'RE SENDING IT.
THE DAMAGED PYLONS--
SLINGSHOT IT.
I NEVER WANTED ANYONE TO GET HURT BECAUSE OF MY ACTIONS.

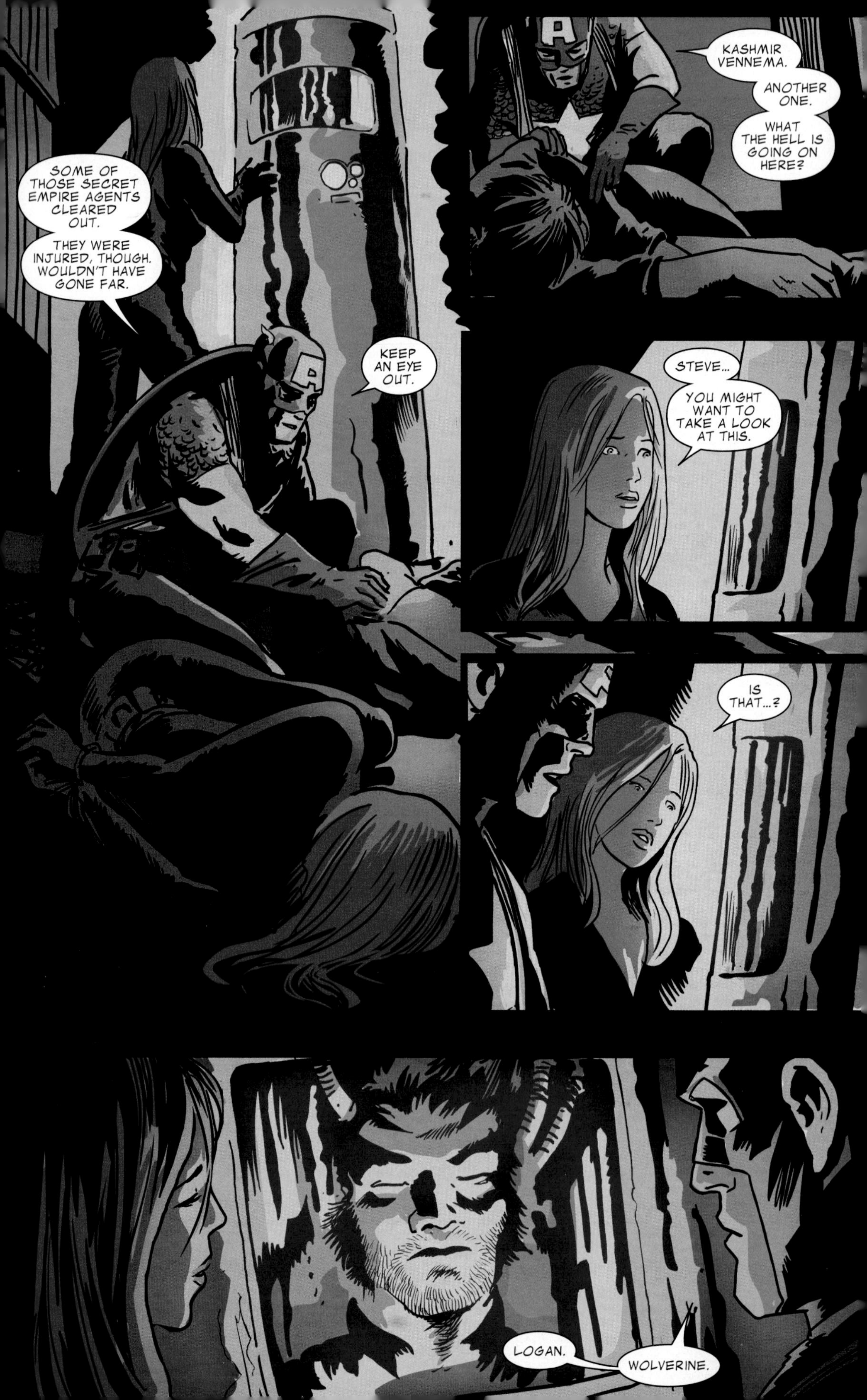
SOME OF THOSE SECRET EMPIRE AGENTS CLEARED OUT.
THEY WERE INJURED, THOUGH. WOULDN'T HAVE GONE FAR.
KEEP AN EYE OUT.
KASHMIR VENNEMA.
ANOTHER ONE.
WHAT THE HELL IS GOING ON HERE?
STEVE...
YOU MIGHT WANT TO TAKE A LOOK AT THIS.
IS THAT...?
LOGAN.
WOLVERINE.

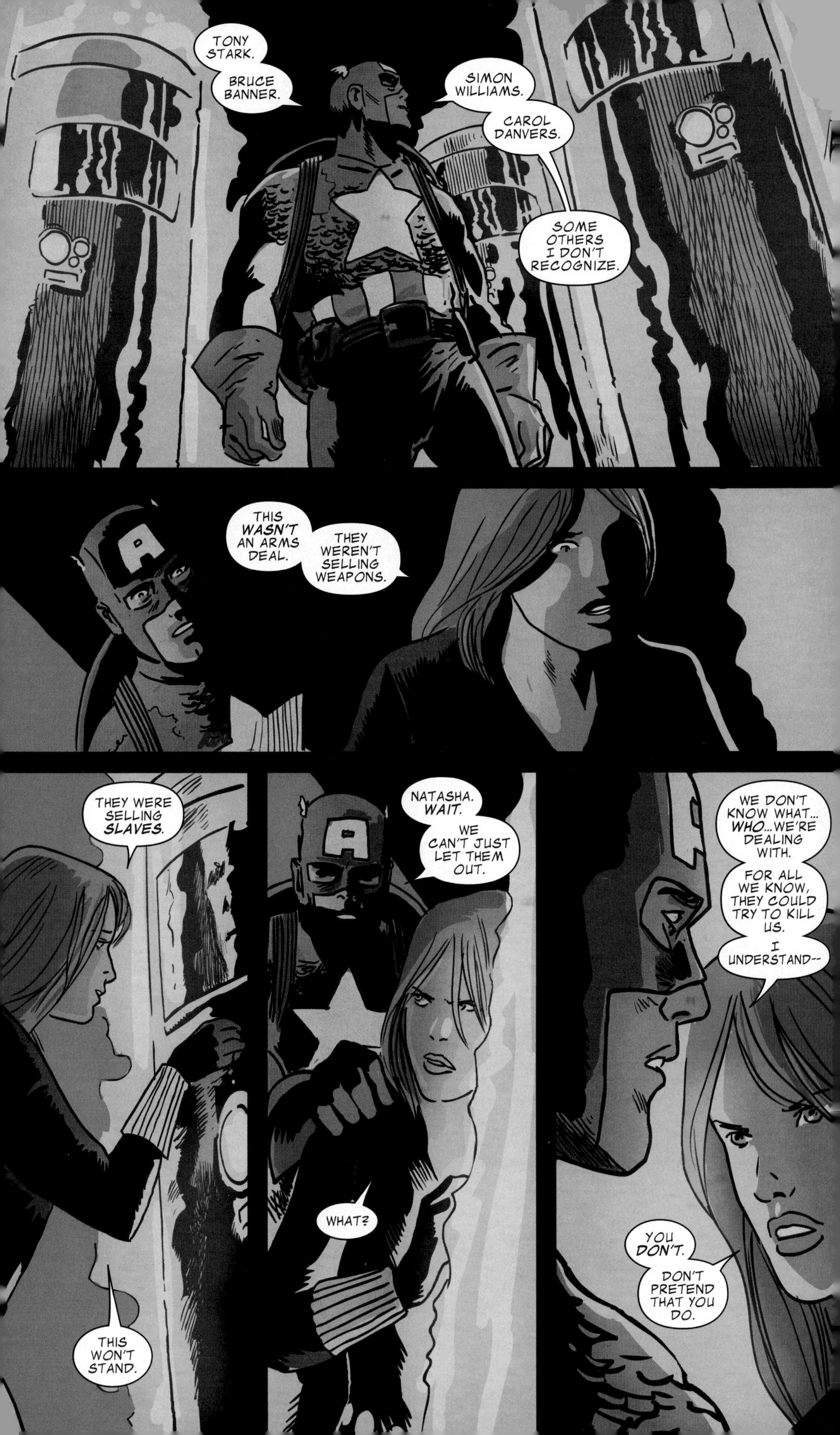
TONY STARK.
BRUCE BANNER.
SIMON WILLIAMS.
CAROL DANVERS.
SOME OTHERS I DON'T RECOGNIZE.
THIS *WASN'T* AN ARMS DEAL.
THEY WEREN'T SELLING WEAPONS.
THEY WERE SELLING *SLAVES*.
THIS WON'T STAND.
NATASHA. *WAIT*.
WE CAN'T JUST LET THEM OUT.
WHAT?
WE DON'T KNOW WHAT... *WHO*...WE'RE DEALING WITH.
FOR ALL WE KNOW, THEY COULD TRY TO KILL US.
I UNDERSTAND--
YOU *DON'T*.
DON'T PRETEND THAT YOU DO.

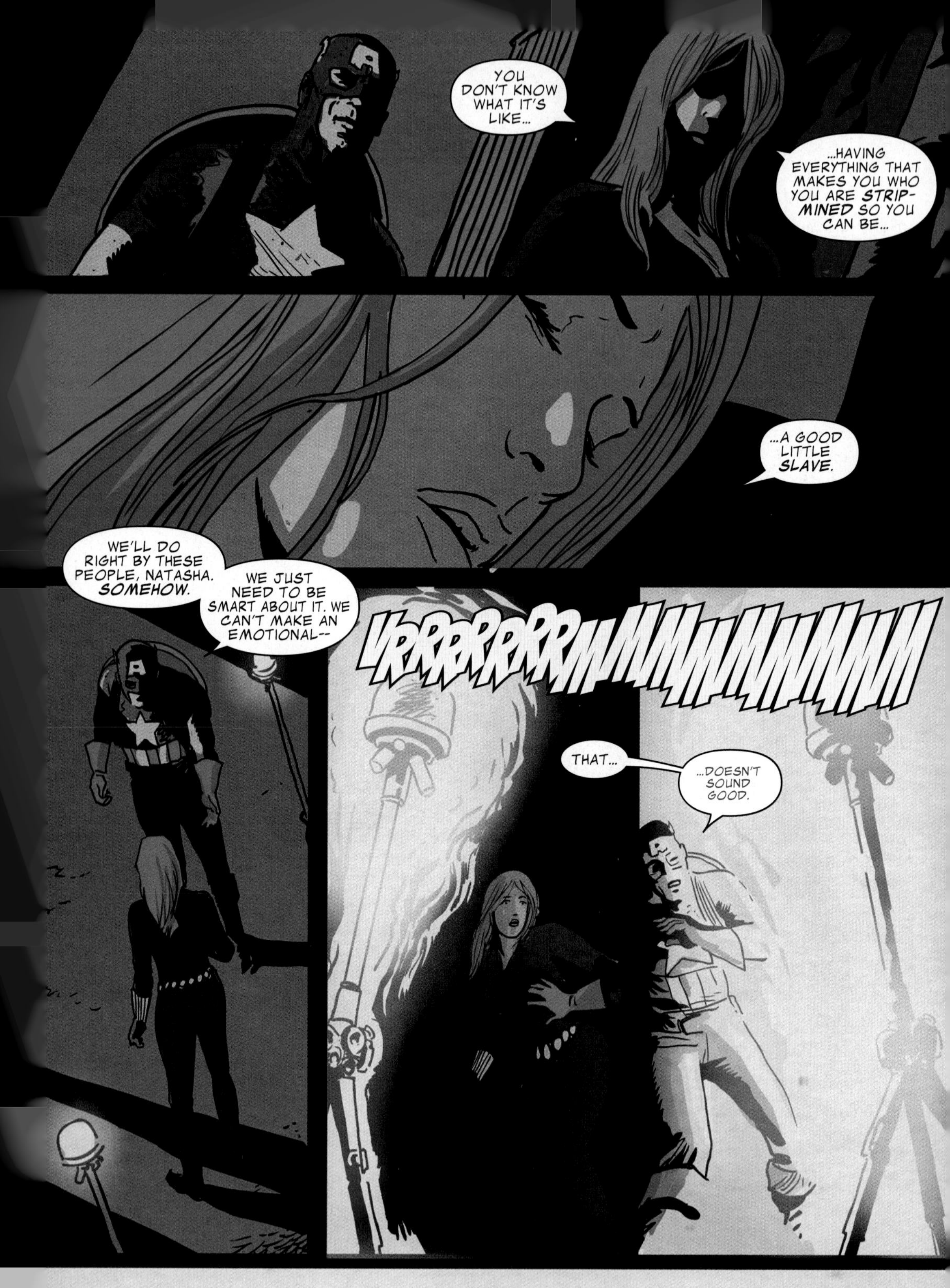
YOU DON'T KNOW WHAT IT'S LIKE...
...HAVING EVERYTHING THAT MAKES YOU WHO YOU ARE STRIP-MINED SO YOU CAN BE...
...A GOOD LITTLE SLAVE.
WE'LL DO RIGHT BY THESE PEOPLE, NATASHA. SOMEHOW.
WE JUST NEED TO BE SMART ABOUT IT. WE CAN'T MAKE AN EMOTIONAL--
VRRRRRRRRMMMMMMMMMMMM
THAT...
...DOESN'T SOUND GOOD.

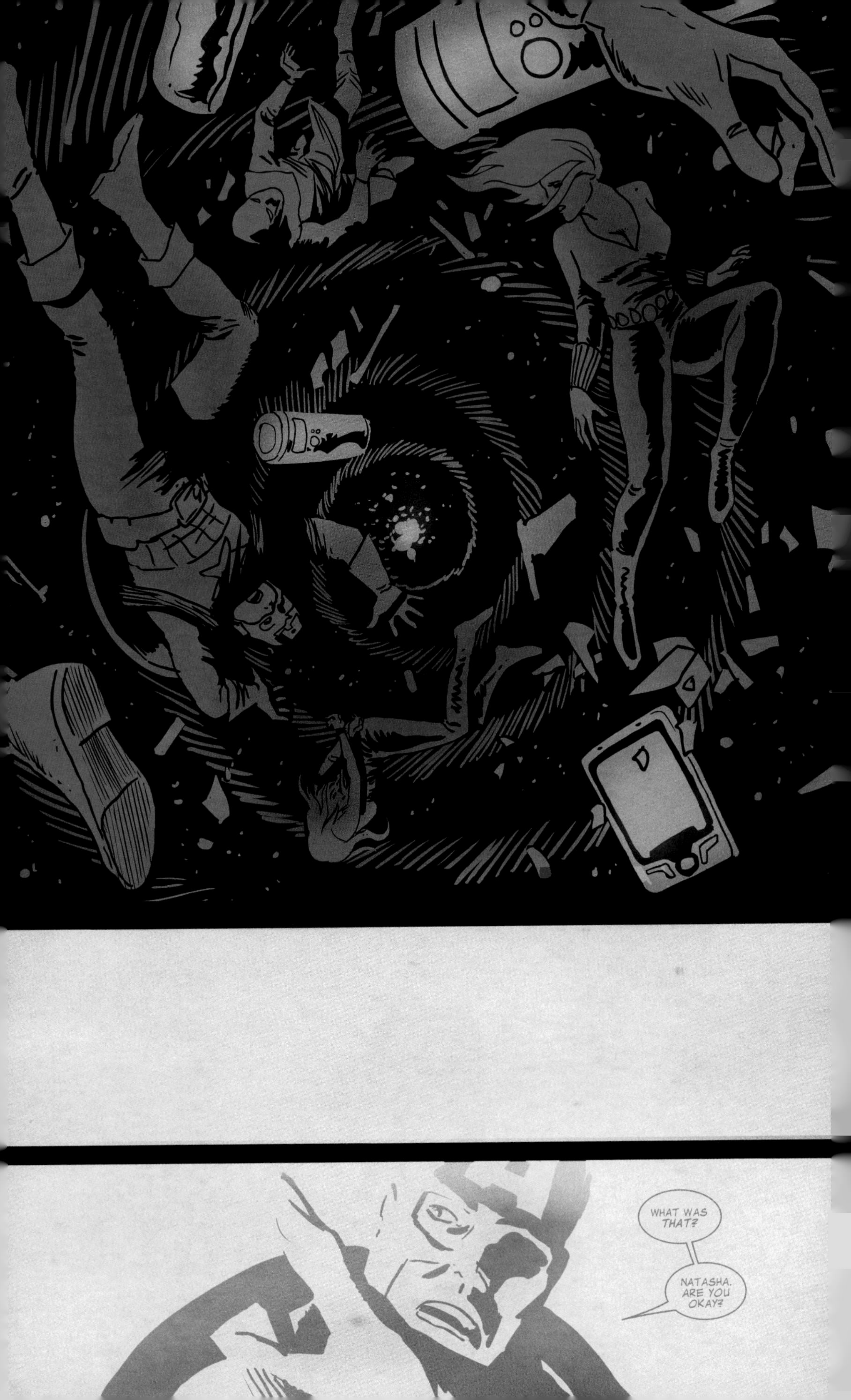
WHAT WAS *THAT?*
NATASHA. ARE YOU *OKAY?*

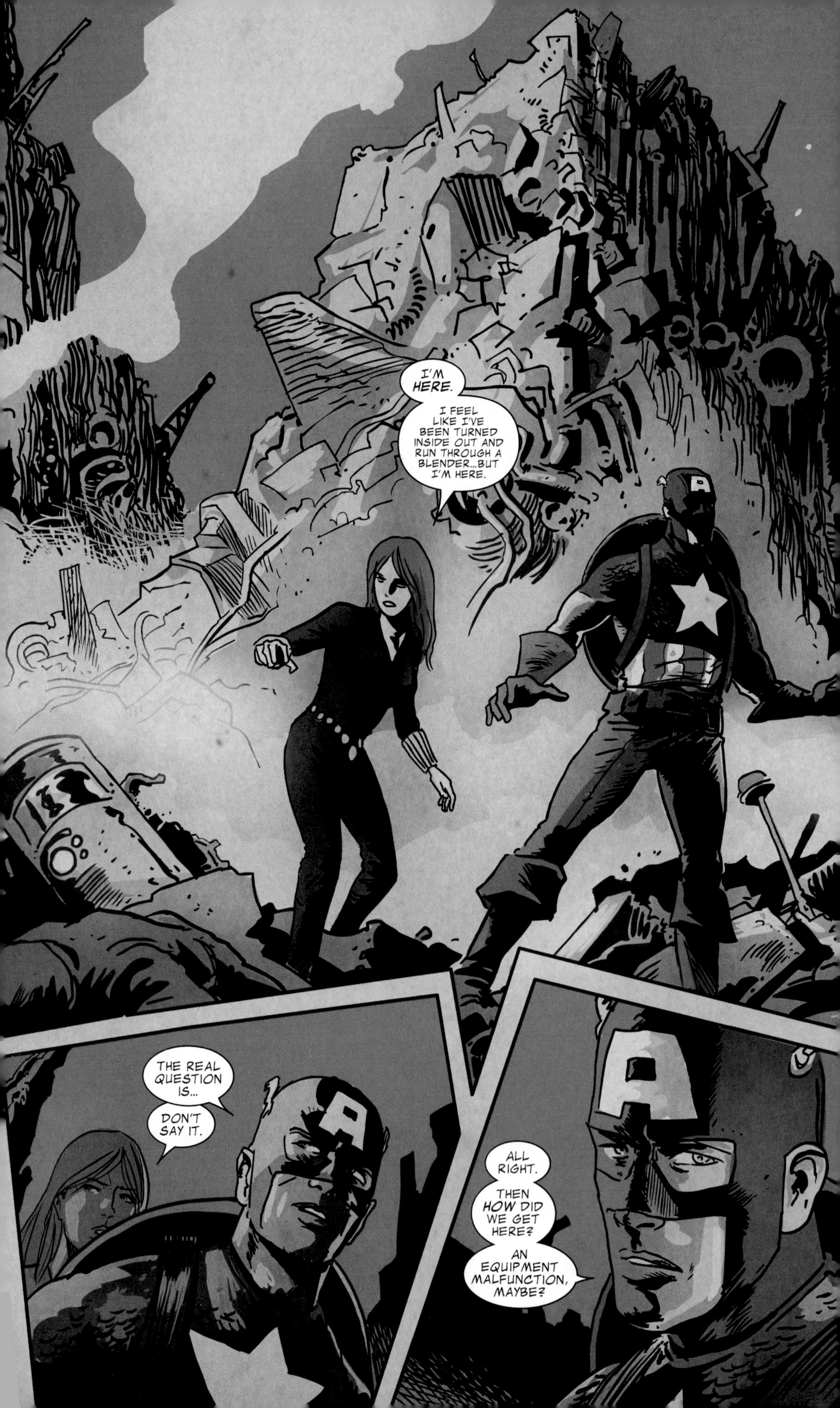
I'M HERE.
I FEEL LIKE I'VE BEEN TURNED INSIDE OUT AND RUN THROUGH A BLENDER...BUT I'M HERE.
THE REAL QUESTION IS...
DON'T SAY IT.
ALL RIGHT.
THEN HOW DID WE GET HERE?
AN EQUIPMENT MALFUNCTION, MAYBE?

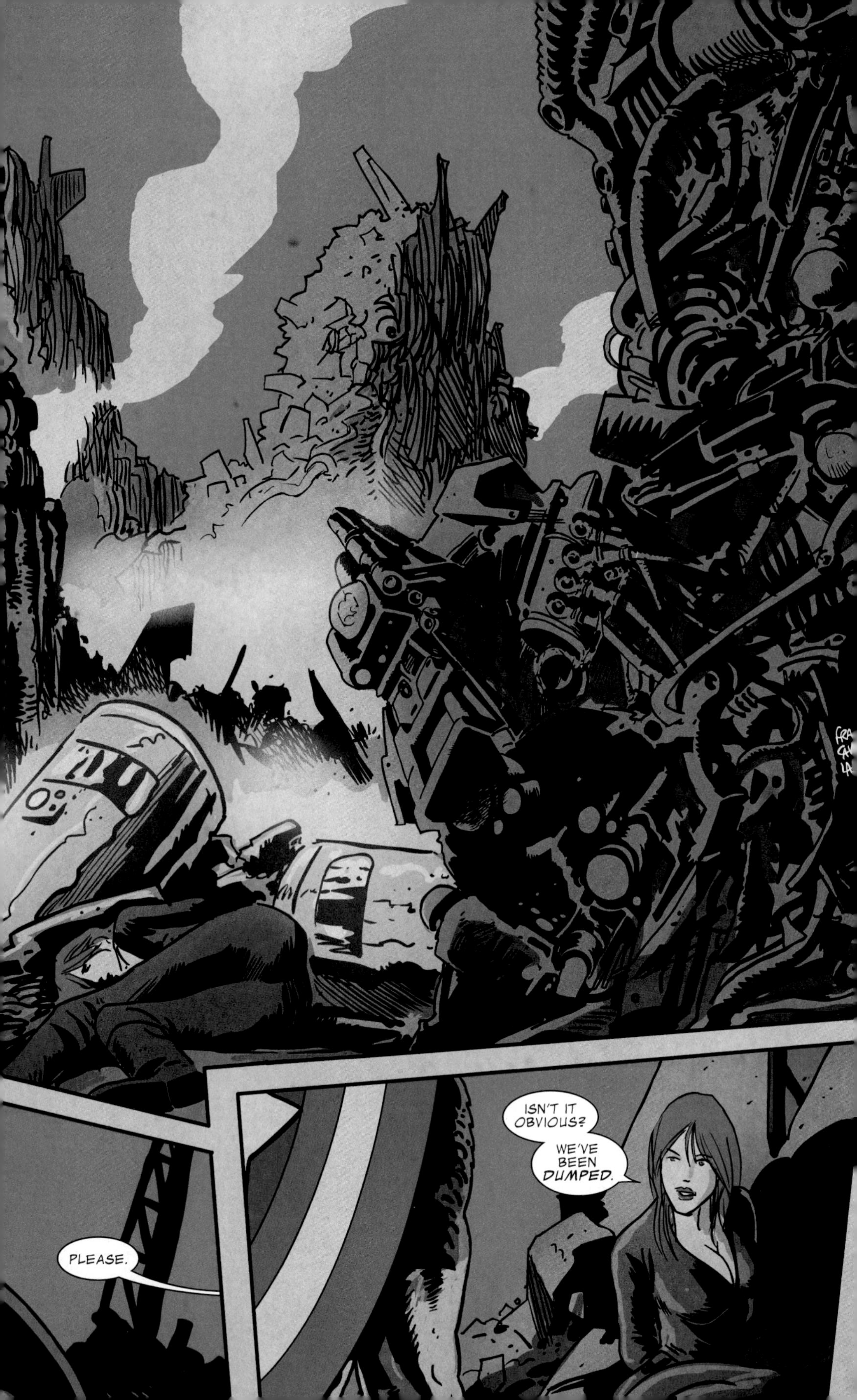
PLEASE.
ISN'T IT OBVIOUS?
WE'VE BEEN DUMPED.

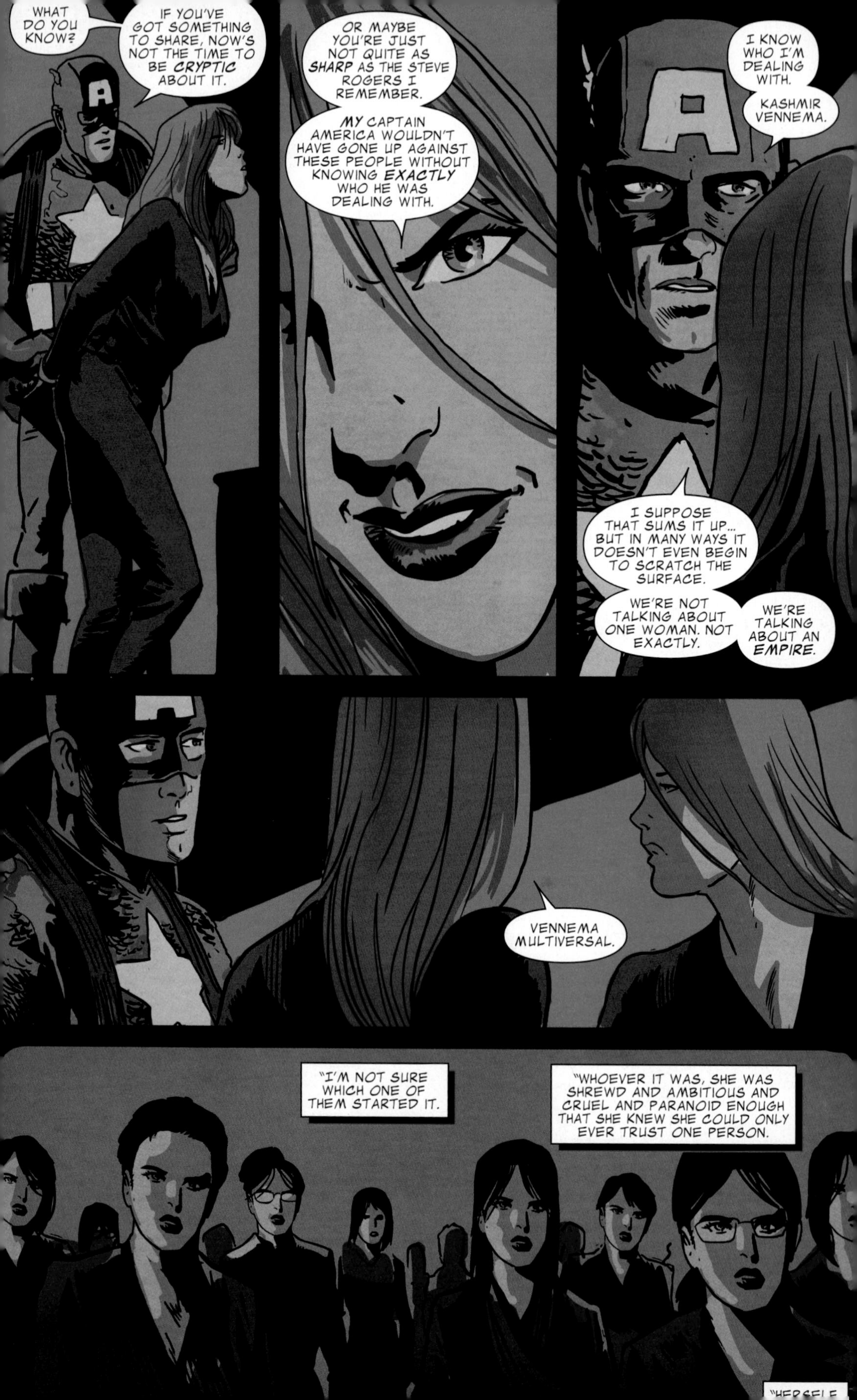
WHAT DO YOU KNOW?
IF YOU'VE GOT SOMETHING TO SHARE, NOW'S NOT THE TIME TO BE *CRYPTIC* ABOUT IT.
OR MAYBE YOU'RE JUST NOT QUITE AS *SHARP* AS THE STEVE ROGERS I REMEMBER.
MY CAPTAIN AMERICA WOULDN'T HAVE GONE UP AGAINST THESE PEOPLE WITHOUT KNOWING *EXACTLY* WHO HE WAS DEALING WITH.
I KNOW WHO I'M DEALING WITH.
KASHMIR VENNEMA.
I SUPPOSE THAT SUMS IT UP... BUT IN MANY WAYS IT DOESN'T EVEN BEGIN TO SCRATCH THE SURFACE.
WE'RE NOT TALKING ABOUT ONE WOMAN. NOT EXACTLY.
WE'RE TALKING ABOUT AN *EMPIRE*.
VENNEMA MULTIVERSAL.
"I'M NOT SURE WHICH ONE OF THEM STARTED IT.
"WHOEVER IT WAS, SHE WAS SHREWD AND AMBITIOUS AND CRUEL AND PARANOID ENOUGH THAT SHE KNEW SHE COULD ONLY EVER TRUST ONE PERSON.

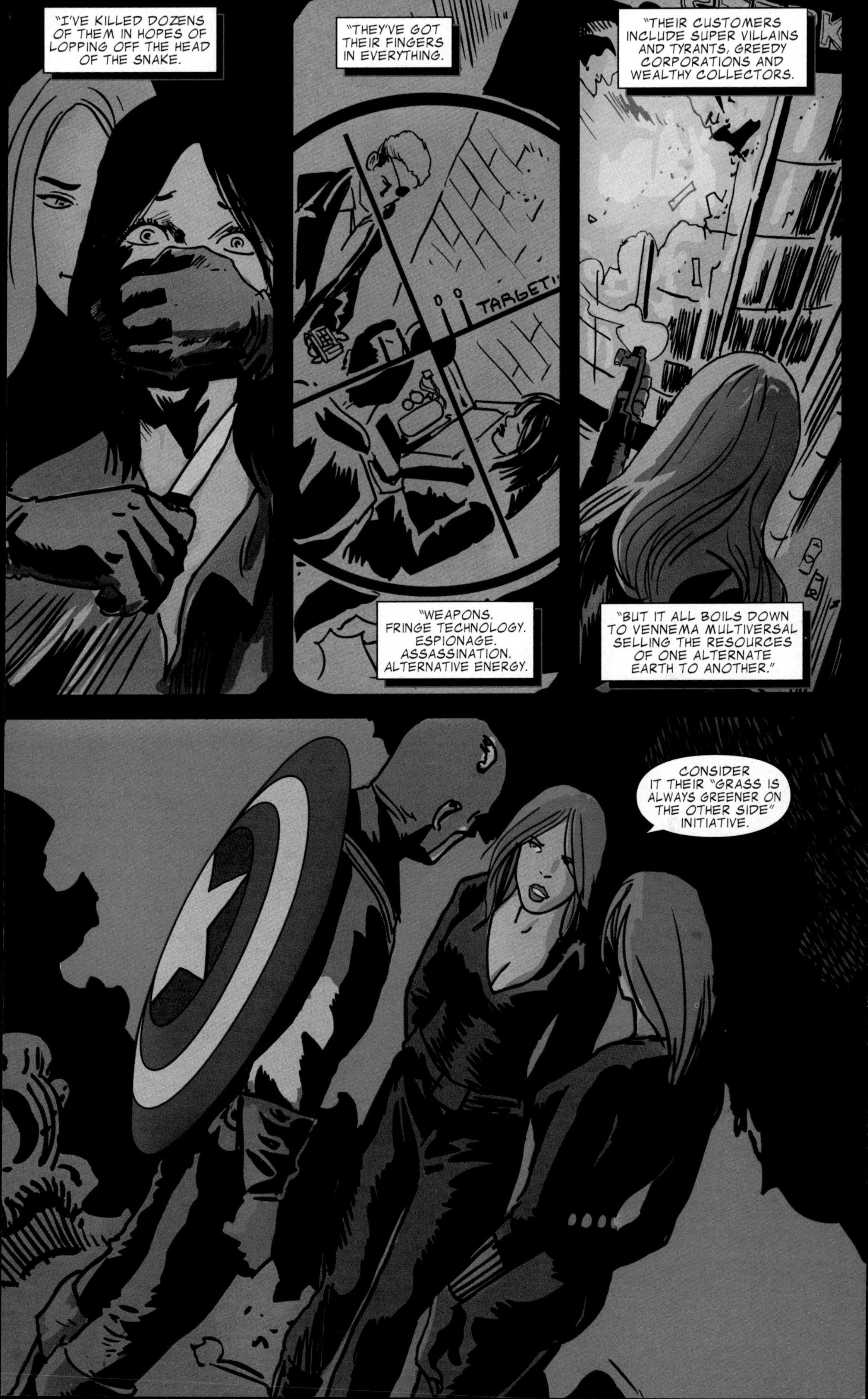
"I'VE KILLED DOZENS OF THEM IN HOPES OF LOPPING OFF THE HEAD OF THE SNAKE.
"THEY'VE GOT THEIR FINGERS IN EVERYTHING.
TARGET
"WEAPONS. FRINGE TECHNOLOGY. ESPIONAGE. ASSASSINATION. ALTERNATIVE ENERGY.
"THEIR CUSTOMERS INCLUDE SUPER VILLAINS AND TYRANTS, GREEDY CORPORATIONS AND WEALTHY COLLECTORS.
"BUT IT ALL BOILS DOWN TO VENNEMA MULTIVERSAL SELLING THE RESOURCES OF ONE ALTERNATE EARTH TO ANOTHER."
CONSIDER IT THEIR "GRASS IS ALWAYS GREENER ON THE OTHER SIDE" INITIATIVE.

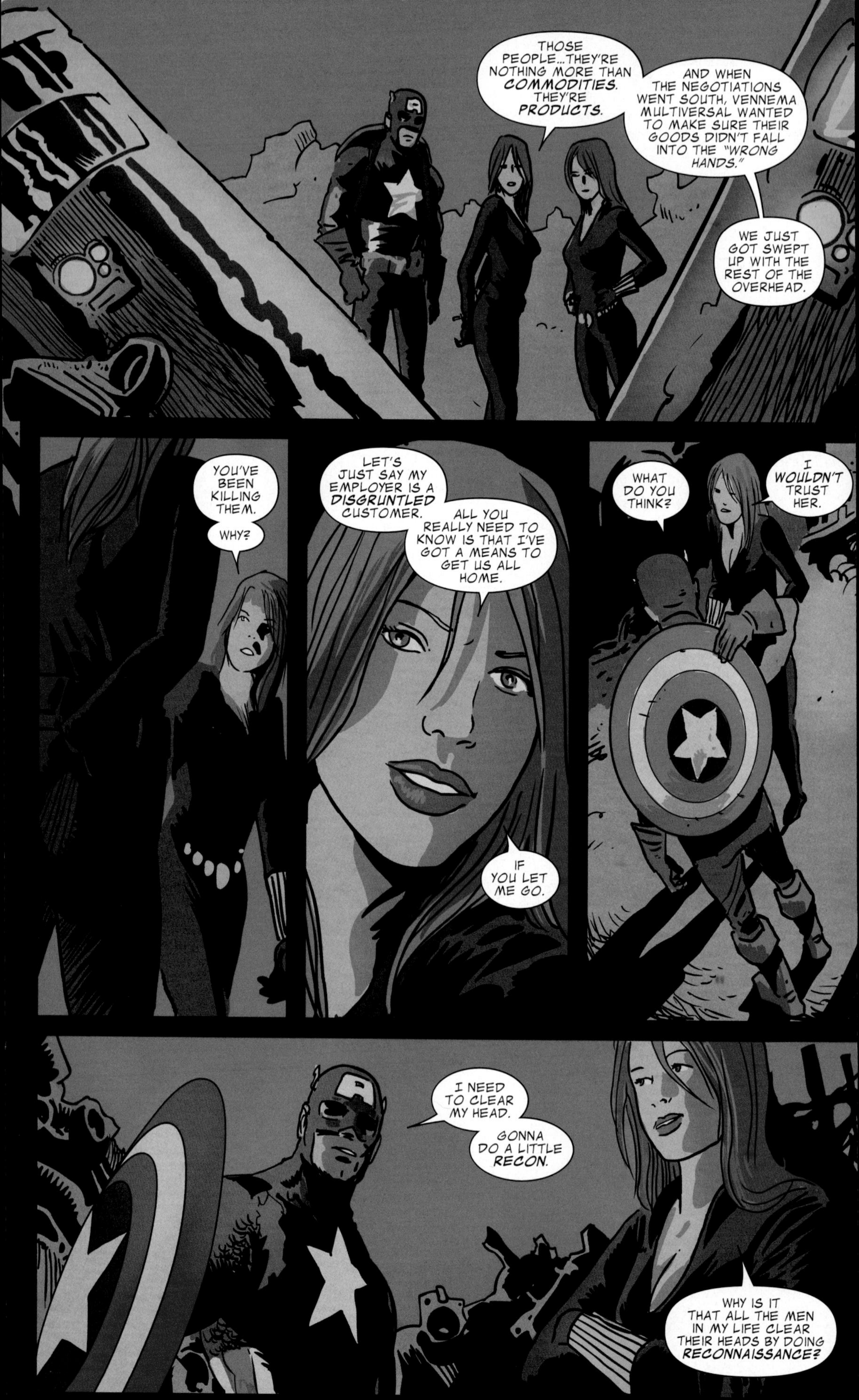
THOSE PEOPLE...THEY'RE NOTHING MORE THAN COMMODITIES. THEY'RE PRODUCTS.
AND WHEN THE NEGOTIATIONS WENT SOUTH, VENNEMA MULTIVERSAL WANTED TO MAKE SURE THEIR GOODS DIDN'T FALL INTO THE "WRONG HANDS."
WE JUST GOT SWEPT UP WITH THE REST OF THE OVERHEAD.
YOU'VE BEEN KILLING THEM.
WHY?
LET'S JUST SAY MY EMPLOYER IS A DISGRUNTLED CUSTOMER.
ALL YOU REALLY NEED TO KNOW IS THAT I'VE GOT A MEANS TO GET US ALL HOME.
IF YOU LET ME GO.
WHAT DO YOU THINK?
I WOULDN'T TRUST HER.
I NEED TO CLEAR MY HEAD.
GONNA DO A LITTLE RECON.
WHY IS IT THAT ALL THE MEN IN MY LIFE CLEAR THEIR HEADS BY DOING RECONNAISSANCE?

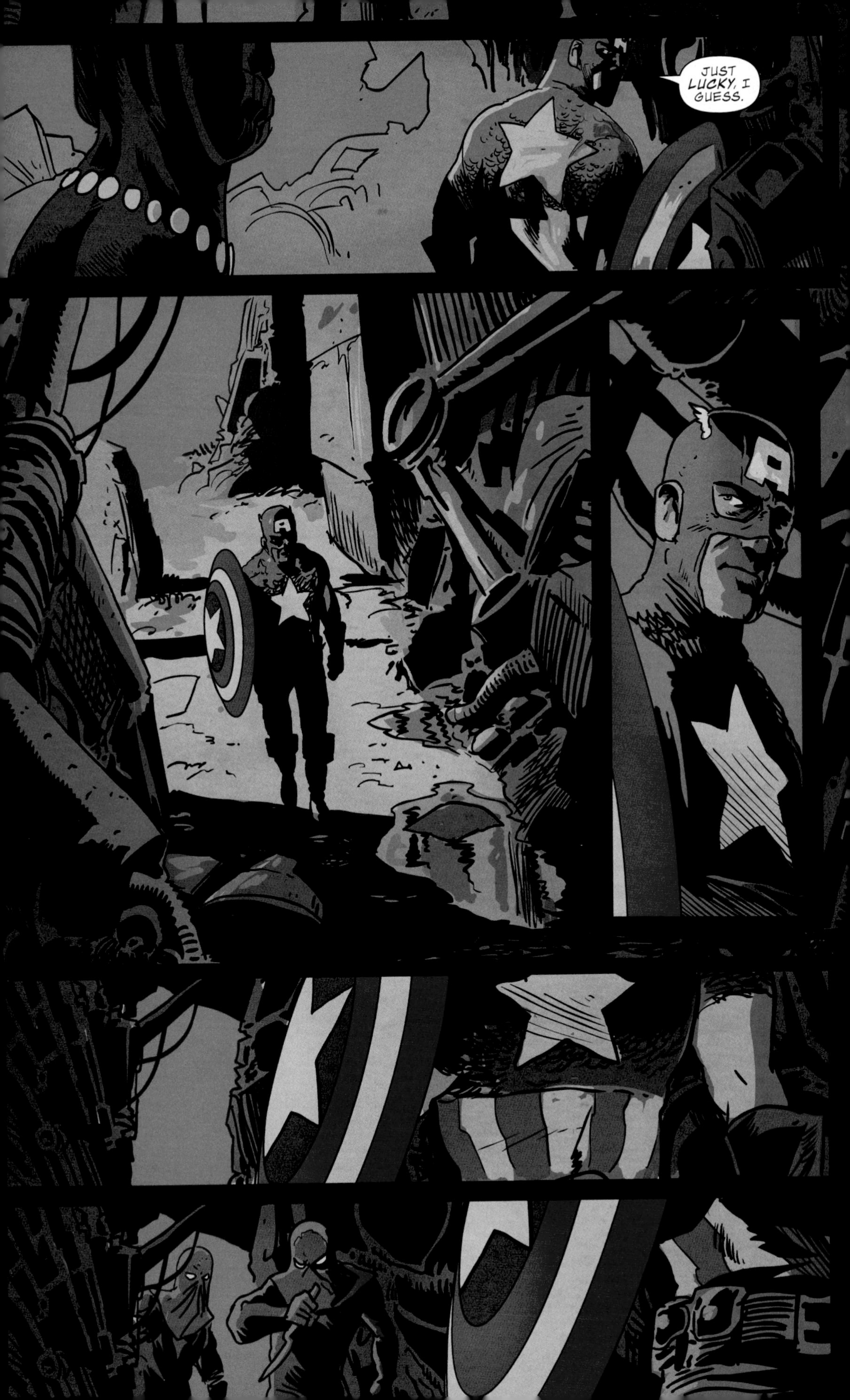
JUST LUCKY, I GUESS.

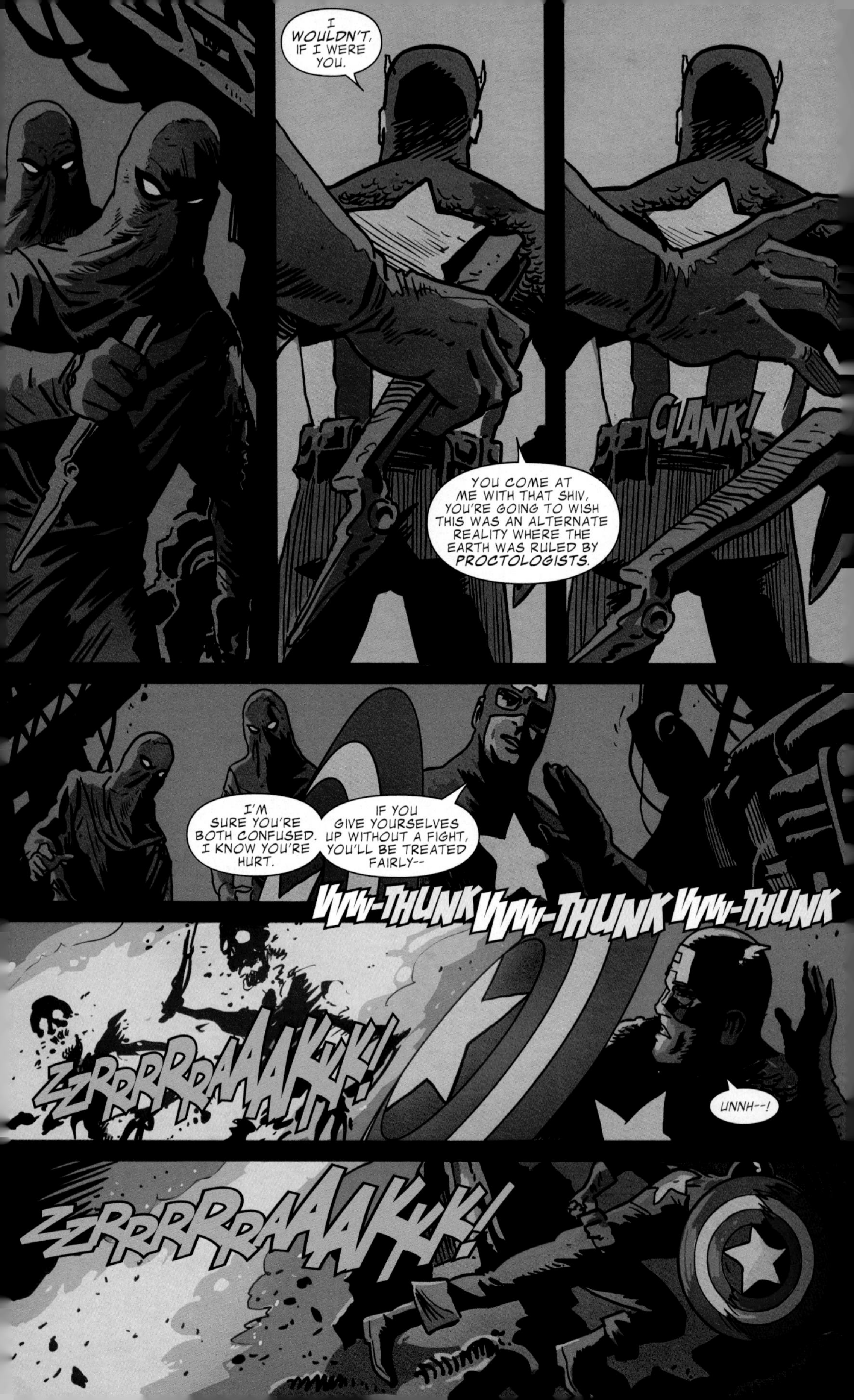
I WOULDN'T, IF I WERE YOU.
CLANK!
YOU COME AT ME WITH THAT SHIV, YOU'RE GOING TO WISH THIS WAS AN ALTERNATE REALITY WHERE THE EARTH WAS RULED BY PROCTOLOGISTS.
I'M SURE YOU'RE BOTH CONFUSED. I KNOW YOU'RE HURT.
IF YOU GIVE YOURSELVES UP WITHOUT A FIGHT, YOU'LL BE TREATED FAIRLY--
VVVV-THUNK VVVV-THUNK VVVV-THUNK
ZZRRRRRAAAKKK!
UNNH--!
ZZRRRRRRAAAKKK!

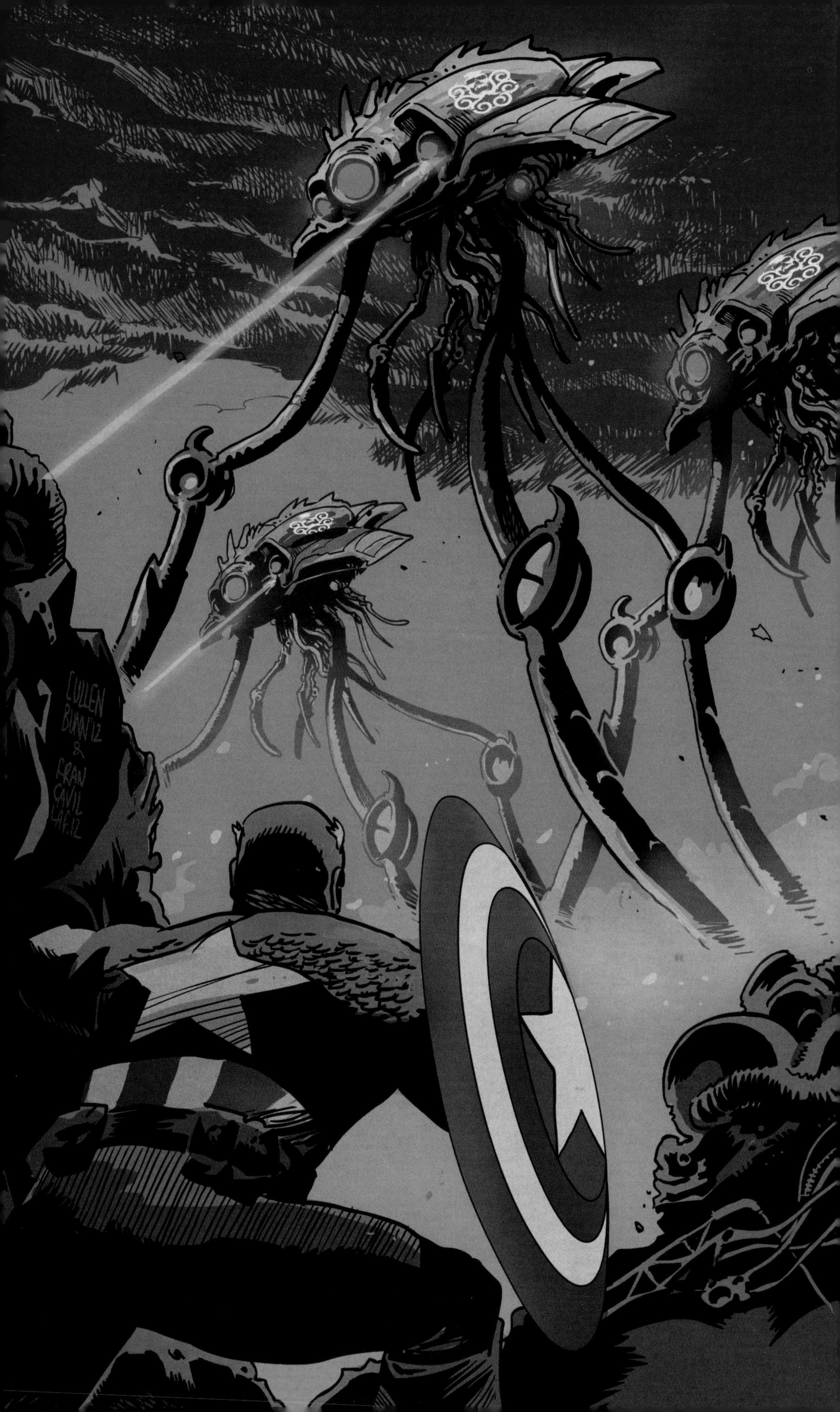
CULLEN BUNN '12
&
FRAN GAVIL LAF.12

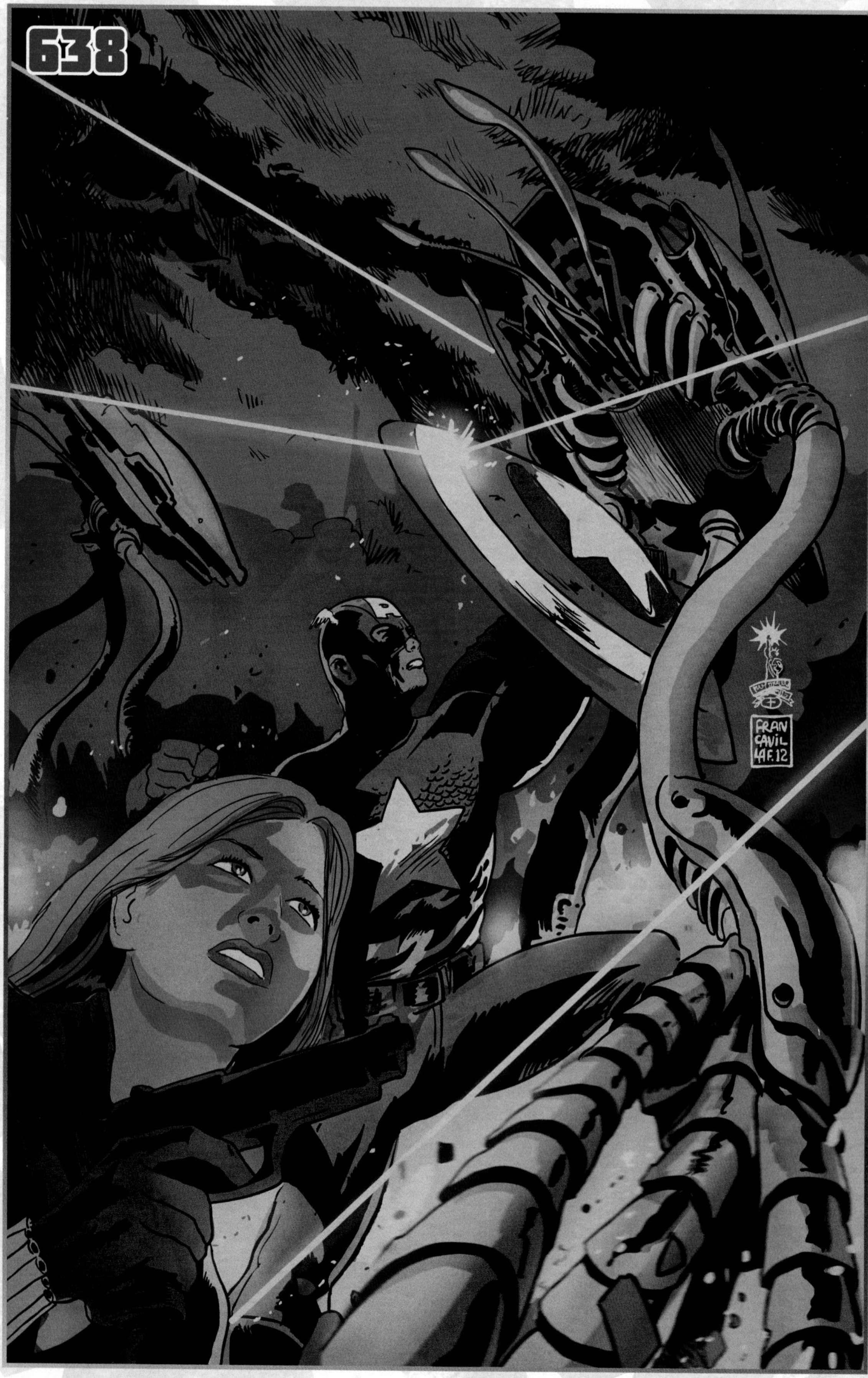
638
FRAN
CAVIL
14F.12

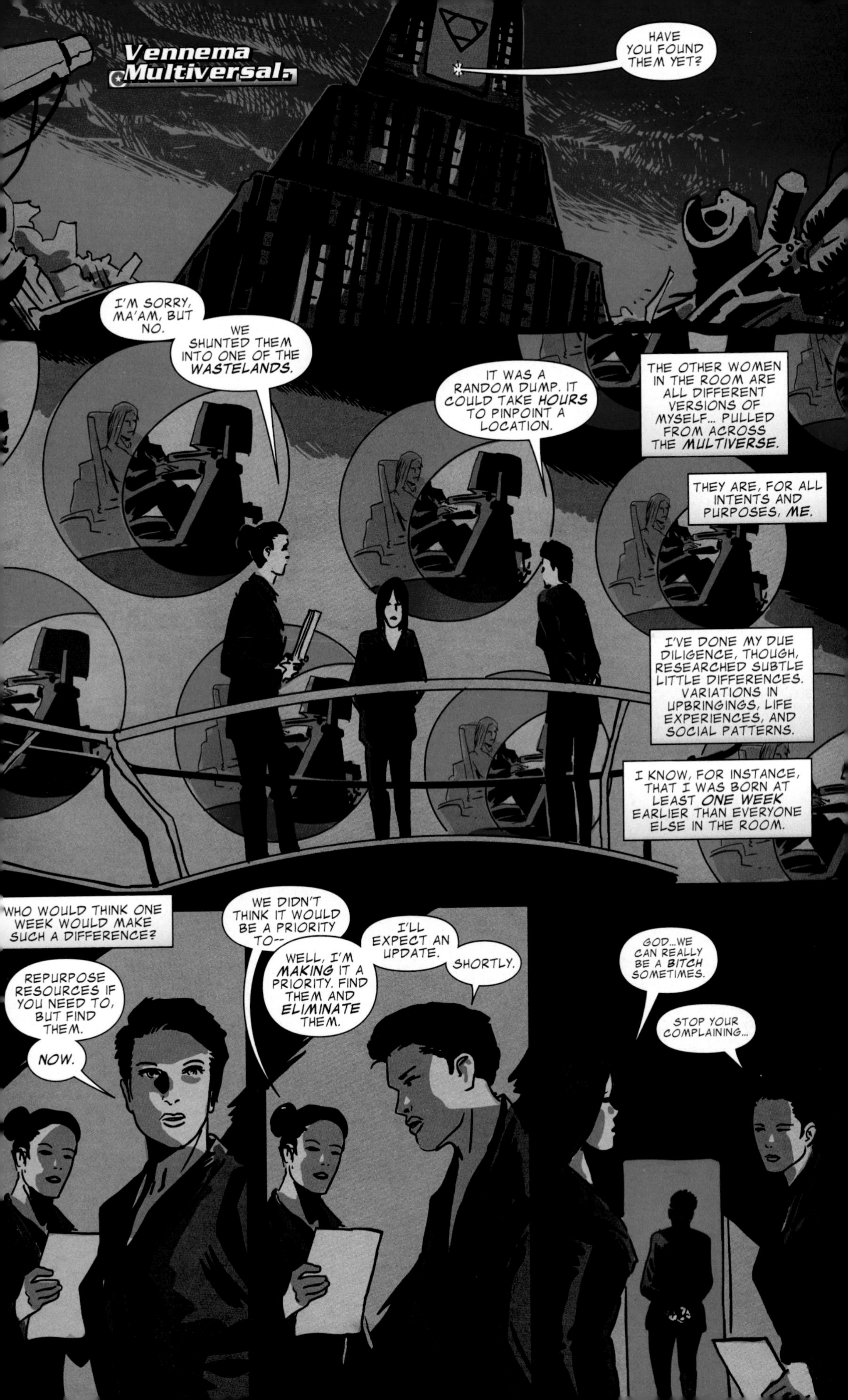
Vennema Multiversal.
HAVE YOU FOUND THEM YET?
I'M SORRY, MA'AM, BUT NO.
WE SHUNTED THEM INTO ONE OF THE WASTELANDS.
IT WAS A RANDOM DUMP. IT COULD TAKE HOURS TO PINPOINT A LOCATION.
THE OTHER WOMEN IN THE ROOM ARE ALL DIFFERENT VERSIONS OF MYSELF... PULLED FROM ACROSS THE MULTIVERSE.
THEY ARE, FOR ALL INTENTS AND PURPOSES, ME.
I'VE DONE MY DUE DILIGENCE, THOUGH, RESEARCHED SUBTLE LITTLE DIFFERENCES. VARIATIONS IN UPBRINGINGS, LIFE EXPERIENCES, AND SOCIAL PATTERNS.
I KNOW, FOR INSTANCE, THAT I WAS BORN AT LEAST ONE WEEK EARLIER THAN EVERYONE ELSE IN THE ROOM.
WHO WOULD THINK ONE WEEK WOULD MAKE SUCH A DIFFERENCE?
REPURPOSE RESOURCES IF YOU NEED TO, BUT FIND THEM.
NOW.
WE DIDN'T THINK IT WOULD BE A PRIORITY TO--
WELL, I'M MAKING IT A PRIORITY. FIND THEM AND ELIMINATE THEM.
I'LL EXPECT AN UPDATE.
SHORTLY.
GOD...WE CAN REALLY BE A BITCH SOMETIMES.
STOP YOUR COMPLAINING...

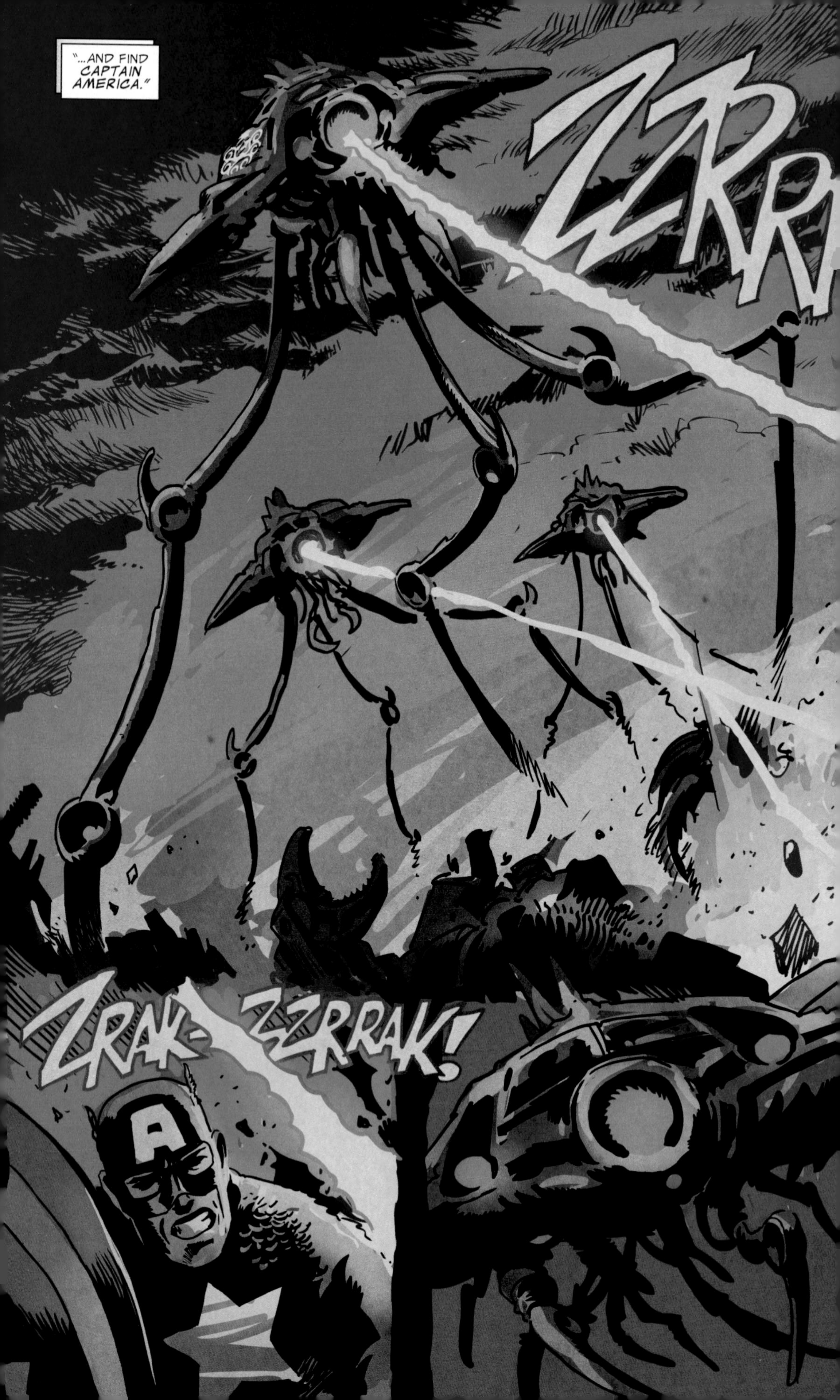

"...AND FIND CAPTAIN AMERICA."
ZZRR
ZRAK-
ZZRRAK!

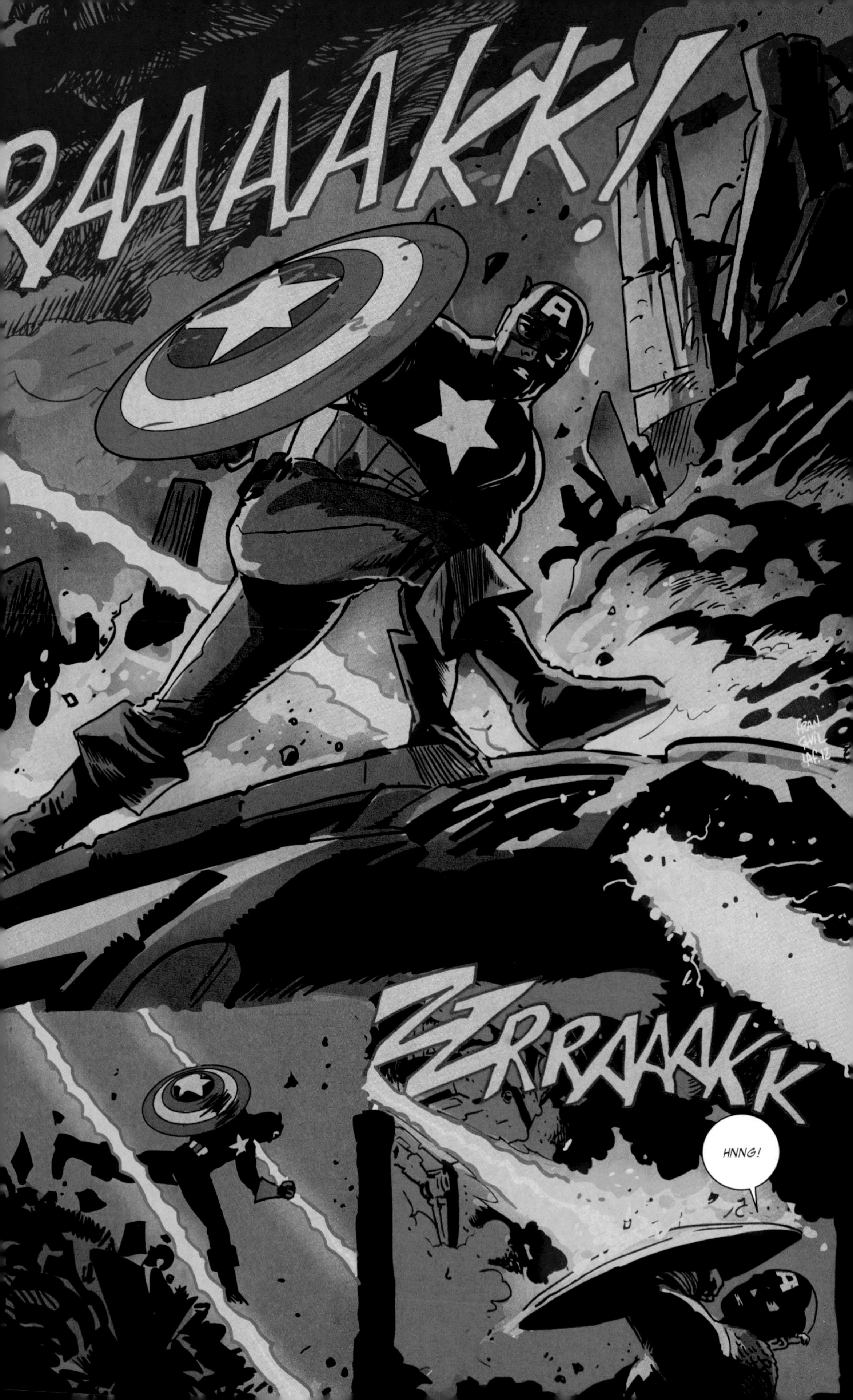
RAAAAKK!
ZZRRAAAKK
HNNG!

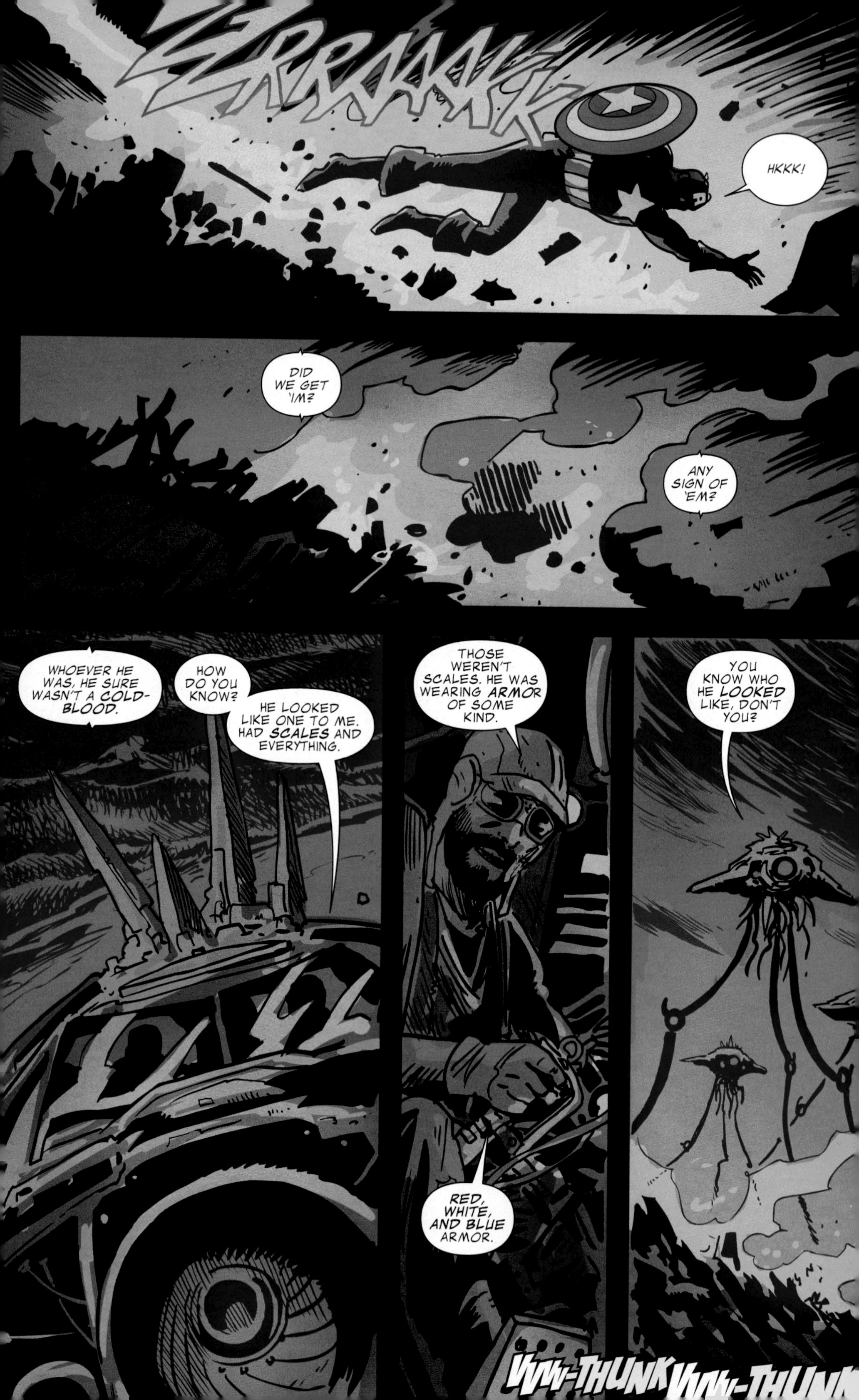
SKRRAAAAKK
HKKK!
DID WE GET 'IM?
ANY SIGN OF 'EM?
WHOEVER HE WAS, HE SURE WASN'T A COLD-BLOOD.
HOW DO YOU KNOW?
HE LOOKED LIKE ONE TO ME. HAD SCALES AND EVERYTHING.
THOSE WEREN'T SCALES. HE WAS WEARING ARMOR OF SOME KIND.
RED, WHITE, AND BLUE ARMOR.
YOU KNOW WHO HE LOOKED LIKE, DON'T YOU?
VVV-THUNK VVV-THUNK

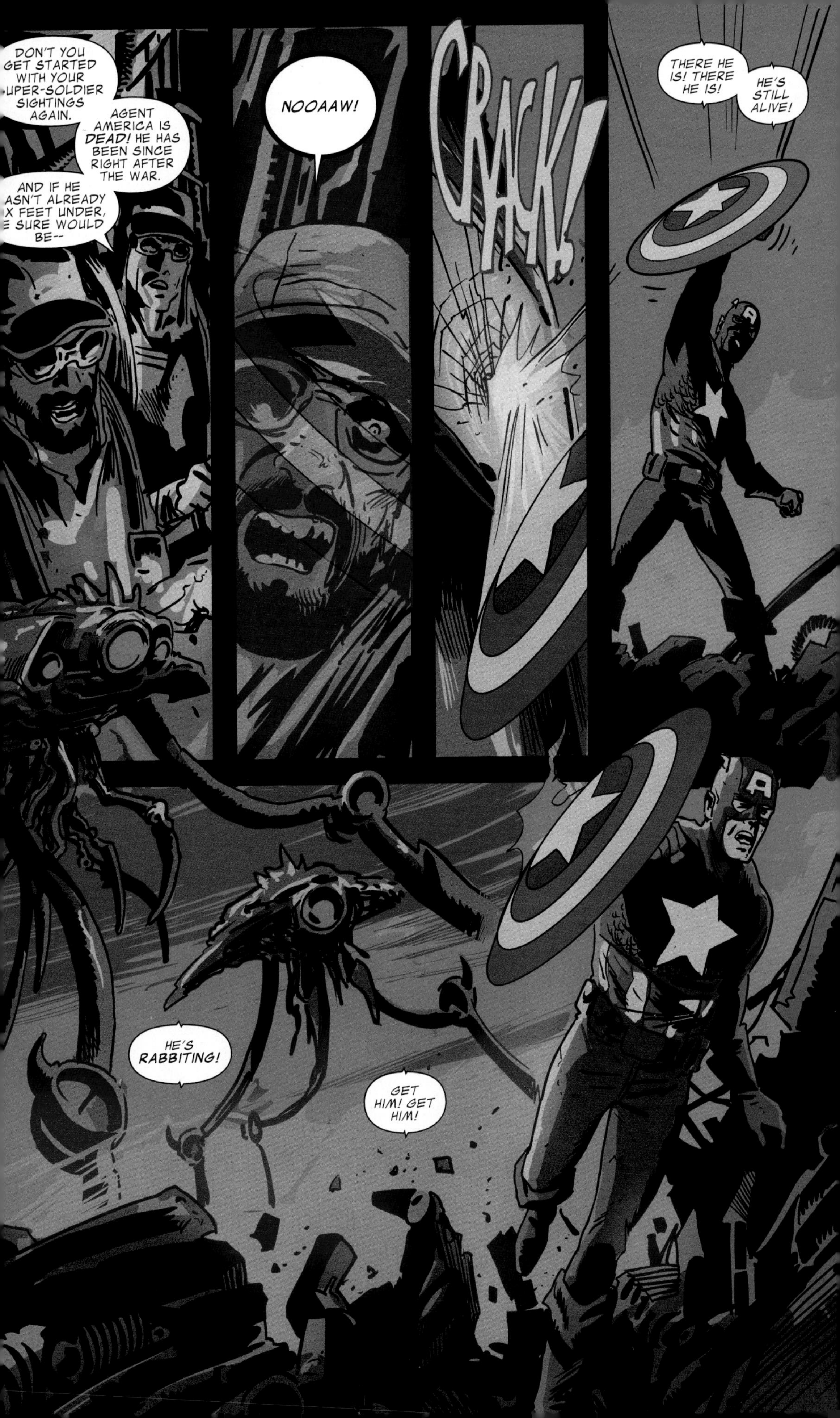
DON'T YOU GET STARTED WITH YOUR UPER-SOLDIER SIGHTINGS AGAIN.
AGENT AMERICA IS DEAD! HE HAS BEEN SINCE RIGHT AFTER THE WAR.
AND IF HE ASN'T ALREADY X FEET UNDER, E SURE WOULD BE--
NOOAAW!
CRACK!
THERE HE IS! THERE HE IS!
HE'S STILL ALIVE!
HE'S RABBITING!
GET HIM! GET HIM!

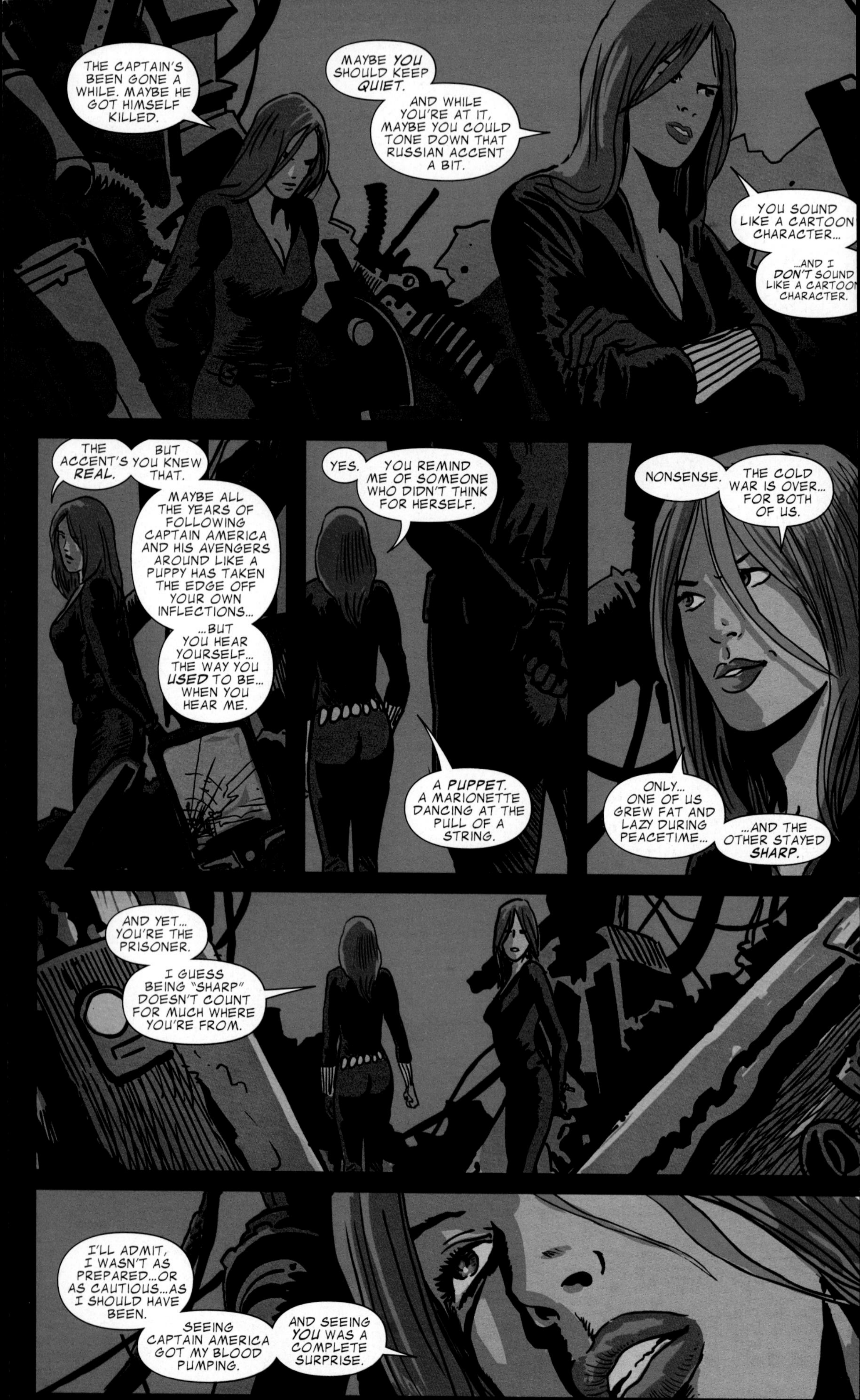
THE CAPTAIN'S BEEN GONE A WHILE. MAYBE HE GOT HIMSELF KILLED.
MAYBE YOU SHOULD KEEP QUIET.
AND WHILE YOU'RE AT IT, MAYBE YOU COULD TONE DOWN THAT RUSSIAN ACCENT A BIT.
YOU SOUND LIKE A CARTOON CHARACTER...
...AND I DON'T SOUND LIKE A CARTOON CHARACTER.
THE ACCENT'S REAL.
BUT YOU KNEW THAT.
MAYBE ALL THE YEARS OF FOLLOWING CAPTAIN AMERICA AND HIS AVENGERS AROUND LIKE A PUPPY HAS TAKEN THE EDGE OFF YOUR OWN INFLECTIONS...
...BUT YOU HEAR YOURSELF... THE WAY YOU USED TO BE... WHEN YOU HEAR ME.
YES.
YOU REMIND ME OF SOMEONE WHO DIDN'T THINK FOR HERSELF.
A PUPPET. A MARIONETTE DANCING AT THE PULL OF A STRING.
NONSENSE.
THE COLD WAR IS OVER... FOR BOTH OF US.
ONLY... ONE OF US GREW FAT AND LAZY DURING PEACETIME...
...AND THE OTHER STAYED SHARP.
AND YET... YOU'RE THE PRISONER.
I GUESS BEING "SHARP" DOESN'T COUNT FOR MUCH WHERE YOU'RE FROM.
I'LL ADMIT, I WASN'T AS PREPARED...OR AS CAUTIOUS...AS I SHOULD HAVE BEEN.
SEEING CAPTAIN AMERICA GOT MY BLOOD PUMPING.
AND SEEING YOU WAS A COMPLETE SURPRISE.

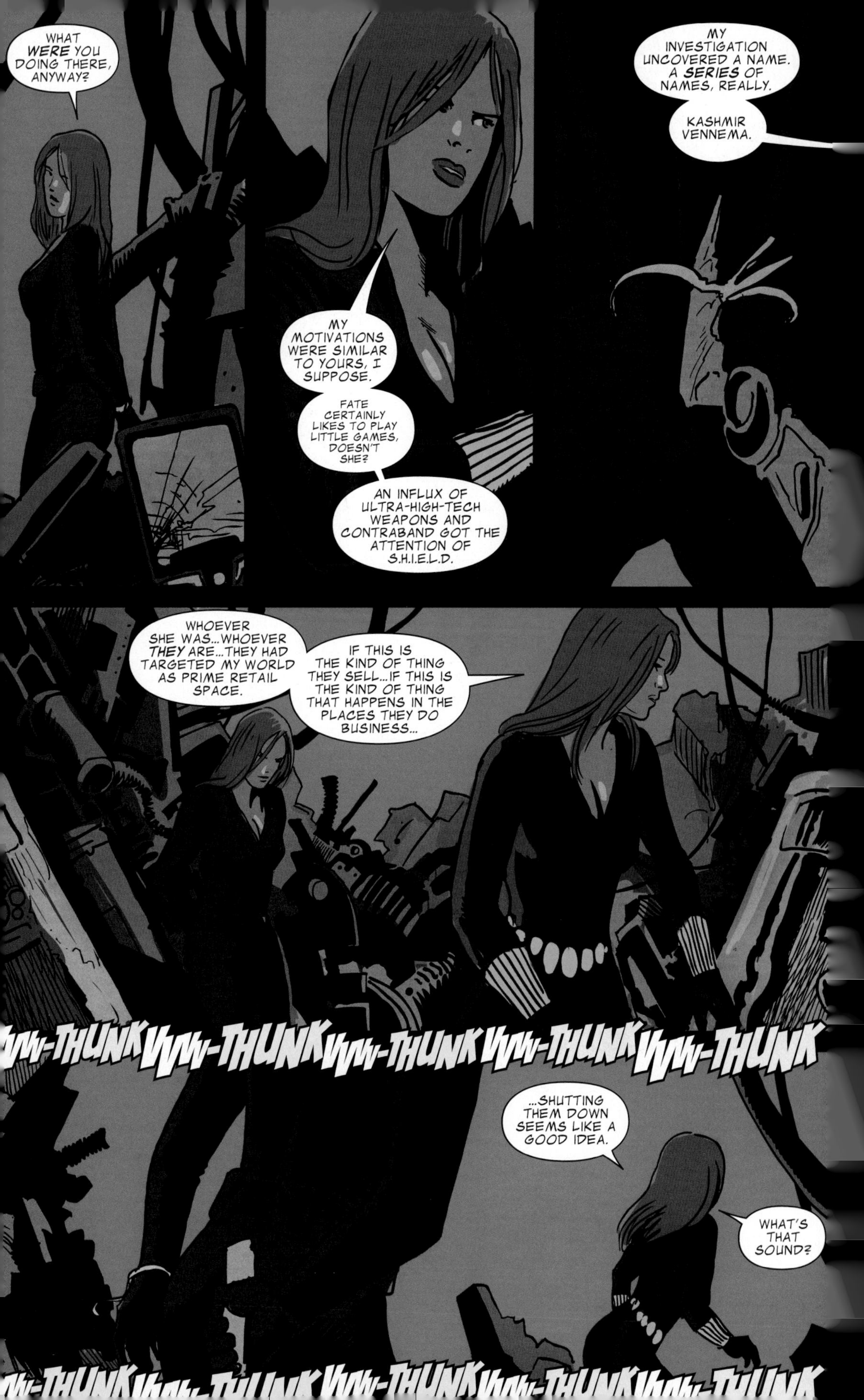
WHAT WERE YOU DOING THERE, ANYWAY?
MY MOTIVATIONS WERE SIMILAR TO YOURS, I SUPPOSE.
FATE CERTAINLY LIKES TO PLAY LITTLE GAMES, DOESN'T SHE?
AN INFLUX OF ULTRA-HIGH-TECH WEAPONS AND CONTRABAND GOT THE ATTENTION OF S.H.I.E.L.D.
MY INVESTIGATION UNCOVERED A NAME. A SERIES OF NAMES, REALLY.
KASHMIR VENNEMA.
WHOEVER SHE WAS...WHOEVER THEY ARE...THEY HAD TARGETED MY WORLD AS PRIME RETAIL SPACE.
IF THIS IS THE KIND OF THING THEY SELL...IF THIS IS THE KIND OF THING THAT HAPPENS IN THE PLACES THEY DO BUSINESS...
VVV-THUNK VVV-THUNK VVV-THUNK VVV-THUNK VVV-THUNK
...SHUTTING THEM DOWN SEEMS LIKE A GOOD IDEA.
WHAT'S THAT SOUND?

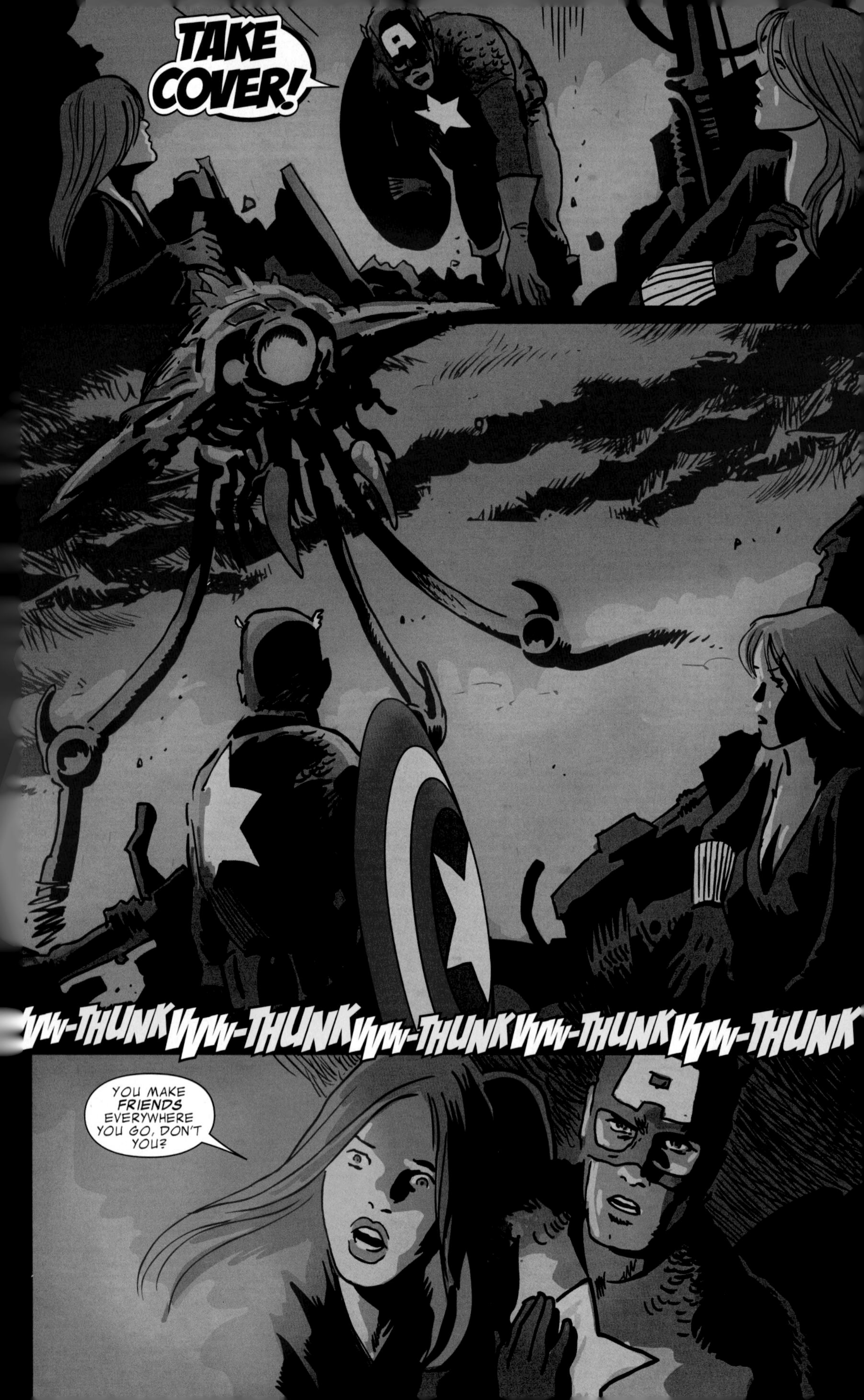
TAKE COVER!
VVV-THUNK VVV-THUNK VVV-THUNK VVV-THUNK VVV-THUNK
YOU MAKE FRIENDS EVERYWHERE YOU GO, DON'T YOU?

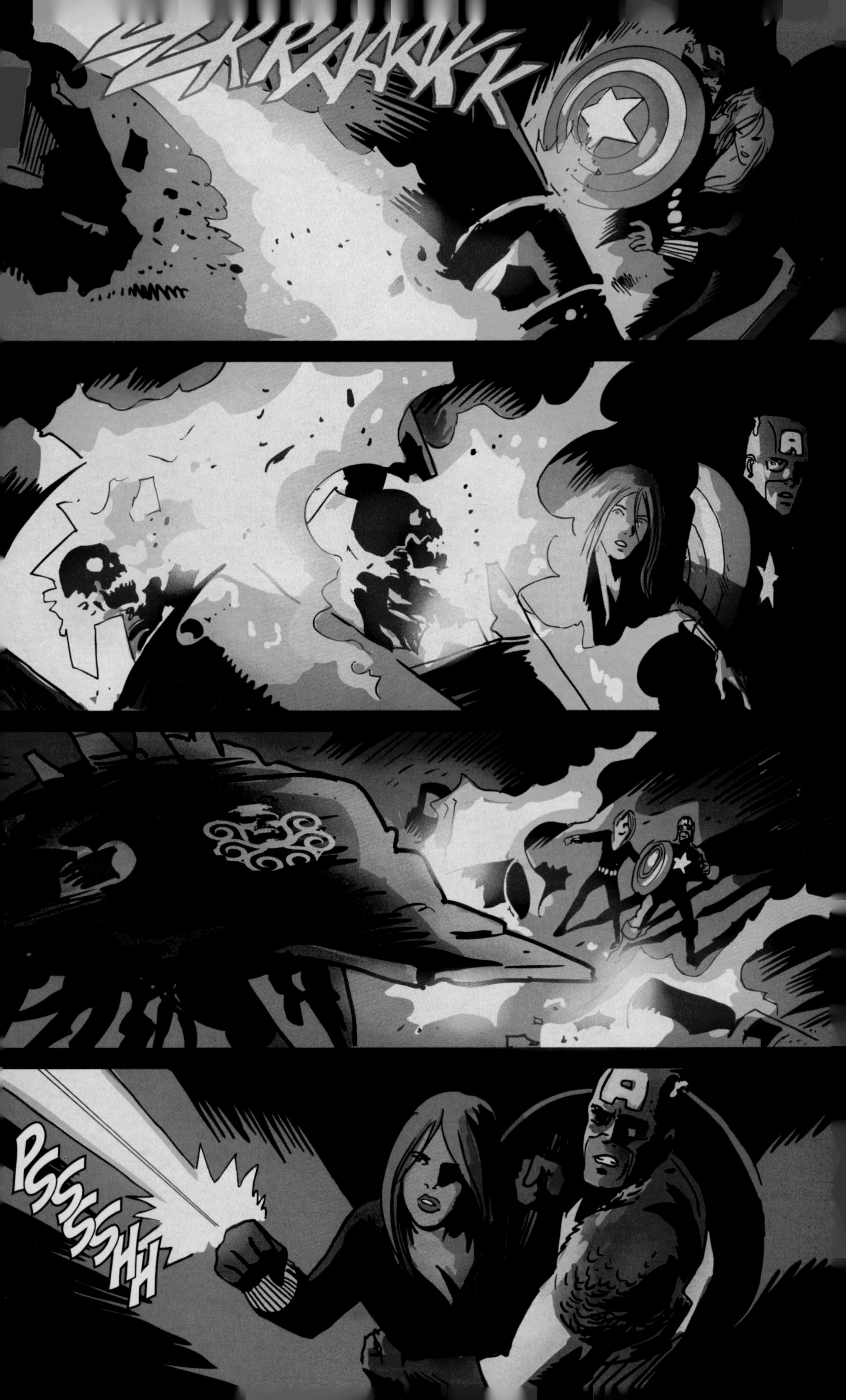
SKRAKKKK
PSSSSHH

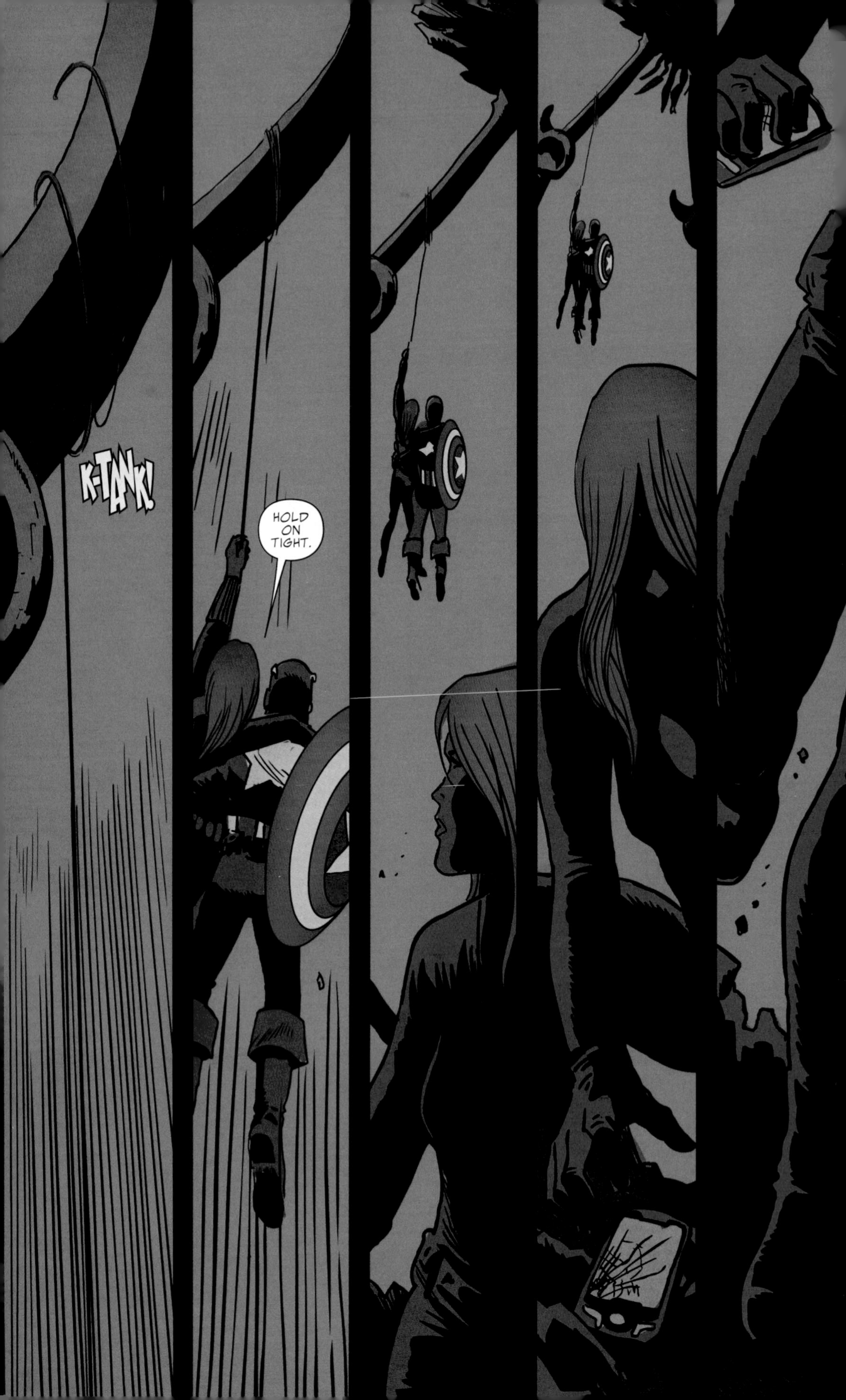
K-TANK!
HOLD ON TIGHT.

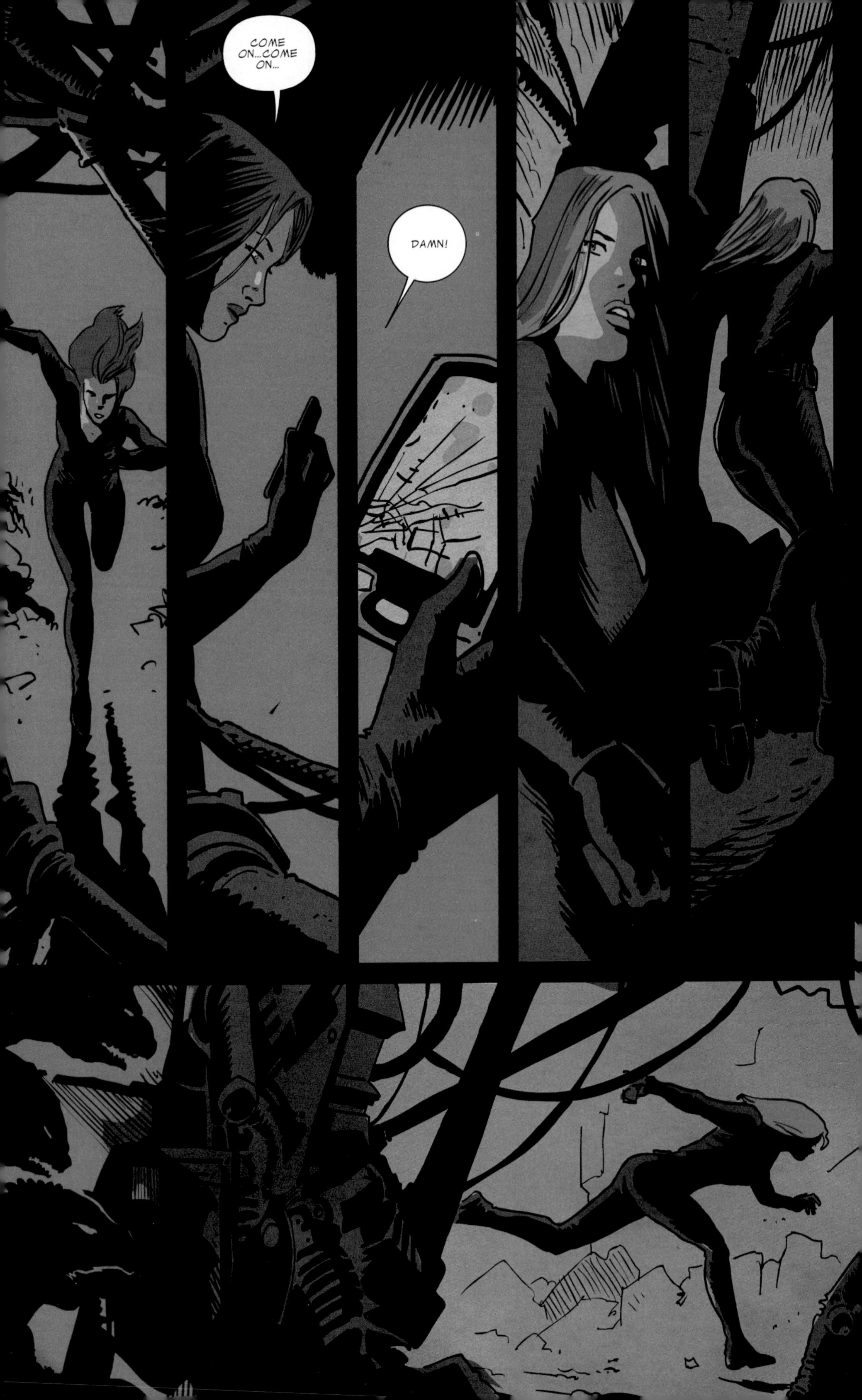
COME ON...COME ON...
DAMN!

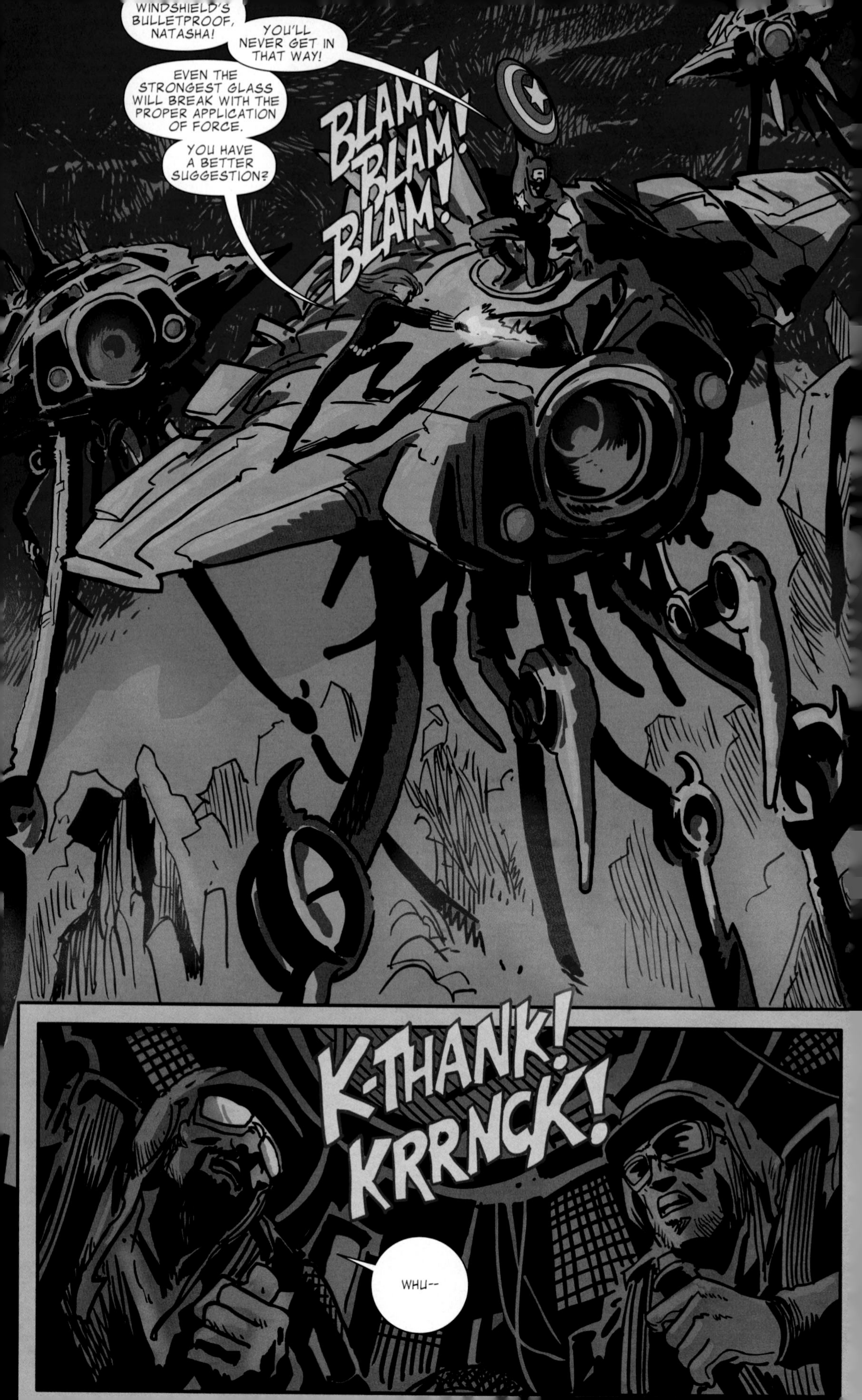
WINDSHIELD'S BULLETPROOF, NATASHA!
YOU'LL NEVER GET IN THAT WAY!
EVEN THE STRONGEST GLASS WILL BREAK WITH THE PROPER APPLICATION OF FORCE.
YOU HAVE A BETTER SUGGESTION?
BLAM! BLAM! BLAM!
K-THANK! KRRNCK!
WHU--

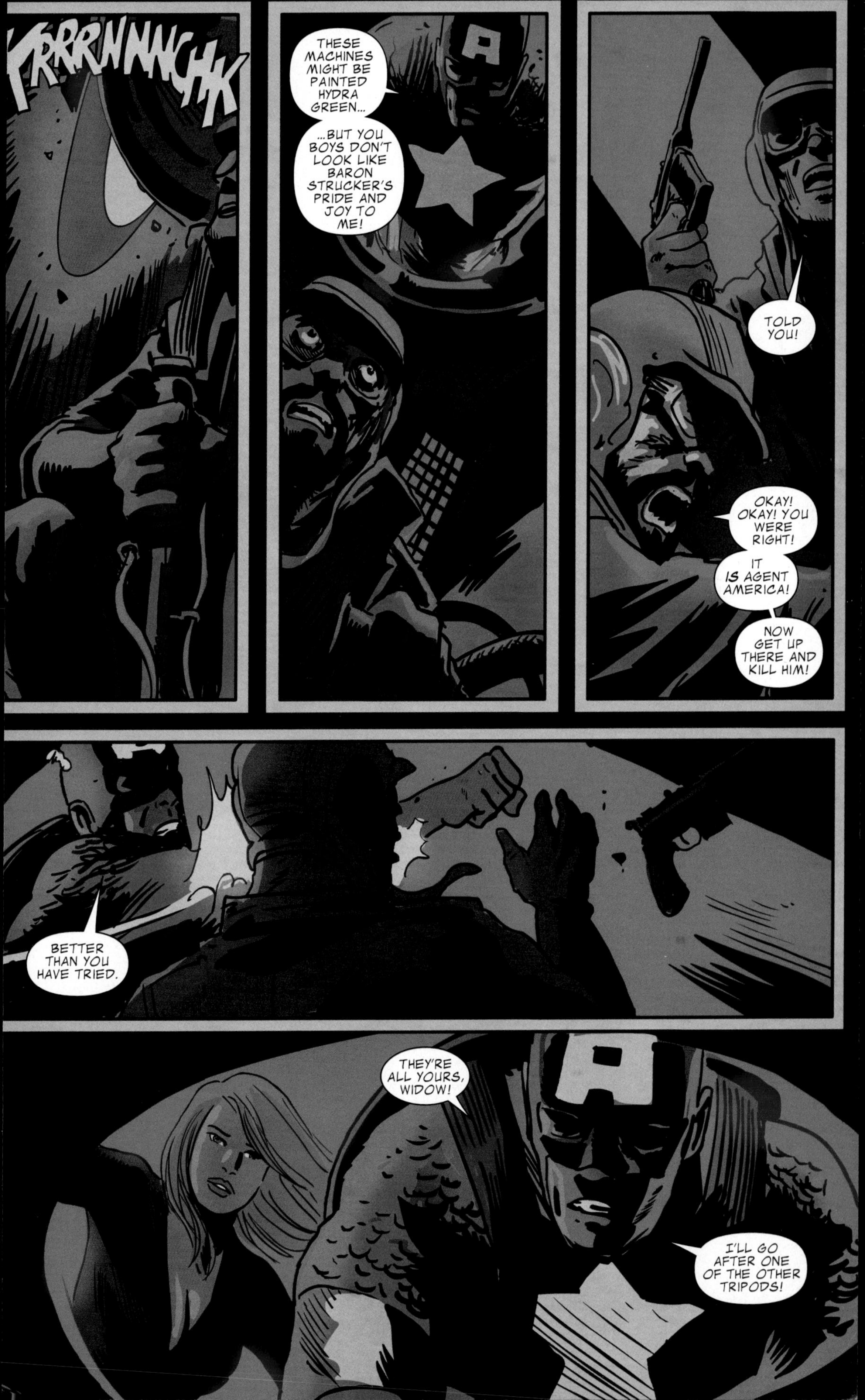
KRRRNNNCHK
THESE MACHINES MIGHT BE PAINTED HYDRA GREEN...
...BUT YOU BOYS DON'T LOOK LIKE BARON STRUCKER'S PRIDE AND JOY TO ME!
TOLD YOU!
OKAY! OKAY! YOU WERE RIGHT!
IT **IS** AGENT AMERICA!
NOW GET UP THERE AND KILL HIM!
BETTER THAN YOU HAVE TRIED.
THEY'RE ALL YOURS, WIDOW!
I'LL GO AFTER ONE OF THE OTHER TRIPODS!

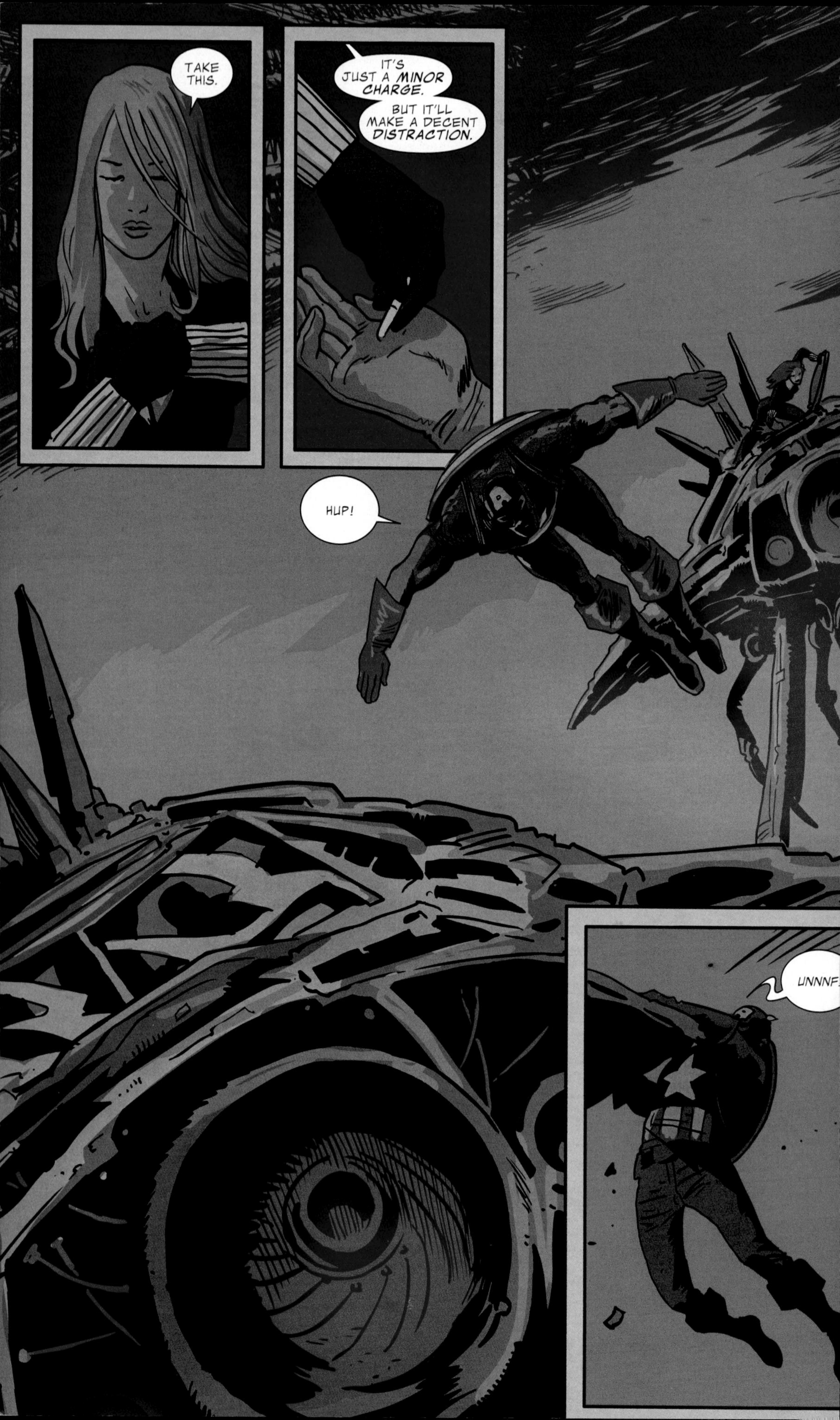
TAKE THIS.
IT'S JUST A MINOR CHARGE.
BUT IT'LL MAKE A DECENT DISTRACTION.
HUP!
UNNNF!

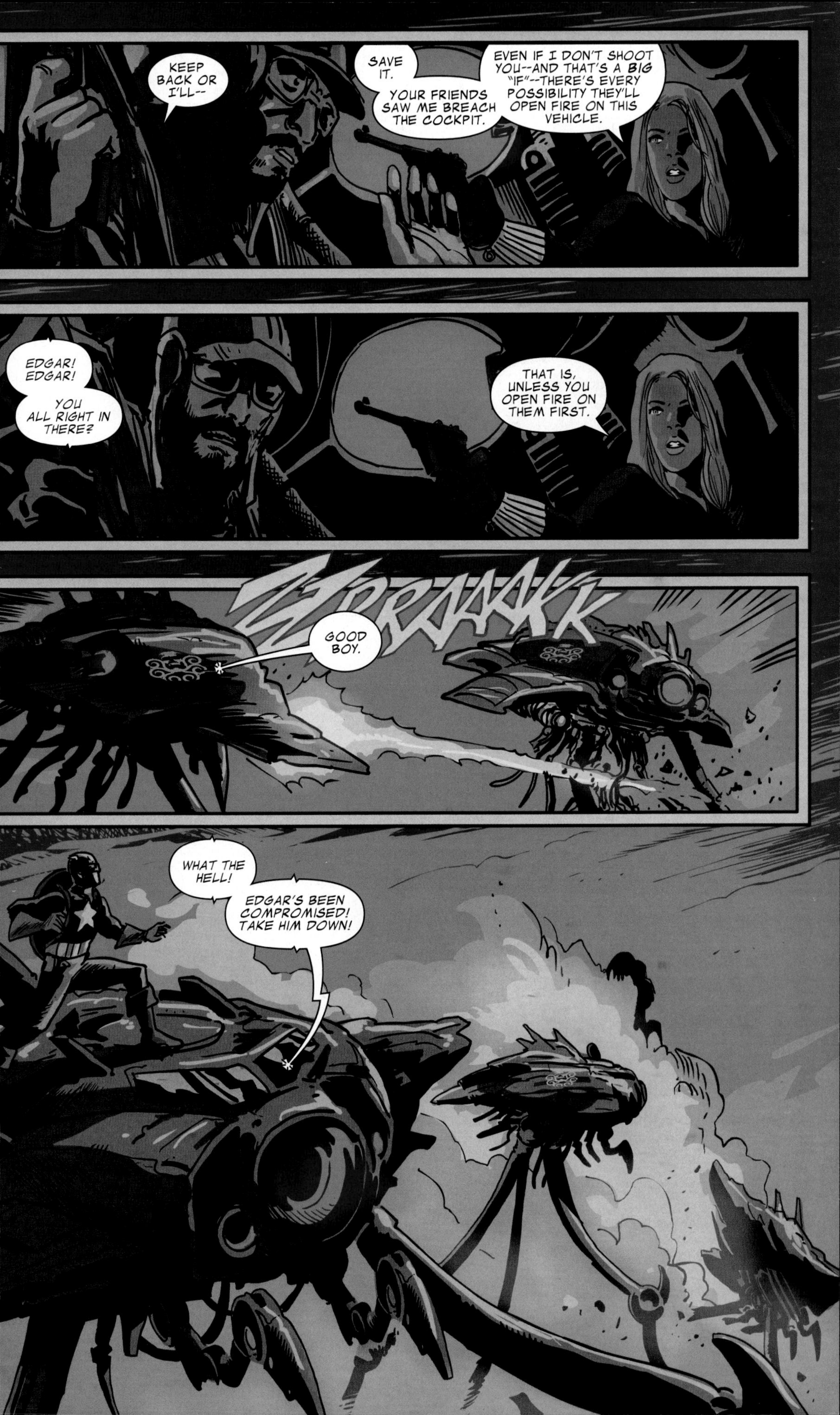
KEEP BACK OR I'LL--
SAVE IT.
YOUR FRIENDS SAW ME BREACH THE COCKPIT.
EVEN IF I DON'T SHOOT YOU--AND THAT'S A BIG "IF"--THERE'S EVERY POSSIBILITY THEY'LL OPEN FIRE ON THIS VEHICLE.
EDGAR! EDGAR!
YOU ALL RIGHT IN THERE?
THAT IS, UNLESS YOU OPEN FIRE ON THEM FIRST.
ZZRRAAKKK
GOOD BOY.
WHAT THE HELL!
EDGAR'S BEEN COMPROMISED! TAKE HIM DOWN!

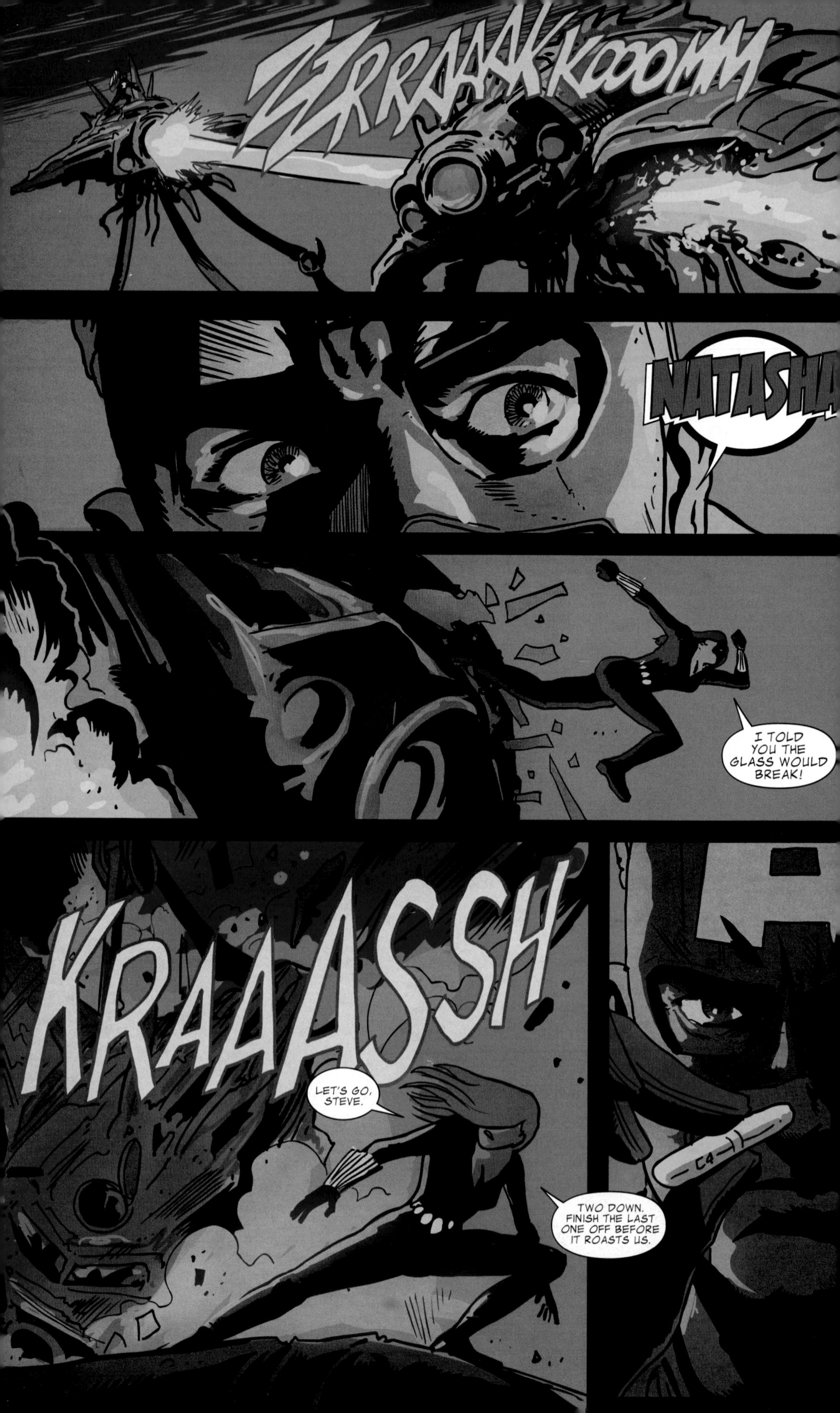

ZZRRAAAK KOOOMM
NATASHA
I TOLD YOU THE GLASS WOULD BREAK!
KRAAASSH
LET'S GO, STEVE.
C4
TWO DOWN. FINISH THE LAST ONE OFF BEFORE IT ROASTS US.

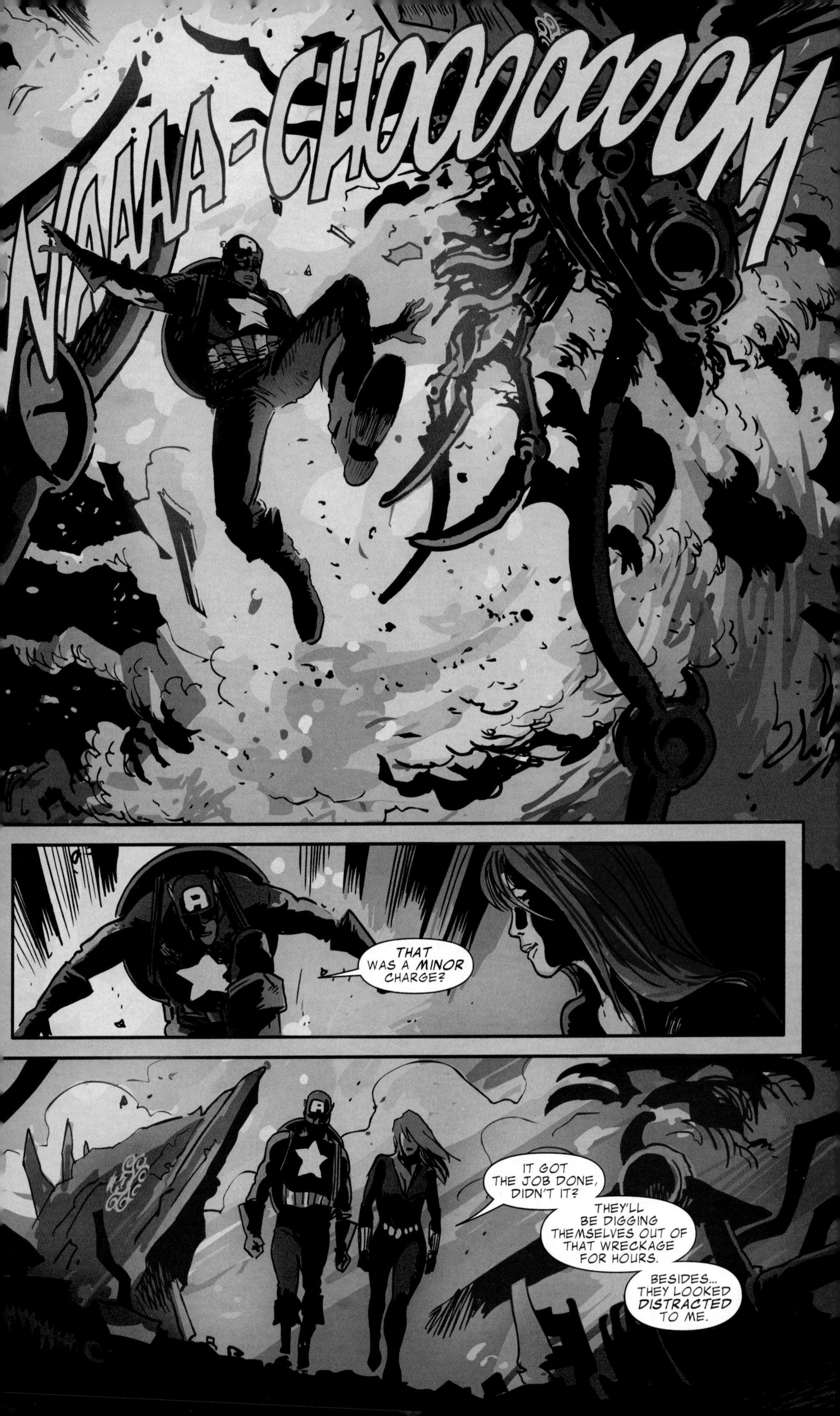

WHAAA-CHOOOOOOM
THAT WAS A MINOR CHARGE?
IT GOT THE JOB DONE, DIDN'T IT?
THEY'LL BE DIGGING THEMSELVES OUT OF THAT WRECKAGE FOR HOURS.
BESIDES... THEY LOOKED DISTRACTED TO ME.

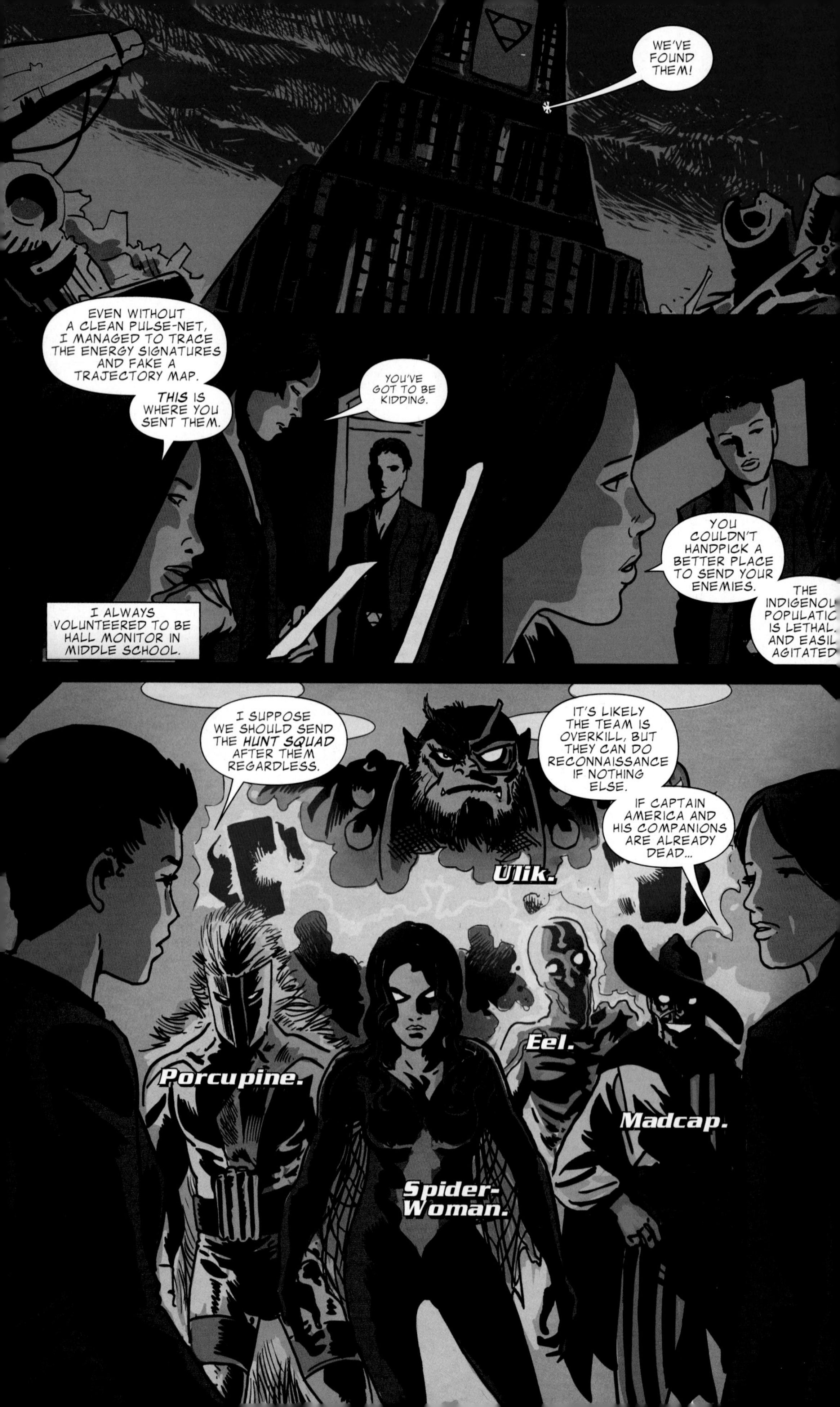
WE'VE FOUND THEM!
EVEN WITHOUT A CLEAN PULSE-NET, I MANAGED TO TRACE THE ENERGY SIGNATURES AND FAKE A TRAJECTORY MAP.
THIS IS WHERE YOU SENT THEM.
I ALWAYS VOLUNTEERED TO BE HALL MONITOR IN MIDDLE SCHOOL.
YOU'VE GOT TO BE KIDDING.
YOU COULDN'T HANDPICK A BETTER PLACE TO SEND YOUR ENEMIES.
I SUPPOSE WE SHOULD SEND THE HUNT SQUAD AFTER THEM REGARDLESS.
IT'S LIKELY THE TEAM IS OVERKILL, BUT THEY CAN DO RECONNAISSANCE IF NOTHING ELSE.
IF CAPTAIN AMERICA AND HIS COMPANIONS ARE ALREADY DEAD...
Ulik.
Porcupine.
Eel.
Madcap.
Spider-Woman.

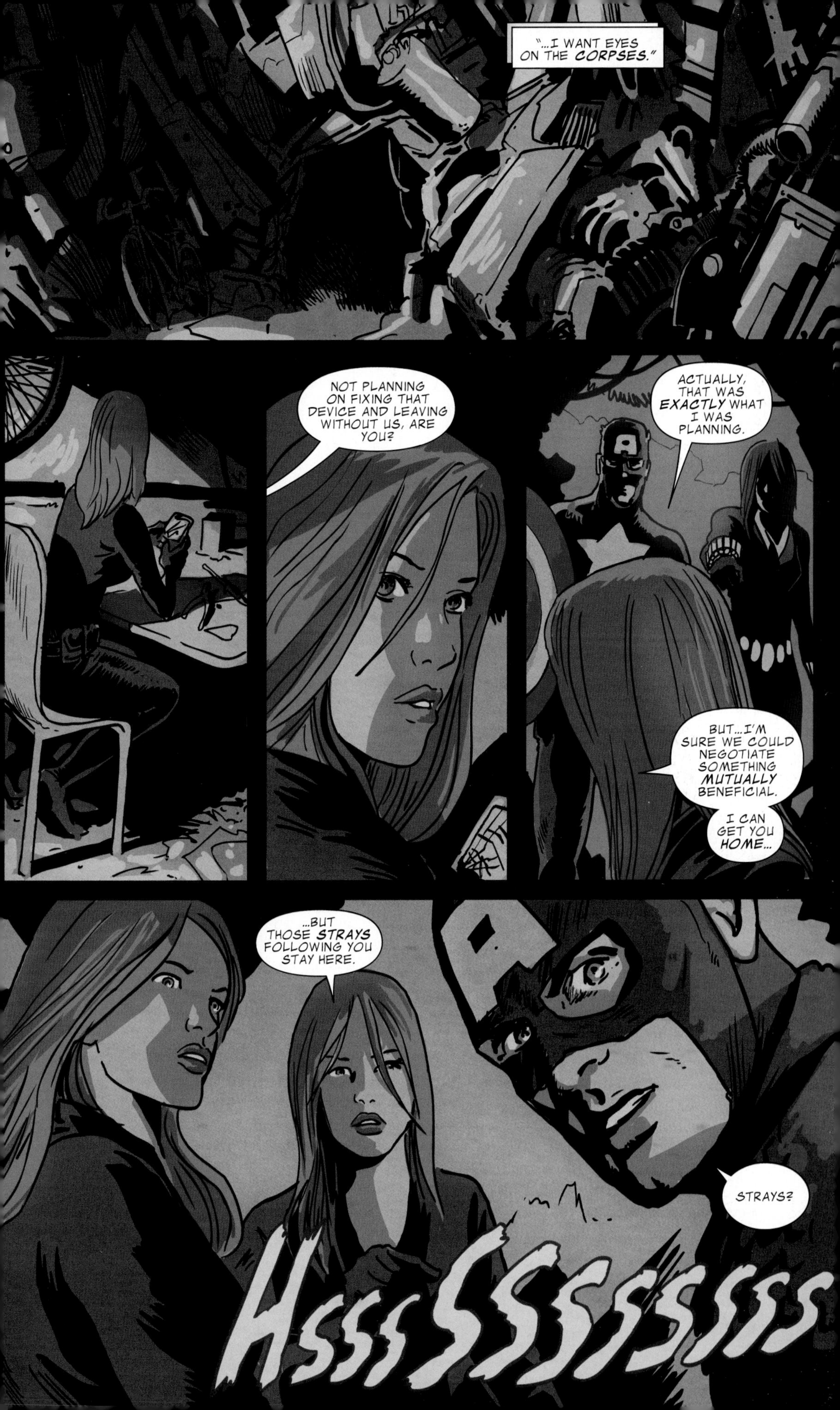

"...I WANT EYES ON THE CORPSES."
NOT PLANNING ON FIXING THAT DEVICE AND LEAVING WITHOUT US, ARE YOU?
ACTUALLY, THAT WAS EXACTLY WHAT I WAS PLANNING.
BUT...I'M SURE WE COULD NEGOTIATE SOMETHING MUTUALLY BENEFICIAL.
I CAN GET YOU HOME...
...BUT THOSE STRAYS FOLLOWING YOU STAY HERE.
STRAYS?
HsssSSSSSSSS

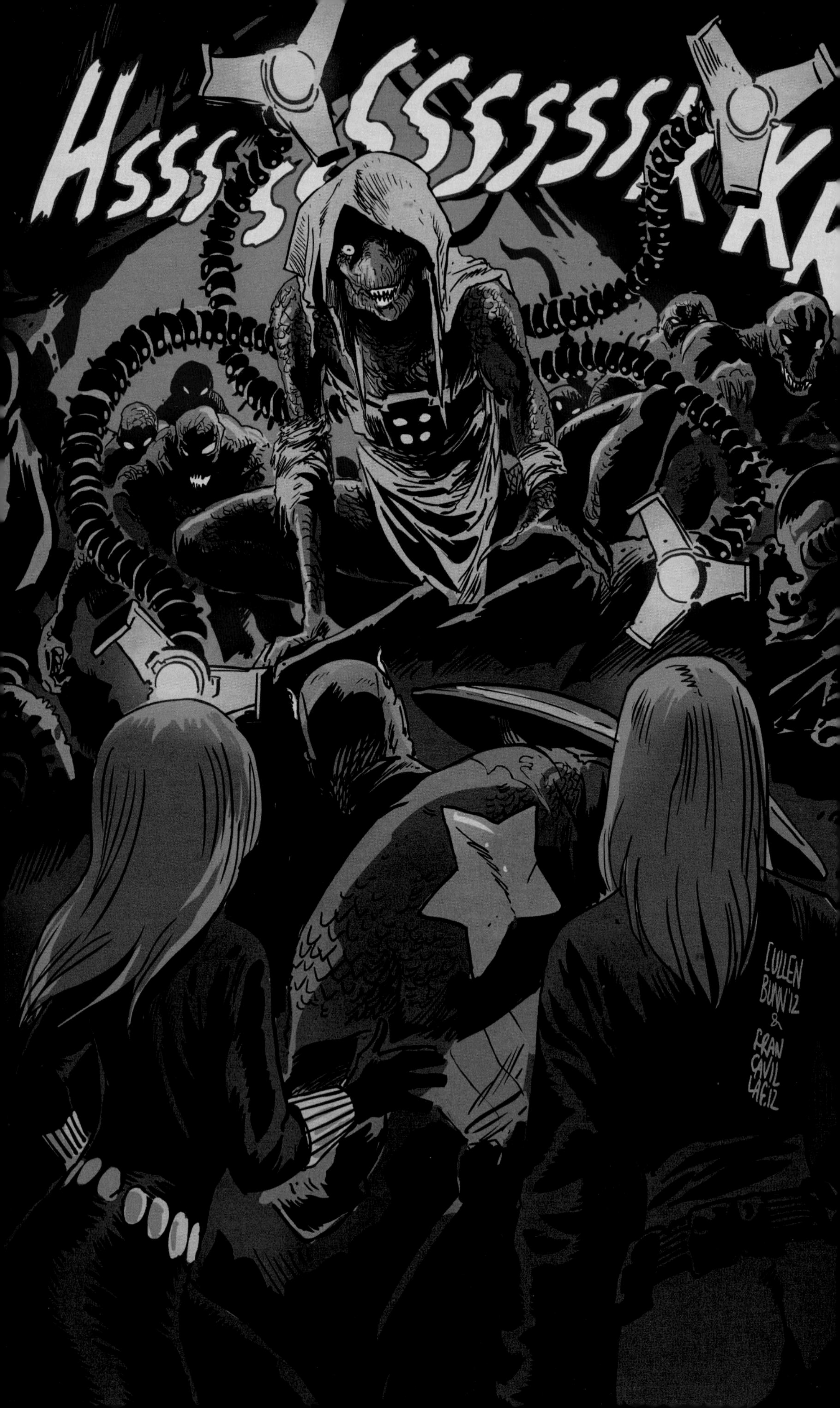

HSSSSSSSSSSKKR
CULLEN BUNN '12 & FRAN CAVILLA F.'12

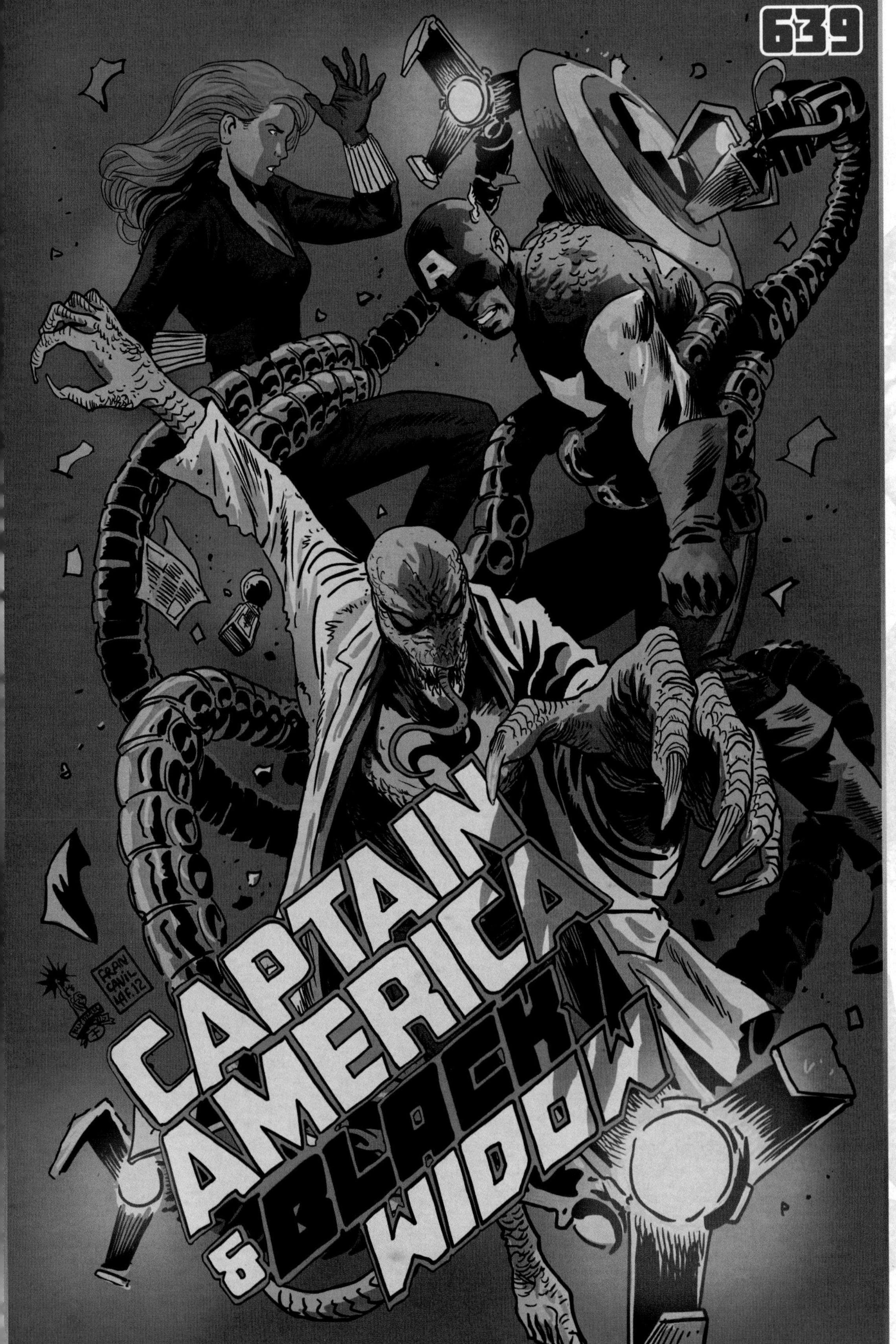
639
CAPTAIN AMERICA
& BLACK WIDOW
FRAN GALVIL

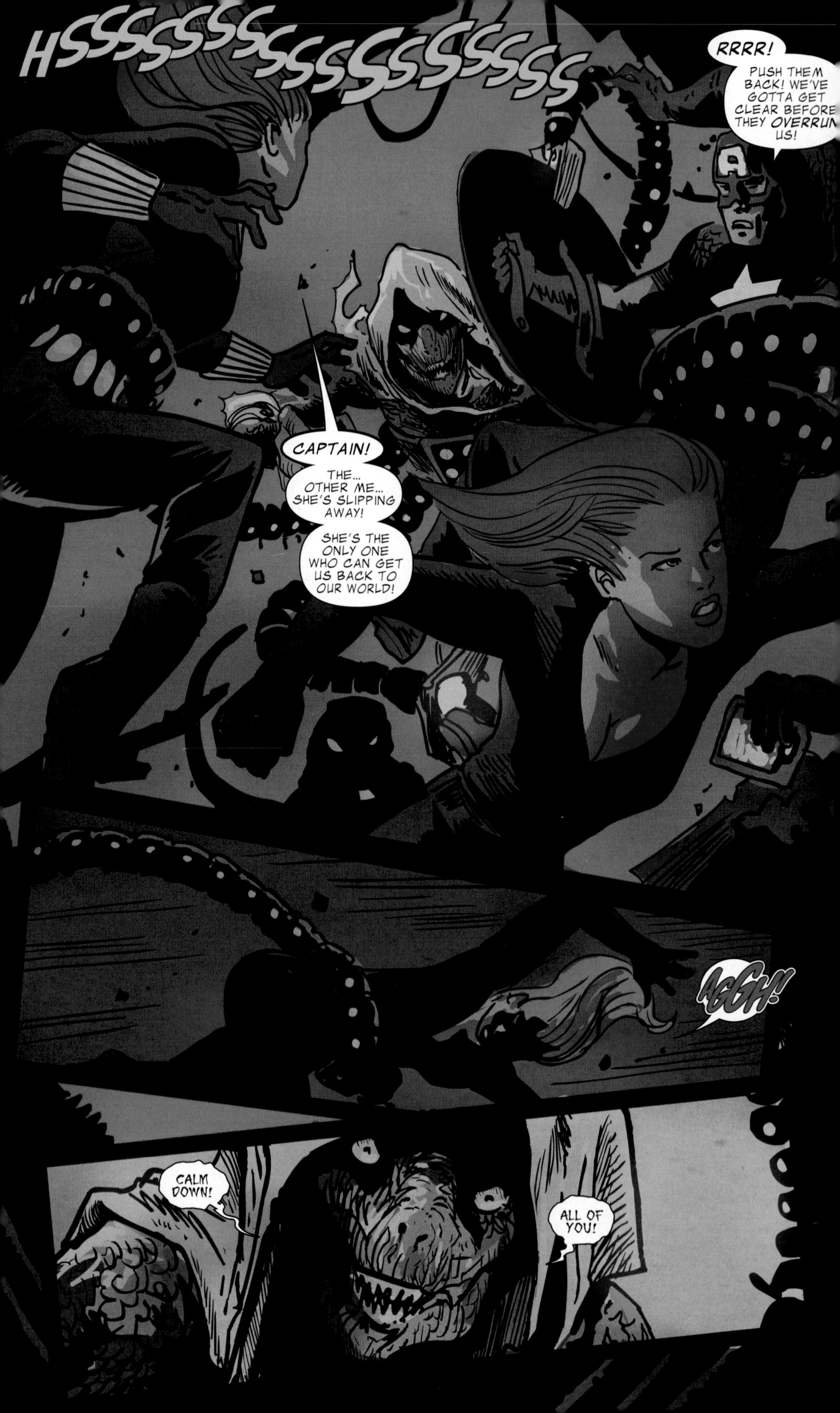
HSSSSSSSSSSSSSSSSSSS
RRRR!
PUSH THEM BACK! WE'VE GOTTA GET CLEAR BEFORE THEY OVERRUN US!
CAPTAIN!
THE... OTHER ME... SHE'S SLIPPING AWAY!
SHE'S THE ONLY ONE WHO CAN GET US BACK TO OUR WORLD!
AGGH!
CALM DOWN!
ALL OF YOU!

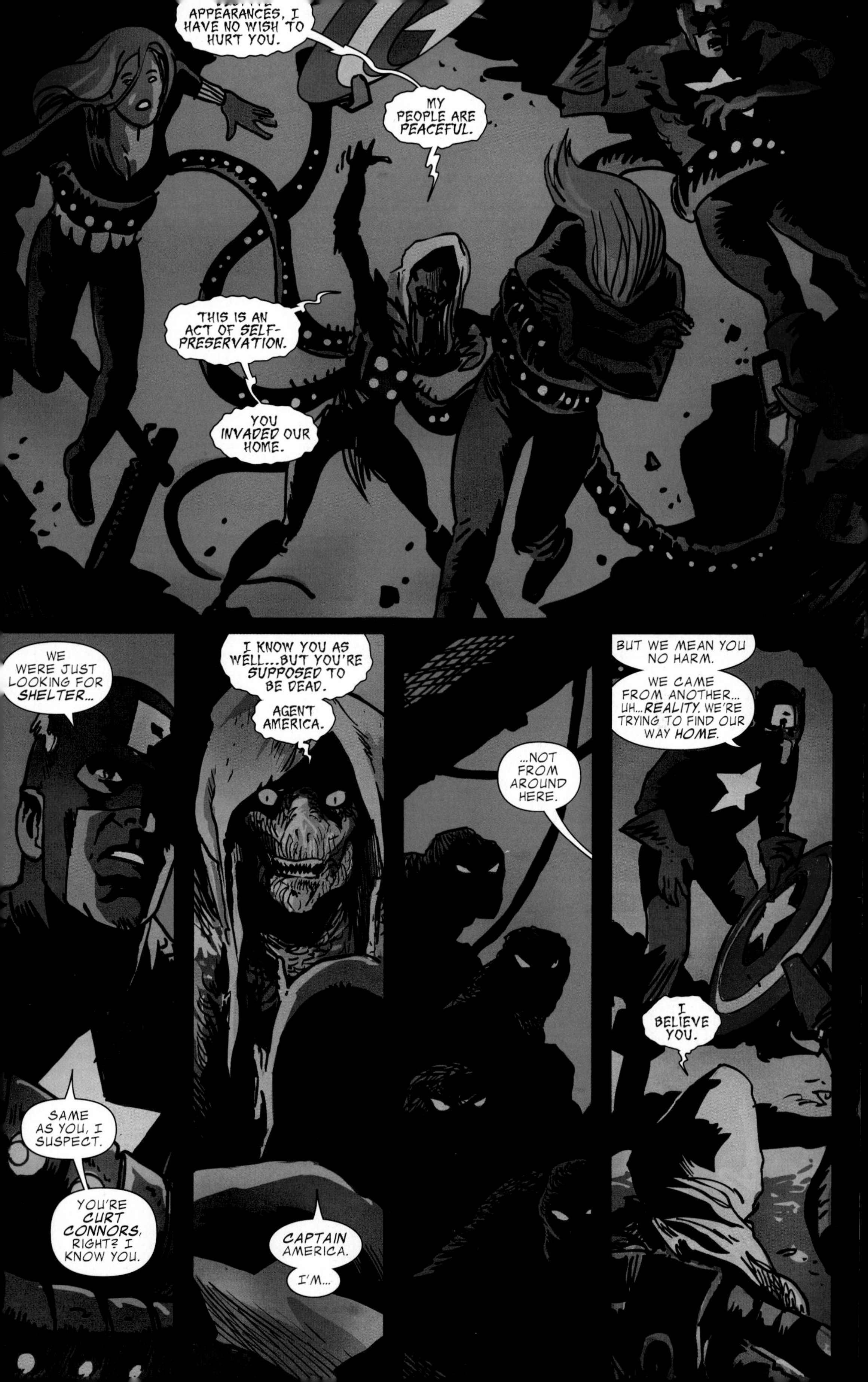
APPEARANCES, I HAVE NO WISH TO HURT YOU.
MY PEOPLE ARE PEACEFUL.
THIS IS AN ACT OF SELF-PRESERVATION.
YOU INVADED OUR HOME.
WE WERE JUST LOOKING FOR SHELTER...
SAME AS YOU, I SUSPECT.
YOU'RE CURT CONNORS, RIGHT? I KNOW YOU.
I KNOW YOU AS WELL...BUT YOU'RE SUPPOSED TO BE DEAD.
AGENT AMERICA.
CAPTAIN AMERICA.
I'M...
...NOT FROM AROUND HERE.
BUT WE MEAN YOU NO HARM.
WE CAME FROM ANOTHER... UH...REALITY. WE'RE TRYING TO FIND OUR WAY HOME.
I BELIEVE YOU.

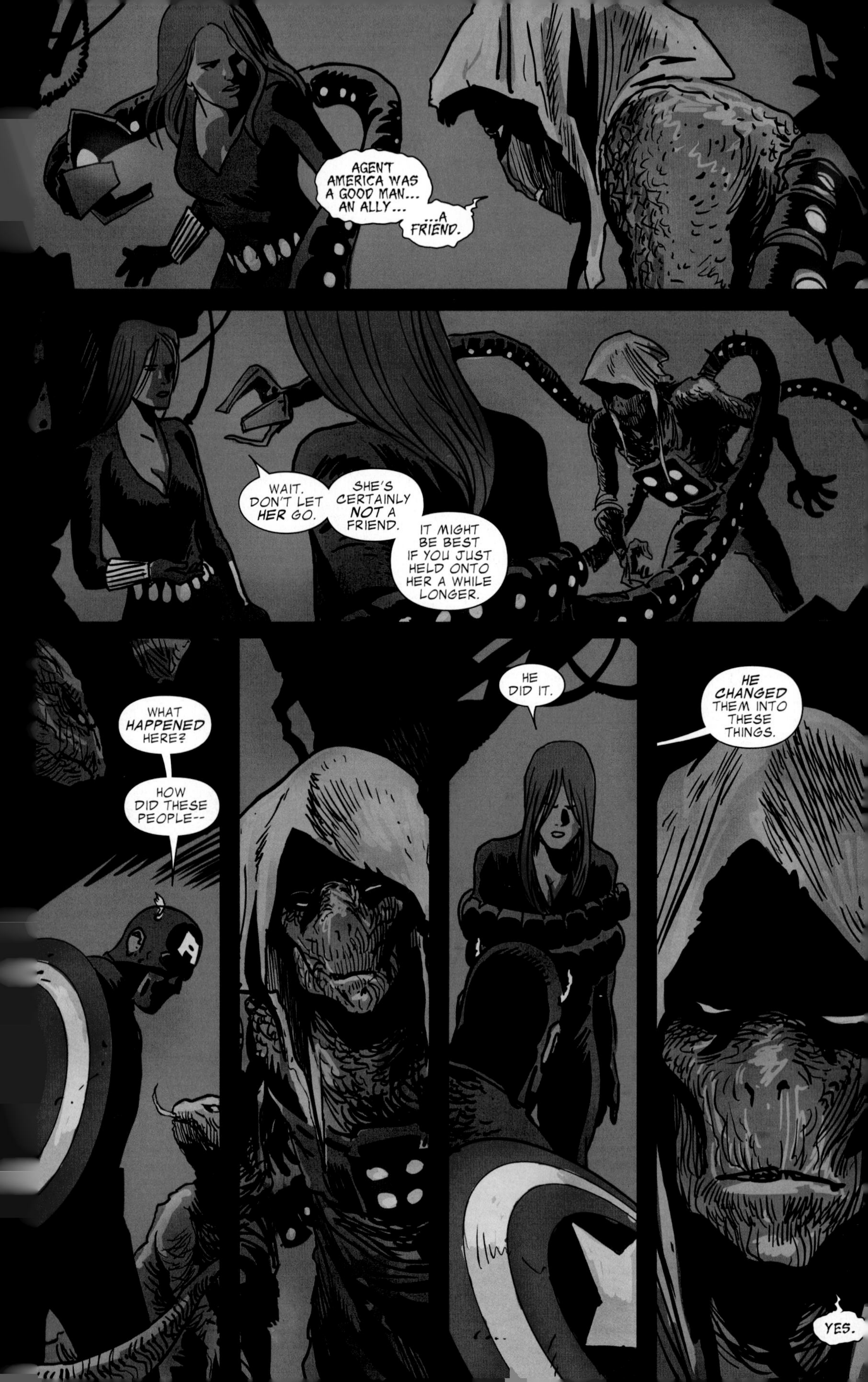

AGENT AMERICA WAS A GOOD MAN... AN ALLY...
...A FRIEND.
WAIT. DON'T LET HER GO.
SHE'S CERTAINLY NOT A FRIEND.
IT MIGHT BE BEST IF YOU JUST HELD ONTO HER A WHILE LONGER.
WHAT HAPPENED HERE?
HOW DID THESE PEOPLE--
HE DID IT.
HE CHANGED THEM INTO THESE THINGS.
YES.

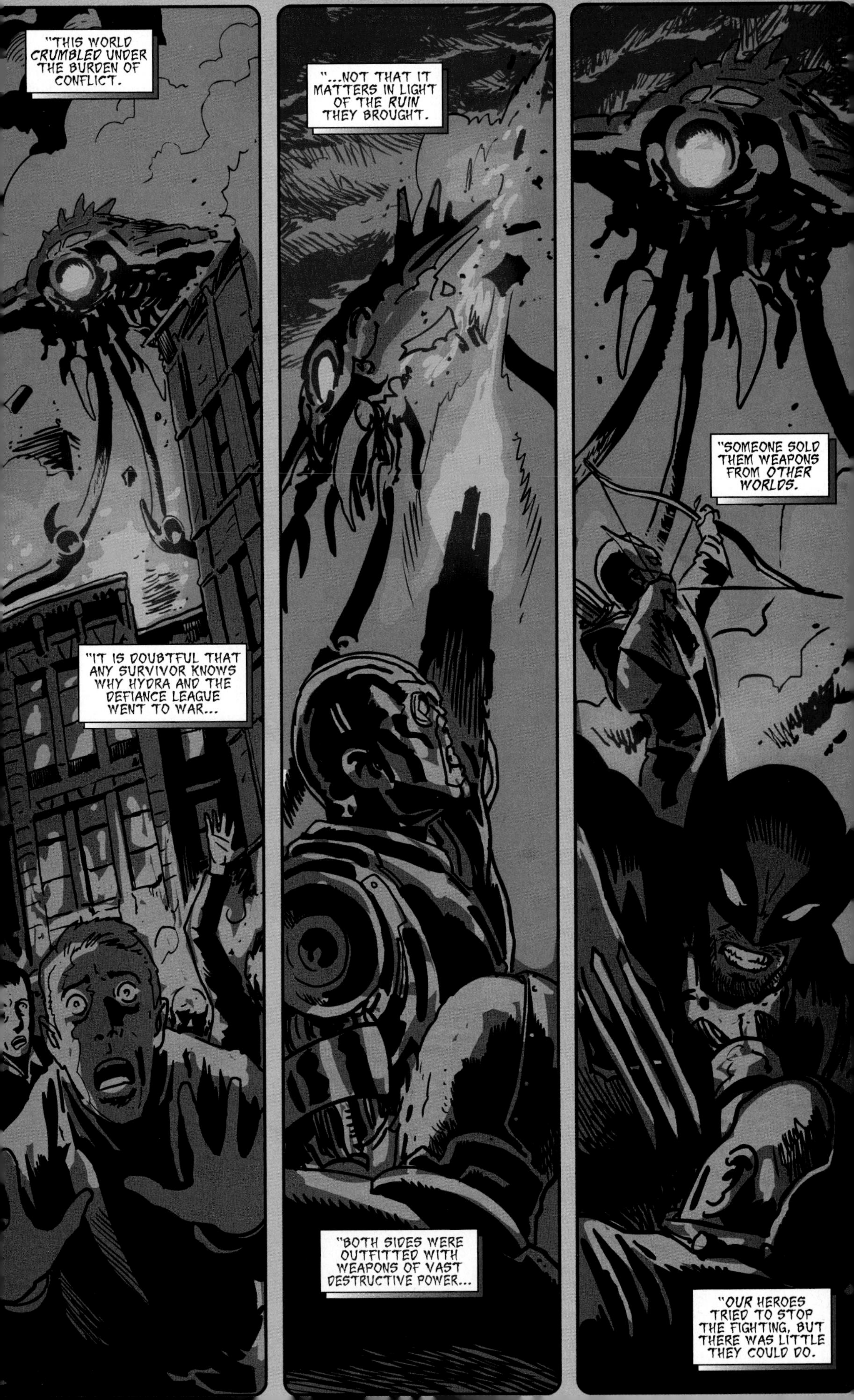
"THIS WORLD CRUMBLED UNDER THE BURDEN OF CONFLICT.
"IT IS DOUBTFUL THAT ANY SURVIVOR KNOWS WHY HYDRA AND THE DEFIANCE LEAGUE WENT TO WAR...
"...NOT THAT IT MATTERS IN LIGHT OF THE RUIN THEY BROUGHT.
"BOTH SIDES WERE OUTFITTED WITH WEAPONS OF VAST DESTRUCTIVE POWER...
"SOMEONE SOLD THEM WEAPONS FROM OTHER WORLDS.
"OUR HEROES TRIED TO STOP THE FIGHTING, BUT THERE WAS LITTLE THEY COULD DO.

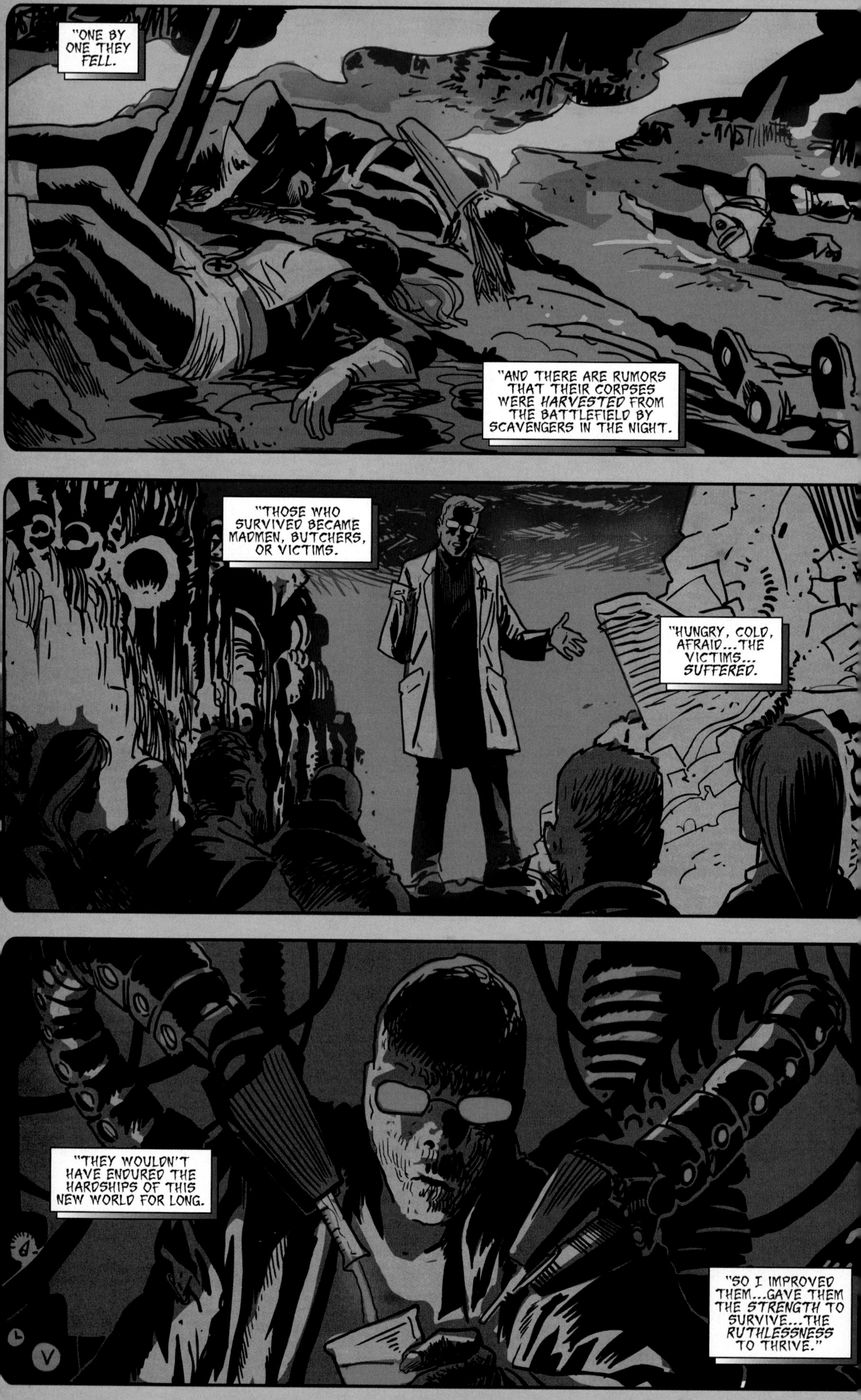
"ONE BY ONE THEY FELL.
"AND THERE ARE RUMORS THAT THEIR CORPSES WERE *HARVESTED* FROM THE BATTLEFIELD BY SCAVENGERS IN THE NIGHT.
"THOSE WHO SURVIVED BECAME MADMEN, BUTCHERS, OR VICTIMS.
"HUNGRY, COLD, AFRAID...THE VICTIMS... SUFFERED.
"THEY WOULDN'T HAVE ENDURED THE HARDSHIPS OF THIS NEW WORLD FOR LONG.
"SO I IMPROVED THEM...GAVE THEM THE *STRENGTH* TO SURVIVE...THE *RUTHLESSNESS* TO THRIVE."

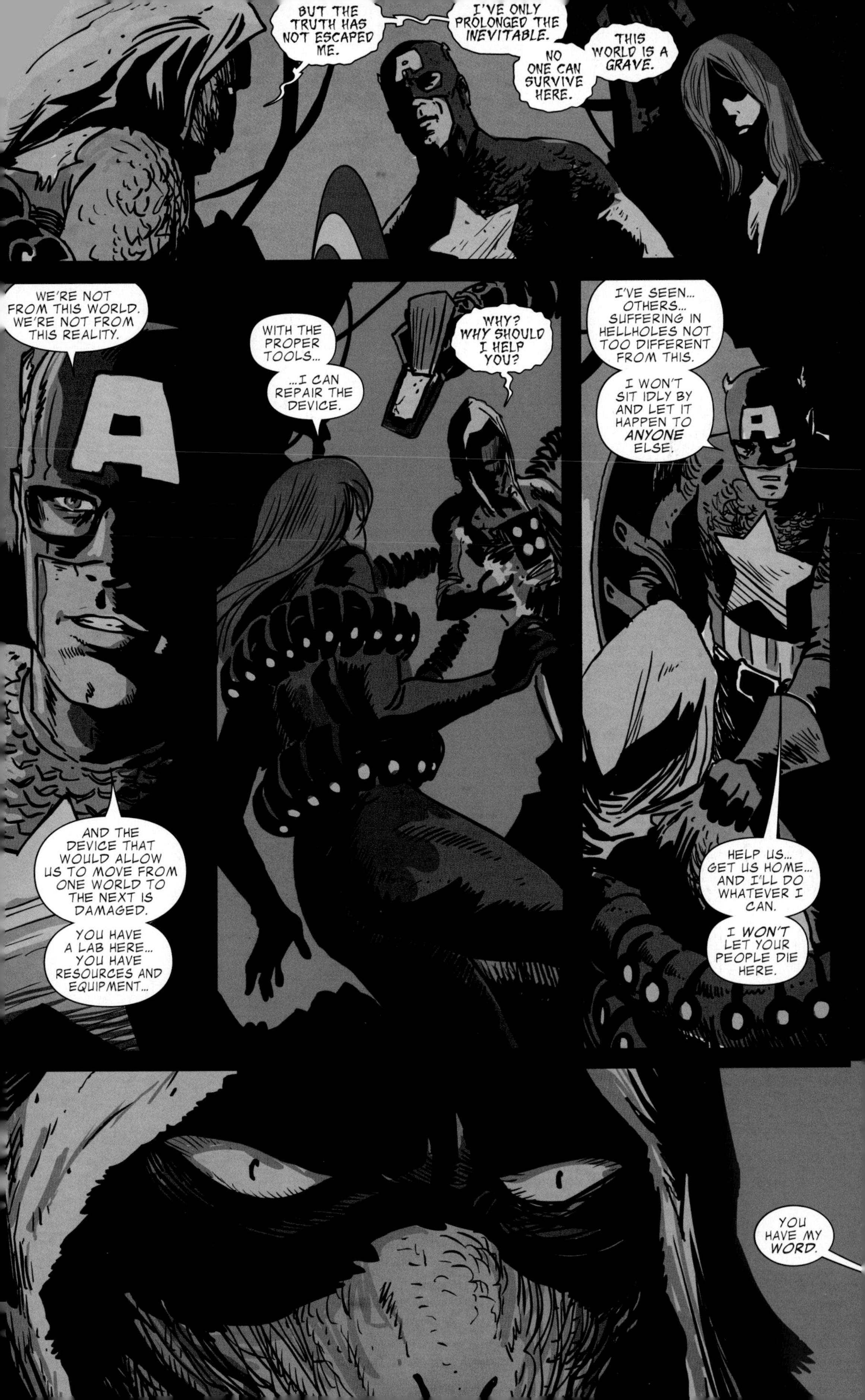
BUT THE TRUTH HAS NOT ESCAPED ME.
I'VE ONLY PROLONGED THE INEVITABLE.
NO ONE CAN SURVIVE HERE.
THIS WORLD IS A GRAVE.
WE'RE NOT FROM THIS WORLD. WE'RE NOT FROM THIS REALITY.
AND THE DEVICE THAT WOULD ALLOW US TO MOVE FROM ONE WORLD TO THE NEXT IS DAMAGED.
YOU HAVE A LAB HERE... YOU HAVE RESOURCES AND EQUIPMENT...
WITH THE PROPER TOOLS...
...I CAN REPAIR THE DEVICE.
WHY? WHY SHOULD I HELP YOU?
I'VE SEEN... OTHERS... SUFFERING IN HELLHOLES NOT TOO DIFFERENT FROM THIS.
I WON'T SIT IDLY BY AND LET IT HAPPEN TO ANYONE ELSE.
HELP US... GET US HOME... AND I'LL DO WHATEVER I CAN.
I WON'T LET YOUR PEOPLE DIE HERE.
YOU HAVE MY WORD.

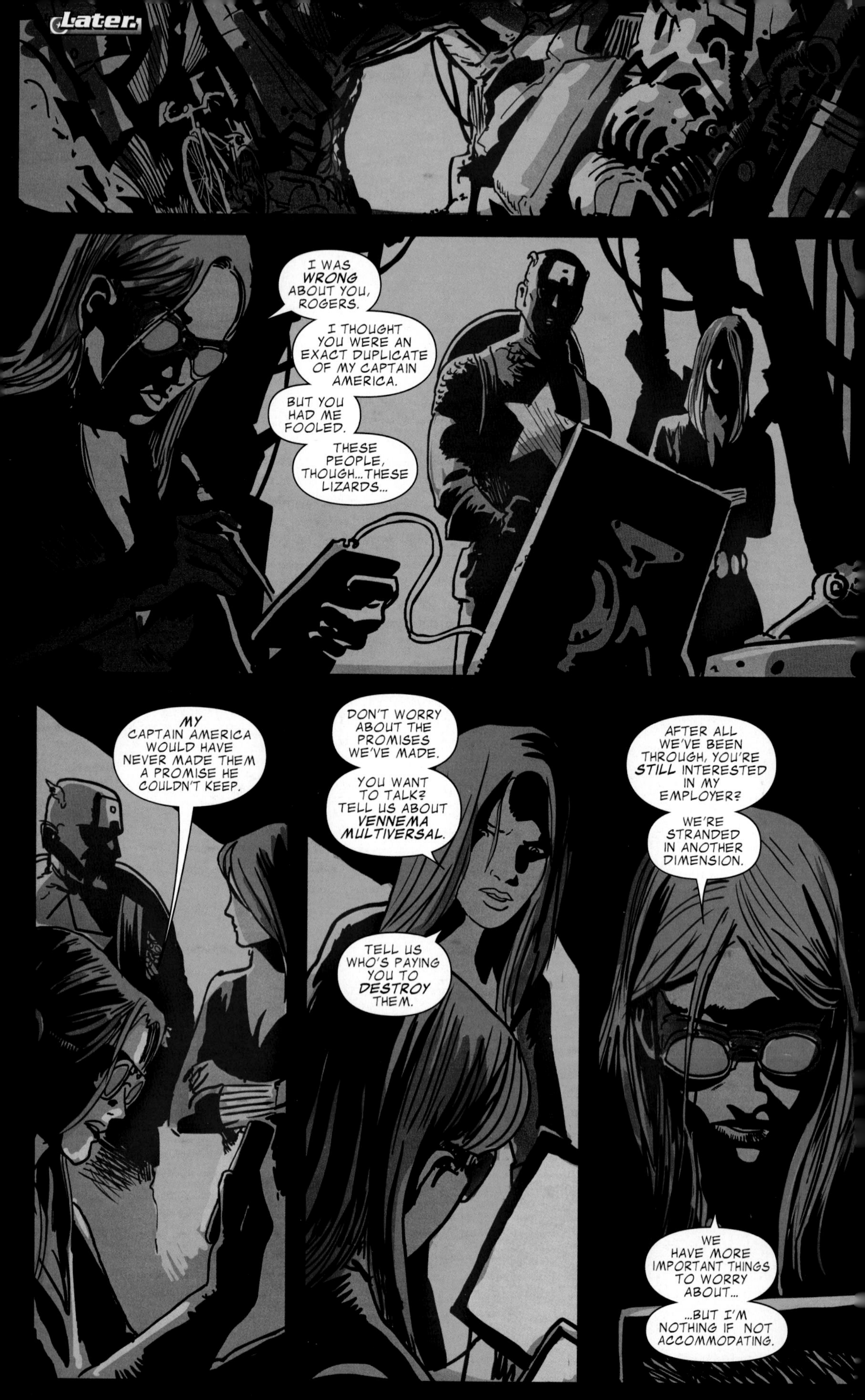
LATER.
I WAS WRONG ABOUT YOU, ROGERS.
I THOUGHT YOU WERE AN EXACT DUPLICATE OF MY CAPTAIN AMERICA.
BUT YOU HAD ME FOOLED.
THESE PEOPLE, THOUGH...THESE LIZARDS...
MY CAPTAIN AMERICA WOULD HAVE NEVER MADE THEM A PROMISE HE COULDN'T KEEP.
DON'T WORRY ABOUT THE PROMISES WE'VE MADE.
YOU WANT TO TALK? TELL US ABOUT VENNEMA MULTIVERSAL.
TELL US WHO'S PAYING YOU TO DESTROY THEM.
AFTER ALL WE'VE BEEN THROUGH, YOU'RE STILL INTERESTED IN MY EMPLOYER?
WE'RE STRANDED IN ANOTHER DIMENSION.
WE HAVE MORE IMPORTANT THINGS TO WORRY ABOUT...
...BUT I'M NOTHING IF NOT ACCOMMODATING.

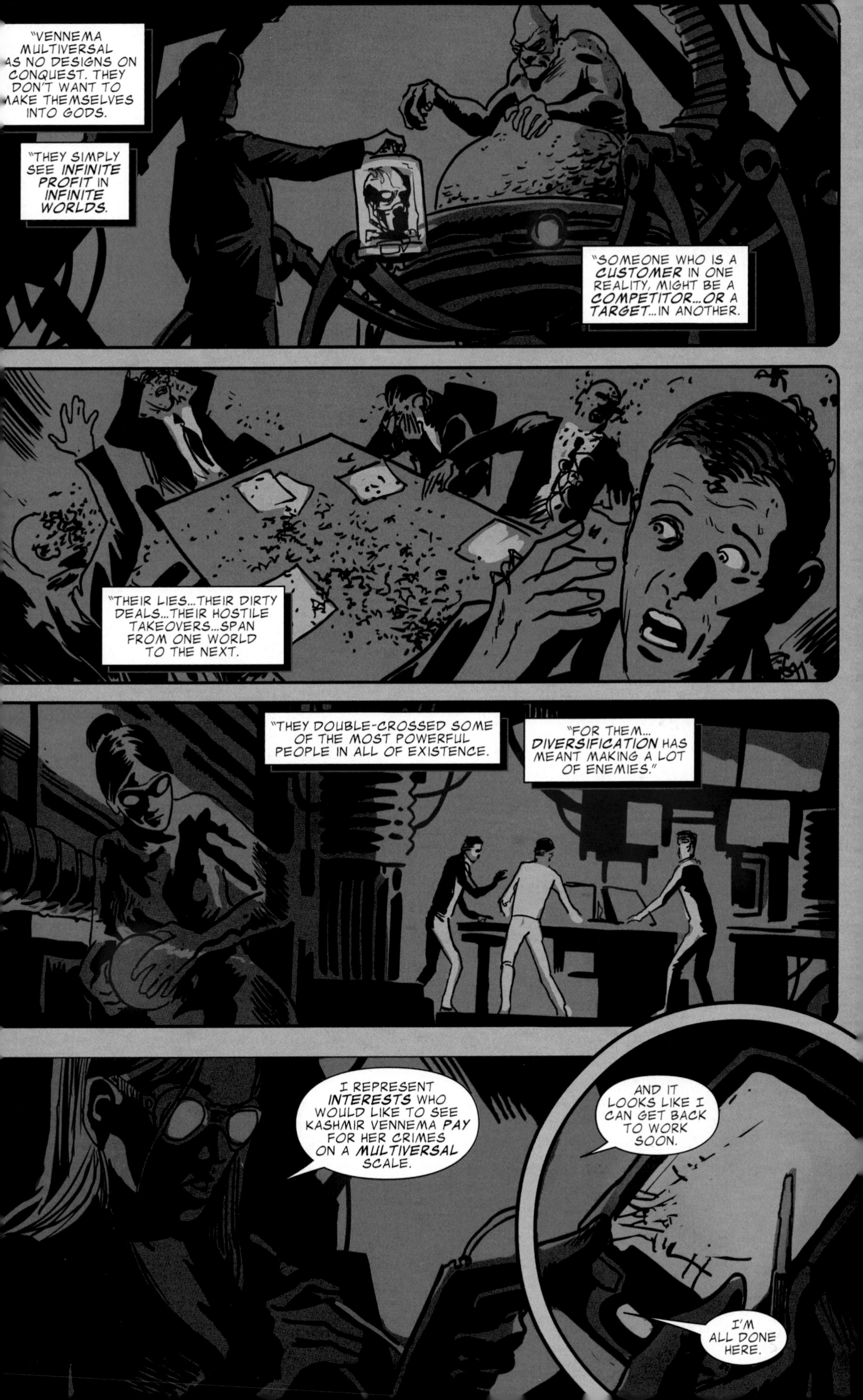
"VENNEMA MULTIVERSAL AS NO DESIGNS ON CONQUEST. THEY DON'T WANT TO AKE THEMSELVES INTO GODS.
"THEY SIMPLY SEE INFINITE PROFIT IN INFINITE WORLDS.
"SOMEONE WHO IS A CUSTOMER IN ONE REALITY, MIGHT BE A COMPETITOR...OR A TARGET...IN ANOTHER.
"THEIR LIES...THEIR DIRTY DEALS...THEIR HOSTILE TAKEOVERS...SPAN FROM ONE WORLD TO THE NEXT.
"THEY DOUBLE-CROSSED SOME OF THE MOST POWERFUL PEOPLE IN ALL OF EXISTENCE.
"FOR THEM... DIVERSIFICATION HAS MEANT MAKING A LOT OF ENEMIES."
I REPRESENT INTERESTS WHO WOULD LIKE TO SEE KASHMIR VENNEMA PAY FOR HER CRIMES ON A MULTIVERSAL SCALE.
AND IT LOOKS LIKE I CAN GET BACK TO WORK SOON.
I'M ALL DONE HERE.

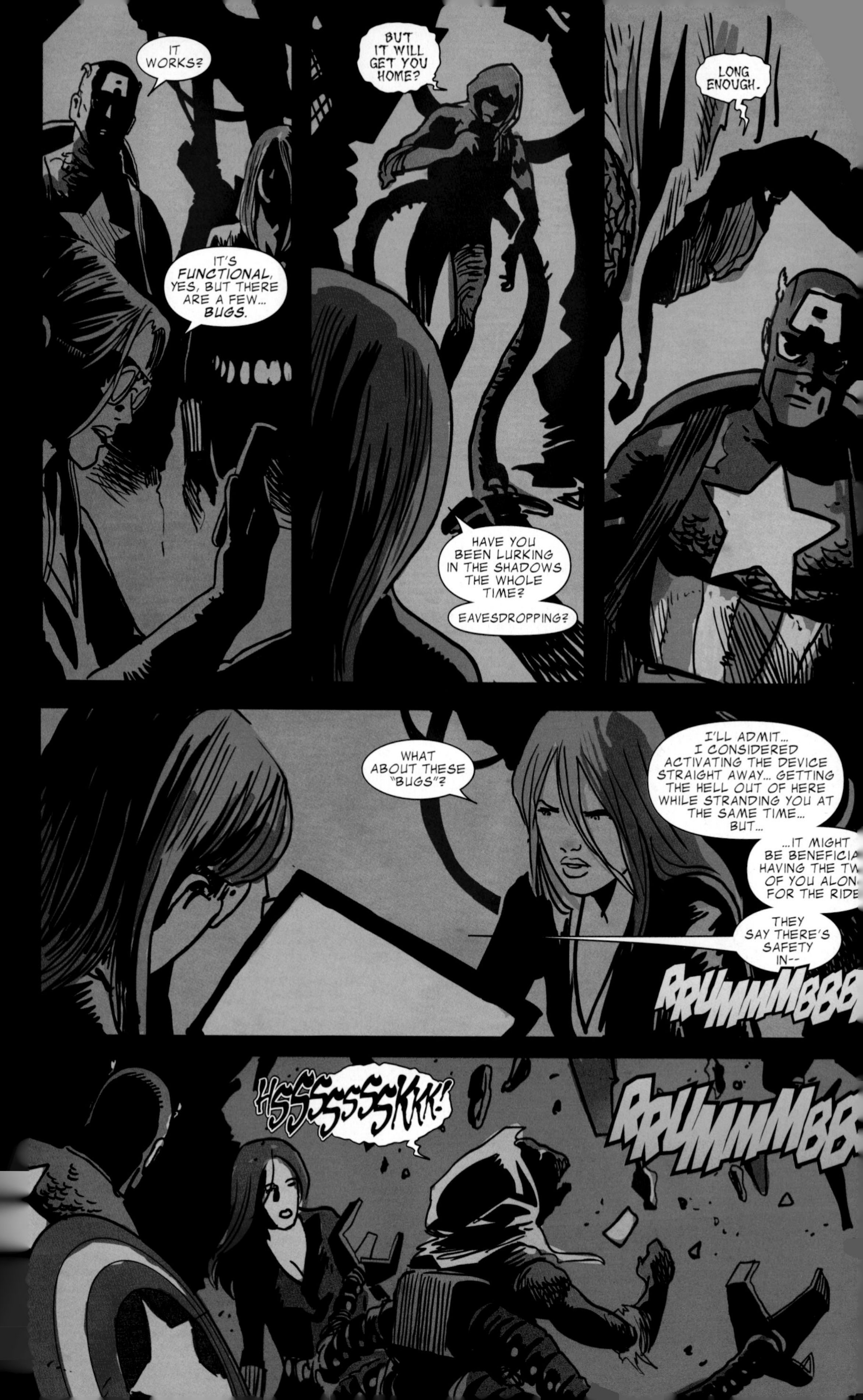
IT WORKS?
IT'S FUNCTIONAL, YES, BUT THERE ARE A FEW... BUGS.
BUT IT WILL GET YOU HOME?
HAVE YOU BEEN LURKING IN THE SHADOWS THE WHOLE TIME?
EAVESDROPPING?
LONG ENOUGH.
WHAT ABOUT THESE "BUGS"?
I'LL ADMIT... I CONSIDERED ACTIVATING THE DEVICE STRAIGHT AWAY... GETTING THE HELL OUT OF HERE WHILE STRANDING YOU AT THE SAME TIME... BUT...
...IT MIGHT BE BENEFICIA HAVING THE TW OF YOU ALON FOR THE RIDE
THEY SAY THERE'S SAFETY IN--
RRUMMMBBB
HSSSSSSKKK!
RRUMMMBBB

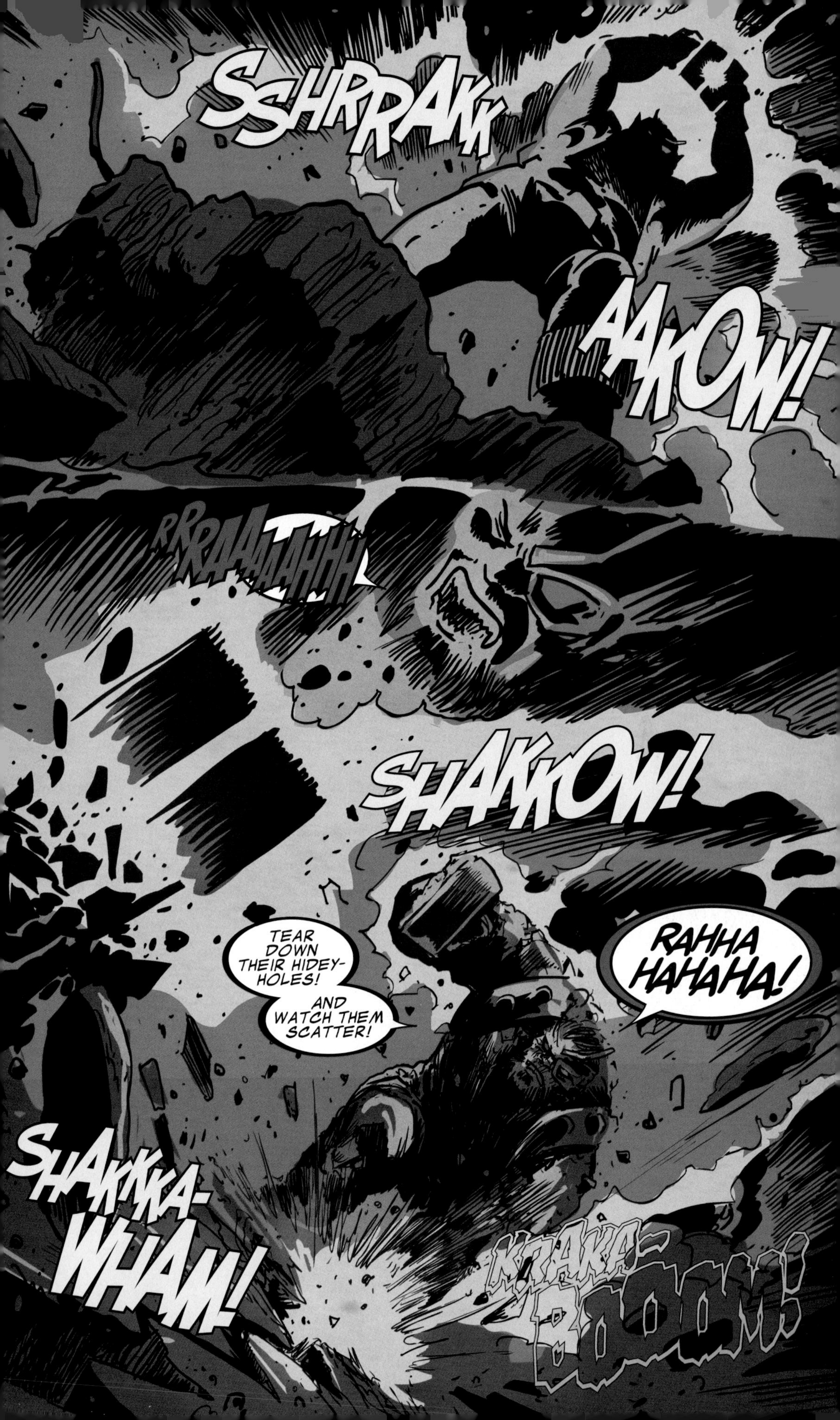
SSHRRAKK
AAKOW!
RRRAAAAAHHH
SHAKKOW!
TEAR DOWN THEIR HIDEY-HOLES!
AND WATCH THEM SCATTER!
RAHHA HAHAHA!
SHAKKKA-WHAM!
KRAKA-BOOOM!

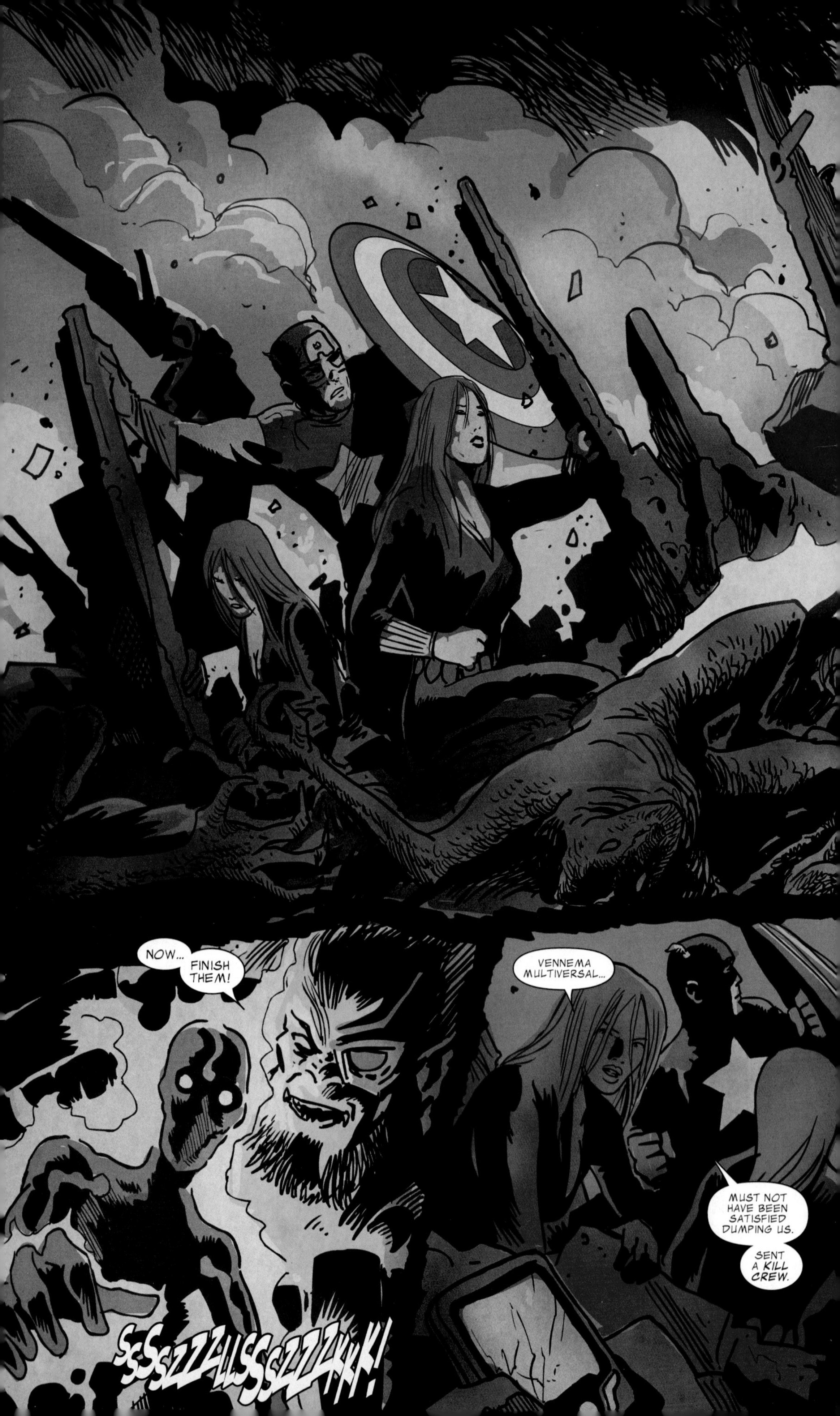
NOW... FINISH THEM!
VENNEMA MULTIVERSAL...
MUST NOT HAVE BEEN SATISFIED DUMPING US.
SENT A KILL CREW.
SSSSZZZZLLSSSSZZZZKKKK!

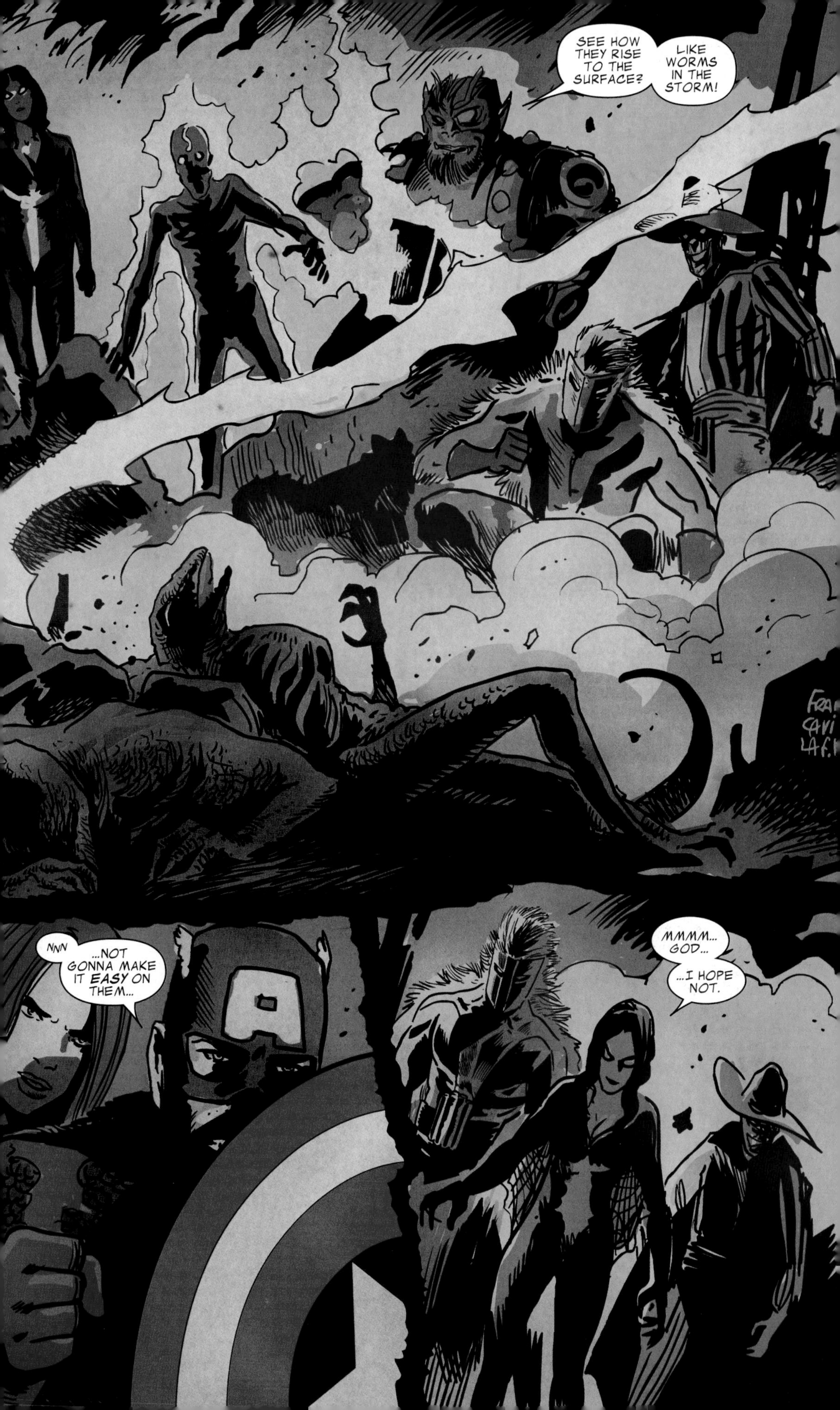
SEE HOW THEY RISE TO THE SURFACE?
LIKE WORMS IN THE STORM!
NNN
...NOT GONNA MAKE IT EASY ON THEM...
MMMM... GOD...
...I HOPE NOT.

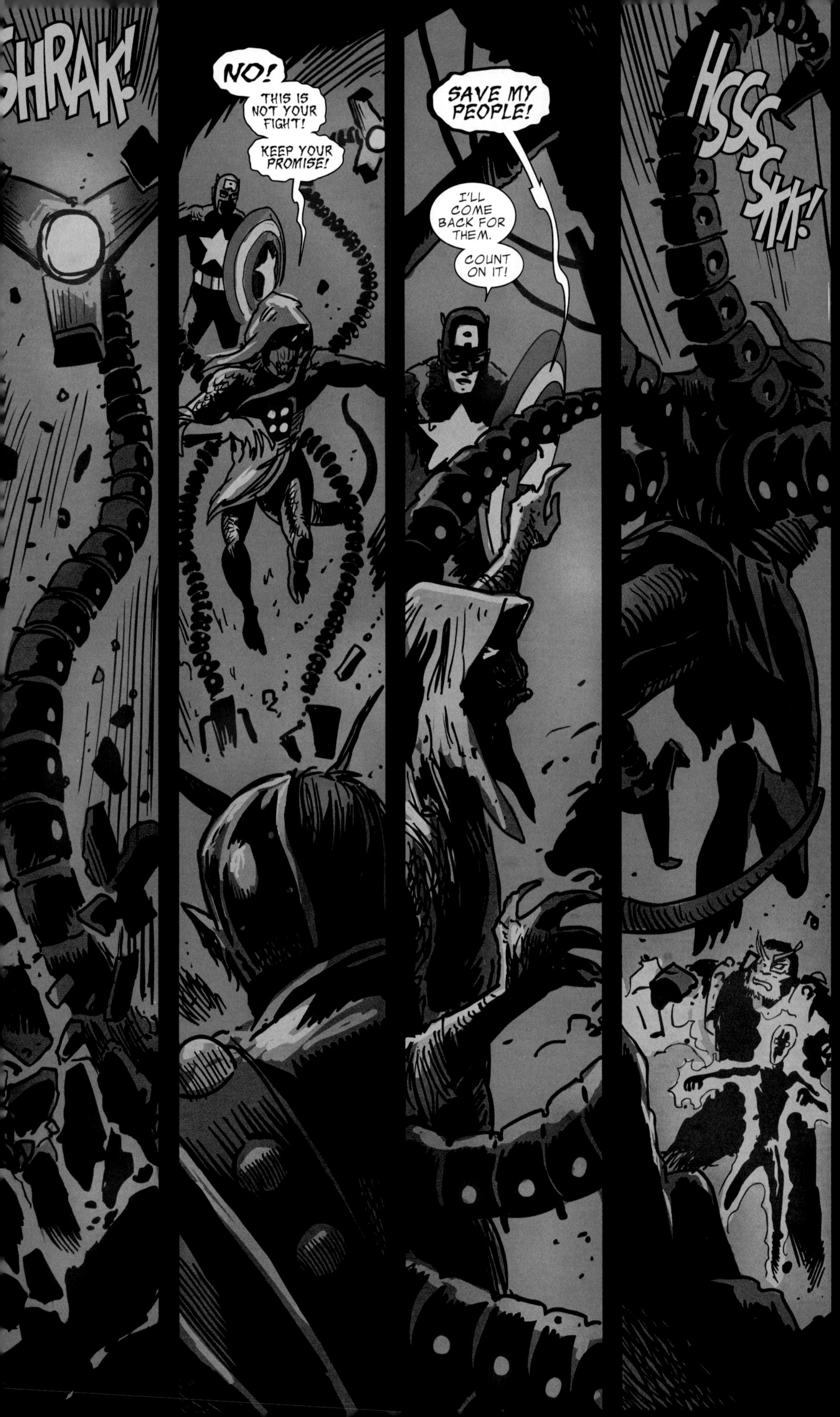
SHRAK!
NO!
THIS IS NOT YOUR FIGHT!
KEEP YOUR PROMISE!
SAVE MY PEOPLE!
I'LL COME BACK FOR THEM.
COUNT ON IT!
HSSSSKK!

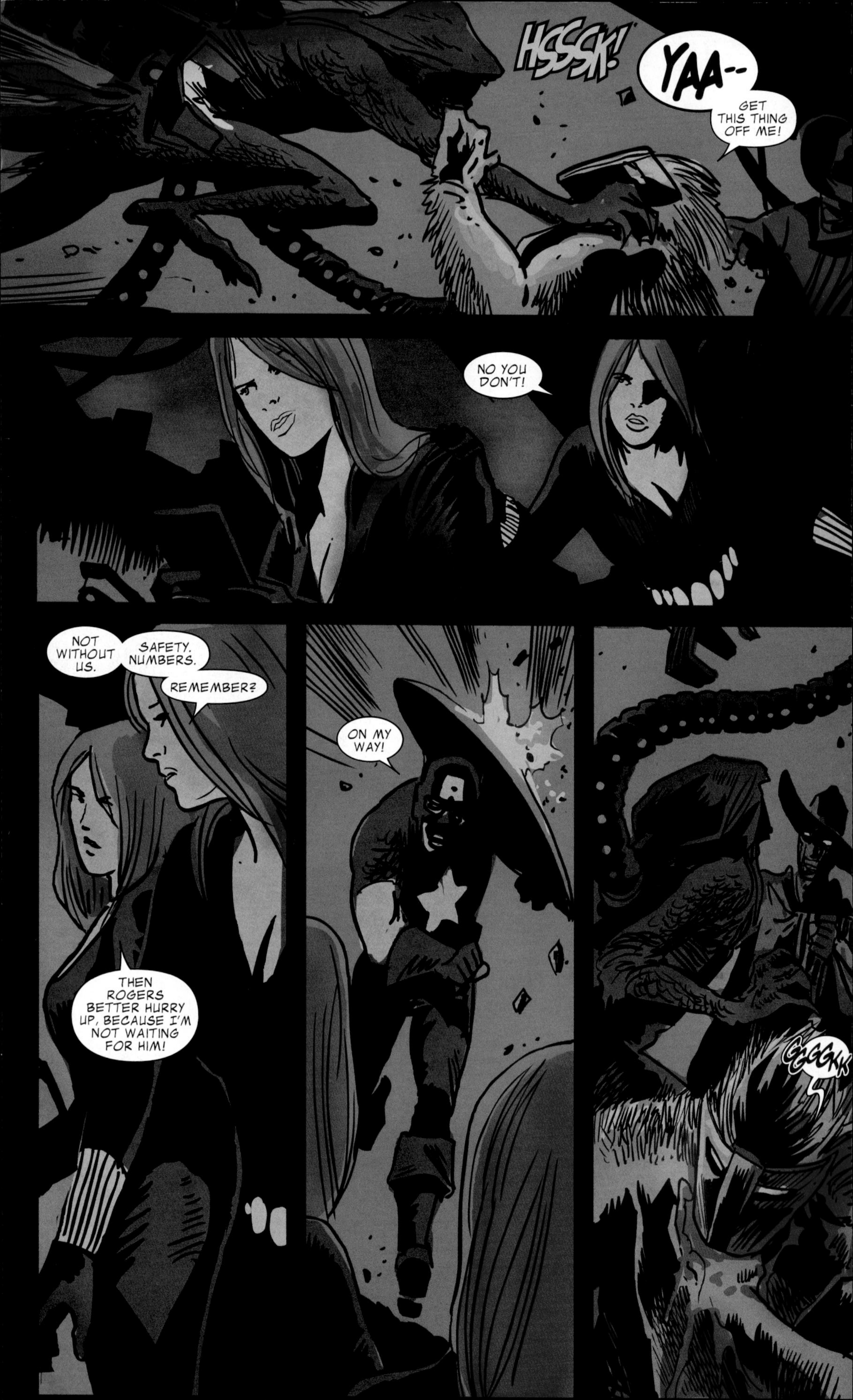
HSSSK!
YAA--
GET THIS THING OFF ME!
NO YOU DON'T!
NOT WITHOUT US.
SAFETY. NUMBERS.
REMEMBER?
THEN ROGERS BETTER HURRY UP, BECAUSE I'M NOT WAITING FOR HIM!
ON MY WAY!
GGGGKK

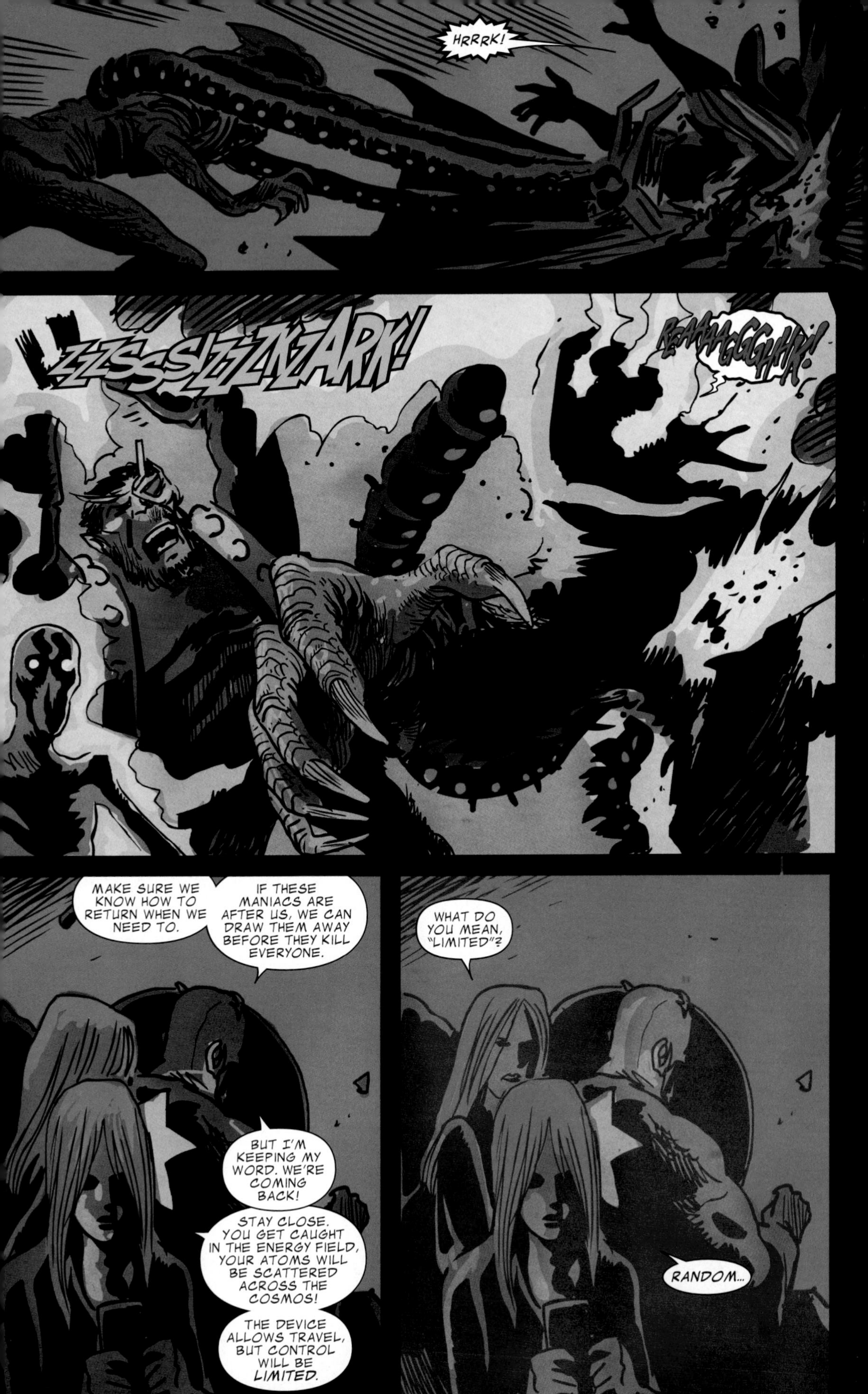
HRRRK!
ZZZSSSIZZZKZARK!
REAAAAGGGHHK!
MAKE SURE WE KNOW HOW TO RETURN WHEN WE NEED TO.
IF THESE MANIACS ARE AFTER US, WE CAN DRAW THEM AWAY BEFORE THEY KILL EVERYONE.
BUT I'M KEEPING MY WORD. WE'RE COMING BACK!
STAY CLOSE. YOU GET CAUGHT IN THE ENERGY FIELD, YOUR ATOMS WILL BE SCATTERED ACROSS THE COSMOS!
THE DEVICE ALLOWS TRAVEL, BUT CONTROL WILL BE LIMITED.
WHAT DO YOU MEAN, "LIMITED"?
RANDOM...

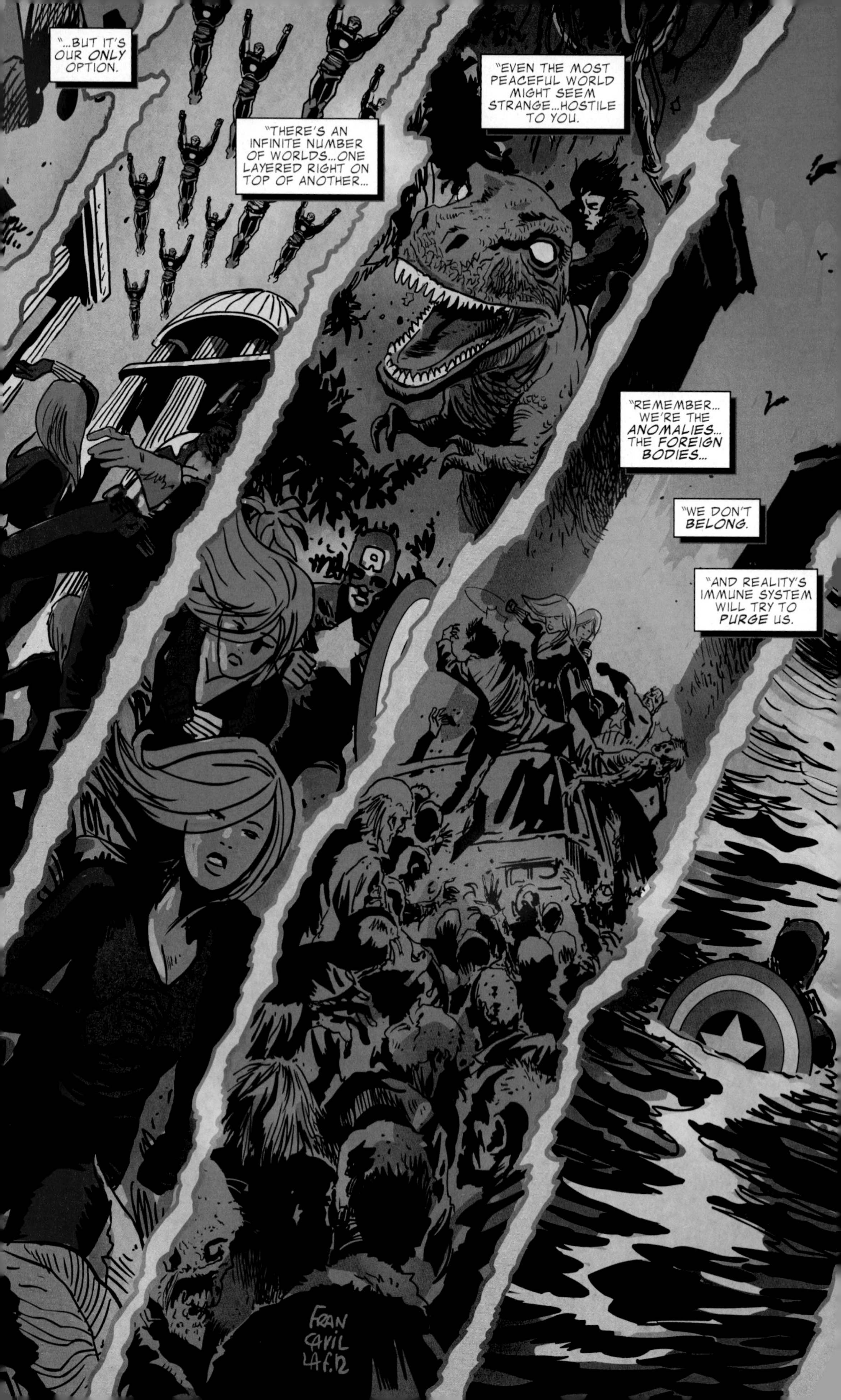
"...BUT IT'S OUR ONLY OPTION.
"THERE'S AN INFINITE NUMBER OF WORLDS...ONE LAYERED RIGHT ON TOP OF ANOTHER...
"EVEN THE MOST PEACEFUL WORLD MIGHT SEEM STRANGE...HOSTILE TO YOU.
"REMEMBER... WE'RE THE ANOMALIES... THE FOREIGN BODIES...
"WE DON'T BELONG.
"AND REALITY'S IMMUNE SYSTEM WILL TRY TO PURGE US.
FRAN CAVIL

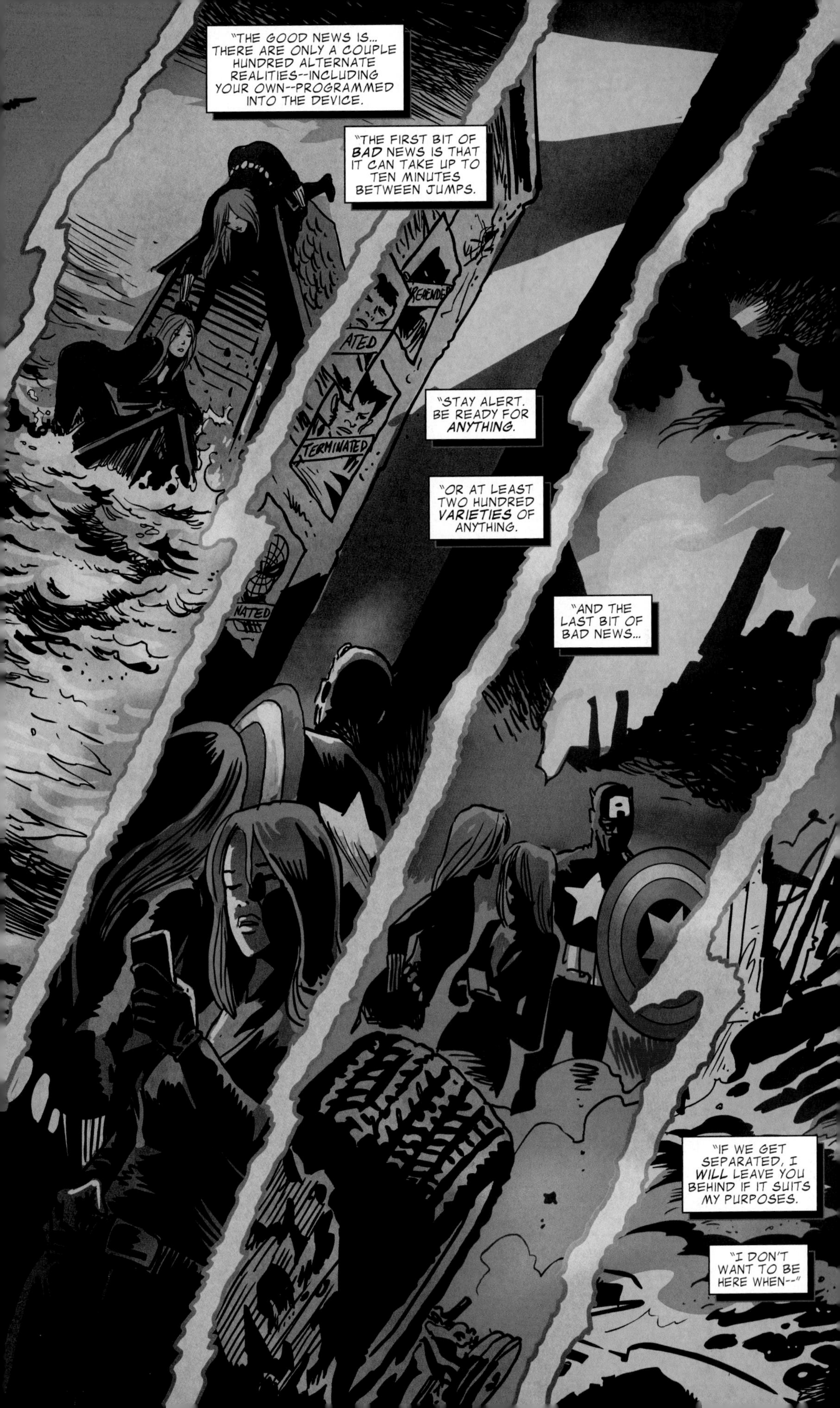
"THE GOOD NEWS IS... THERE ARE ONLY A COUPLE HUNDRED ALTERNATE REALITIES--INCLUDING YOUR OWN--PROGRAMMED INTO THE DEVICE.
"THE FIRST BIT OF BAD NEWS IS THAT IT CAN TAKE UP TO TEN MINUTES BETWEEN JUMPS.
SURRENDER
ATED
TERMINATED
NATED
"STAY ALERT. BE READY FOR ANYTHING.
"OR AT LEAST TWO HUNDRED VARIETIES OF ANYTHING.
"AND THE LAST BIT OF BAD NEWS...
"IF WE GET SEPARATED, I WILL LEAVE YOU BEHIND IF IT SUITS MY PURPOSES.
"I DON'T WANT TO BE HERE WHEN--"

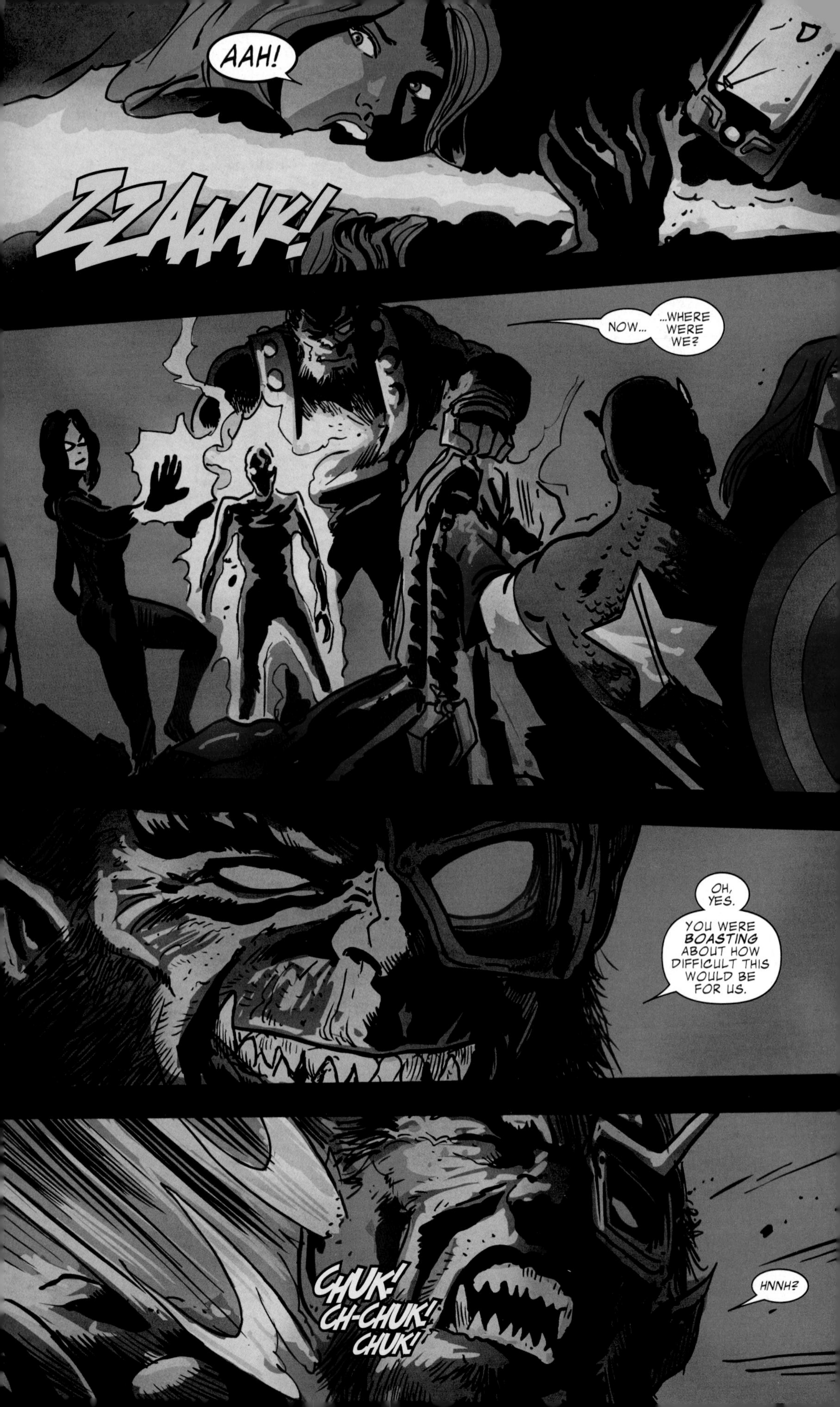
AAH!
ZZZAAAK!
NOW...
...WHERE WERE WE?
OH, YES.
YOU WERE BOASTING ABOUT HOW DIFFICULT THIS WOULD BE FOR US.
CHUK! CH-CHUK! CHUK!
HNNH?

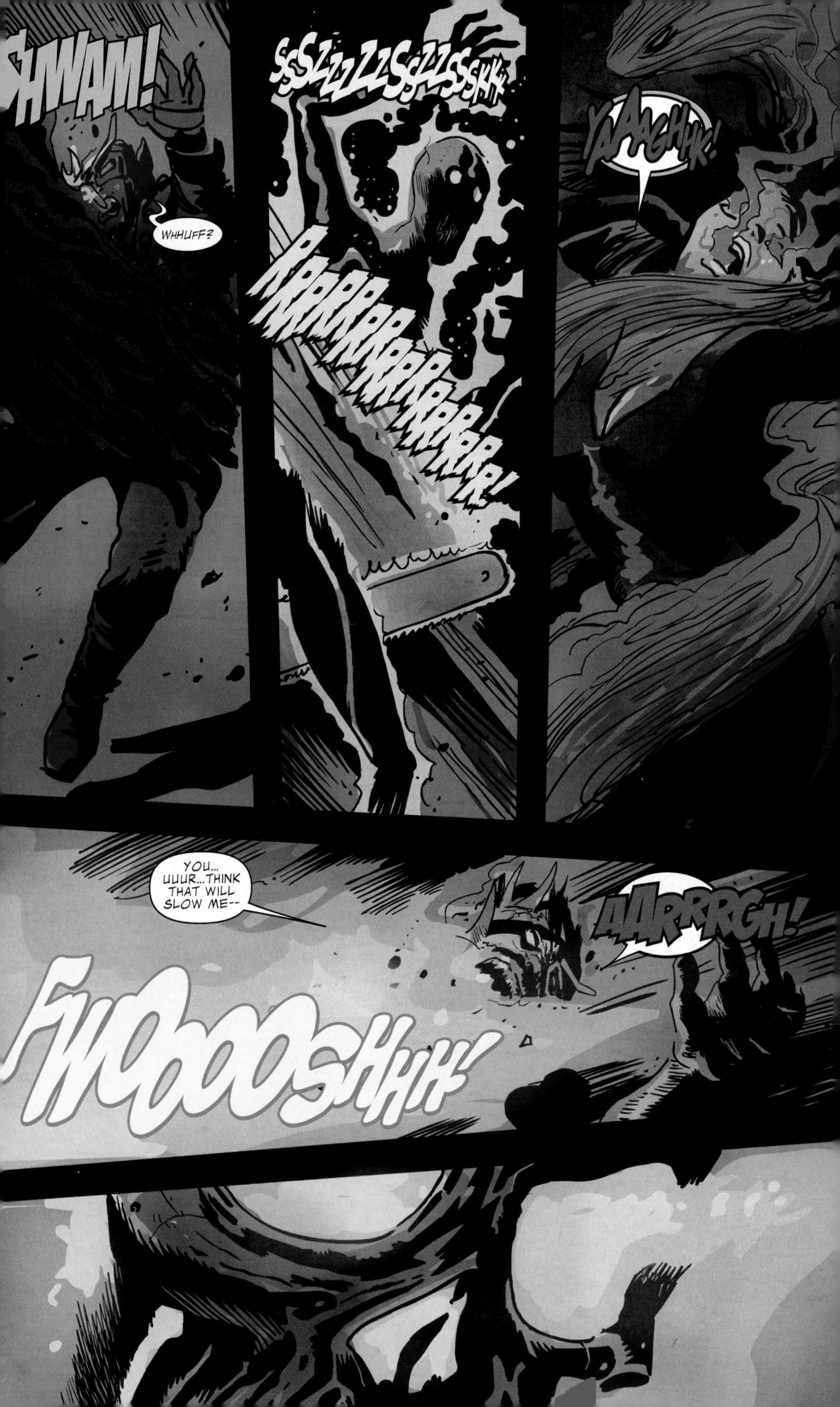
SHWAM!
WHHUFF?
SSSZZZZZSSZZZSSSKKT
RRRRRRRRRRRRRRRRR!
YAAAGHHK!
YOU... UUUR...THINK THAT WILL SLOW ME--
AARRRGH!
FWOOOOSHHH!

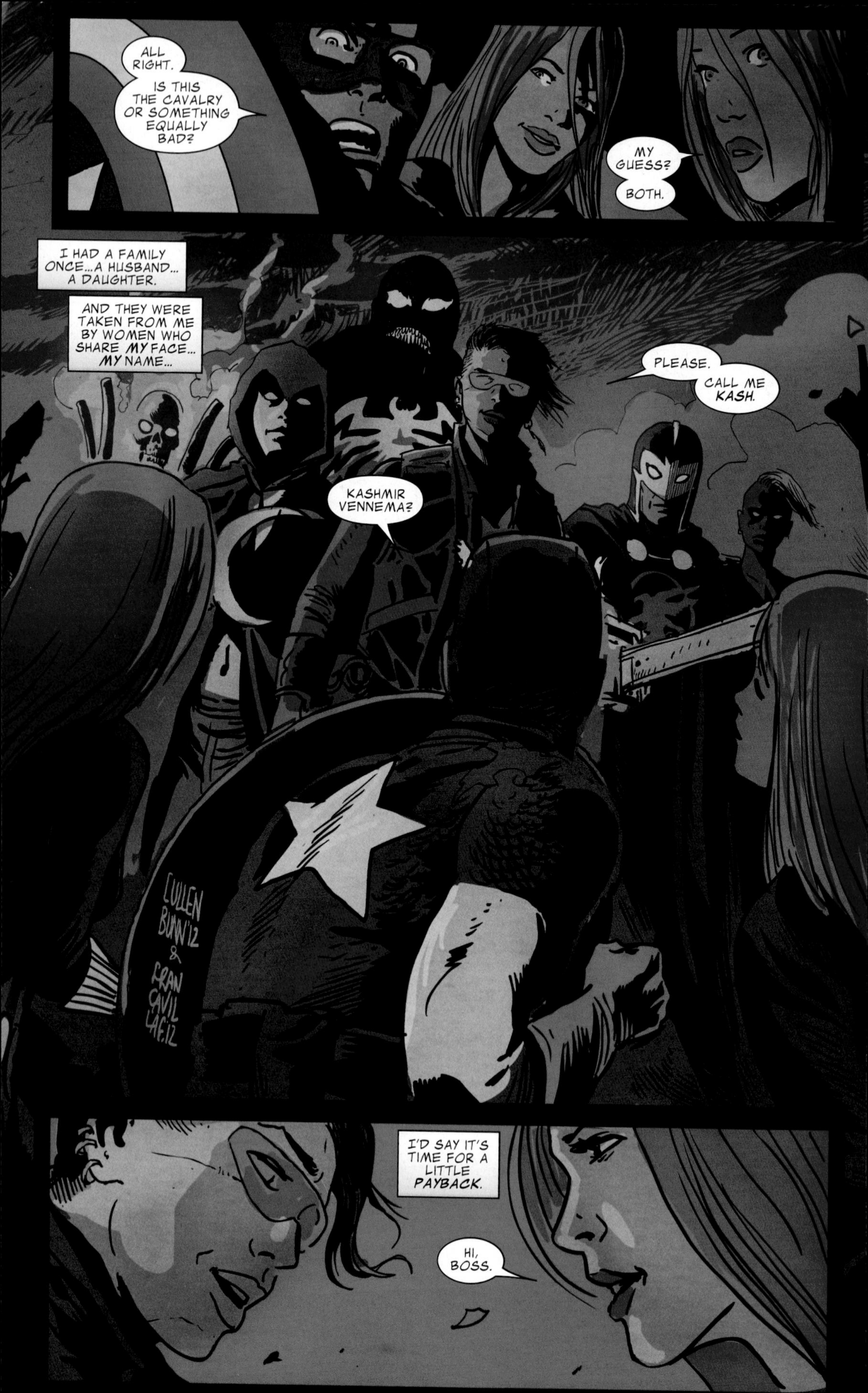
ALL RIGHT.
IS THIS THE CAVALRY OR SOMETHING EQUALLY BAD?
MY GUESS?
BOTH.
I HAD A FAMILY ONCE...A HUSBAND... A DAUGHTER.
AND THEY WERE TAKEN FROM ME BY WOMEN WHO SHARE MY FACE... MY NAME...
KASHMIR VENNEMA?
PLEASE.
CALL ME KASH.
CULLEN BUNN '12 & FRAN CAVILLA '12
I'D SAY IT'S TIME FOR A LITTLE PAYBACK.
HI, BOSS.

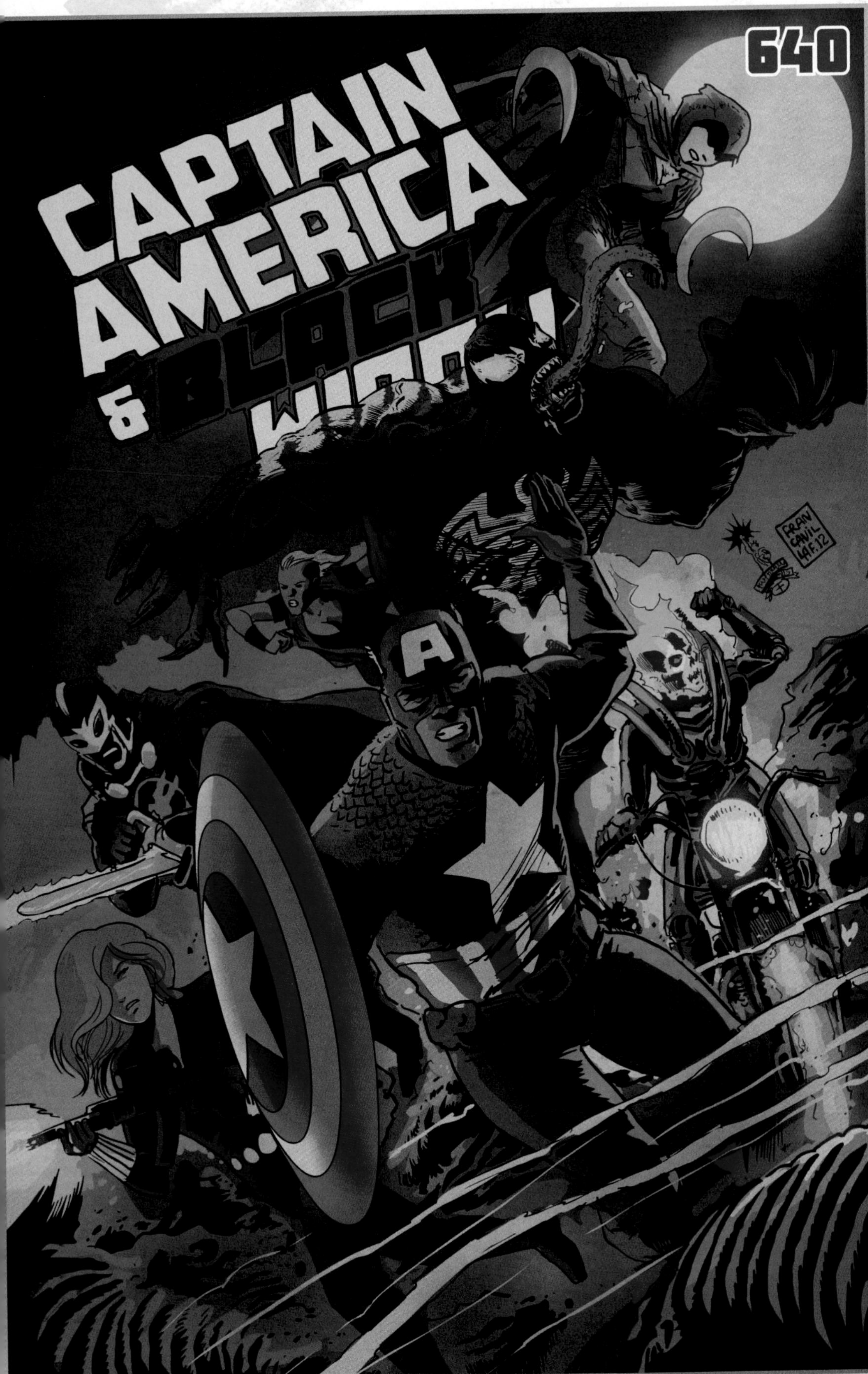
640
CAPTAIN AMERICA
&

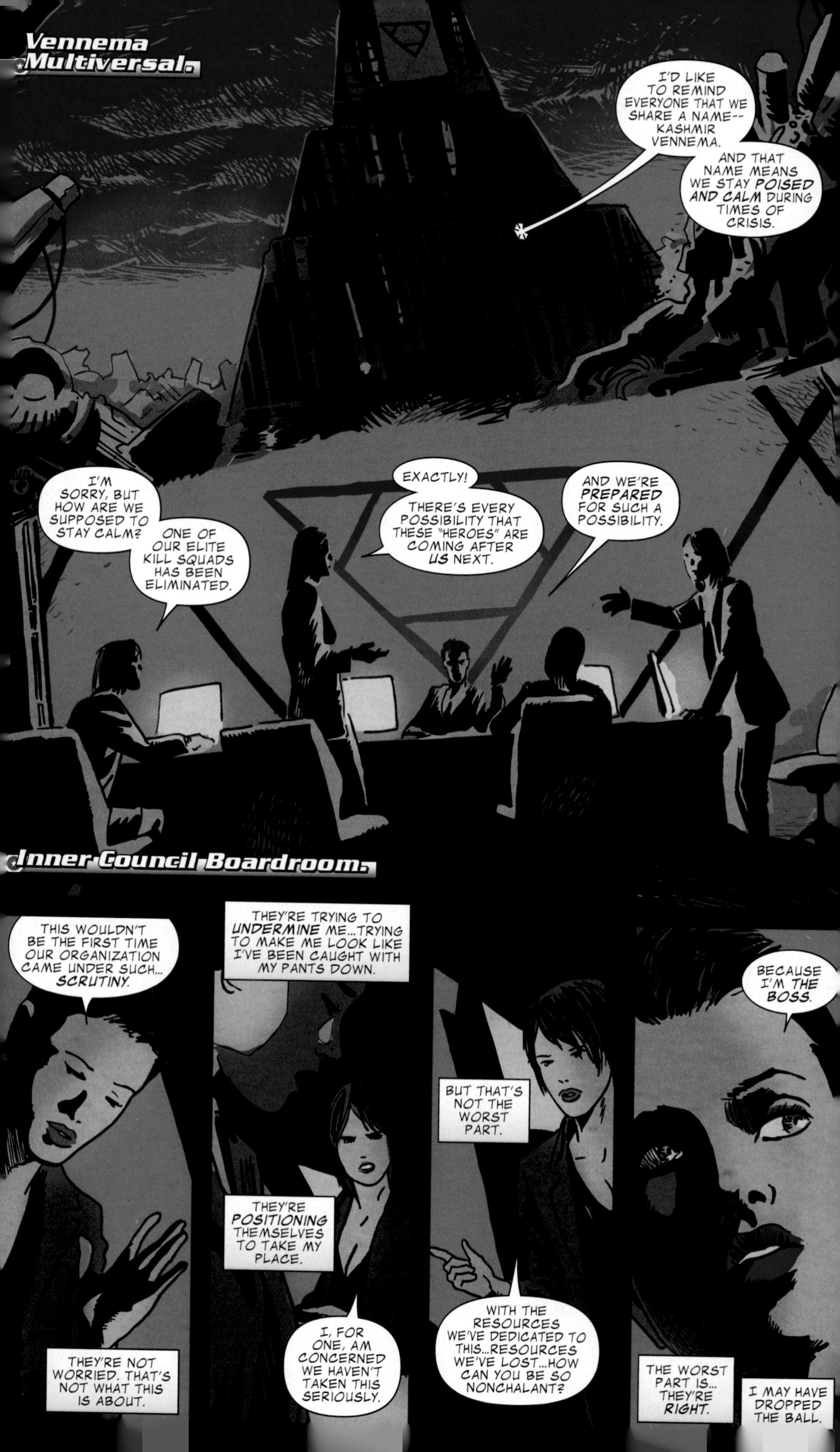
Vennema Multiversal.
I'D LIKE TO REMIND EVERYONE THAT WE SHARE A NAME-- KASHMIR VENNEMA.
AND THAT NAME MEANS WE STAY POISED AND CALM DURING TIMES OF CRISIS.
I'M SORRY, BUT HOW ARE WE SUPPOSED TO STAY CALM?
ONE OF OUR ELITE KILL SQUADS HAS BEEN ELIMINATED.
EXACTLY!
THERE'S EVERY POSSIBILITY THAT THESE "HEROES" ARE COMING AFTER US NEXT.
AND WE'RE PREPARED FOR SUCH A POSSIBILITY.
Inner Council Boardroom.
THIS WOULDN'T BE THE FIRST TIME OUR ORGANIZATION CAME UNDER SUCH... SCRUTINY.
THEY'RE NOT WORRIED. THAT'S NOT WHAT THIS IS ABOUT.
THEY'RE TRYING TO UNDERMINE ME...TRYING TO MAKE ME LOOK LIKE I'VE BEEN CAUGHT WITH MY PANTS DOWN.
THEY'RE POSITIONING THEMSELVES TO TAKE MY PLACE.
I, FOR ONE, AM CONCERNED WE HAVEN'T TAKEN THIS SERIOUSLY.
BUT THAT'S NOT THE WORST PART.
WITH THE RESOURCES WE'VE DEDICATED TO THIS...RESOURCES WE'VE LOST...HOW CAN YOU BE SO NONCHALANT?
BECAUSE I'M THE BOSS.
THE WORST PART IS... THEY'RE RIGHT.
I MAY HAVE DROPPED THE BALL.

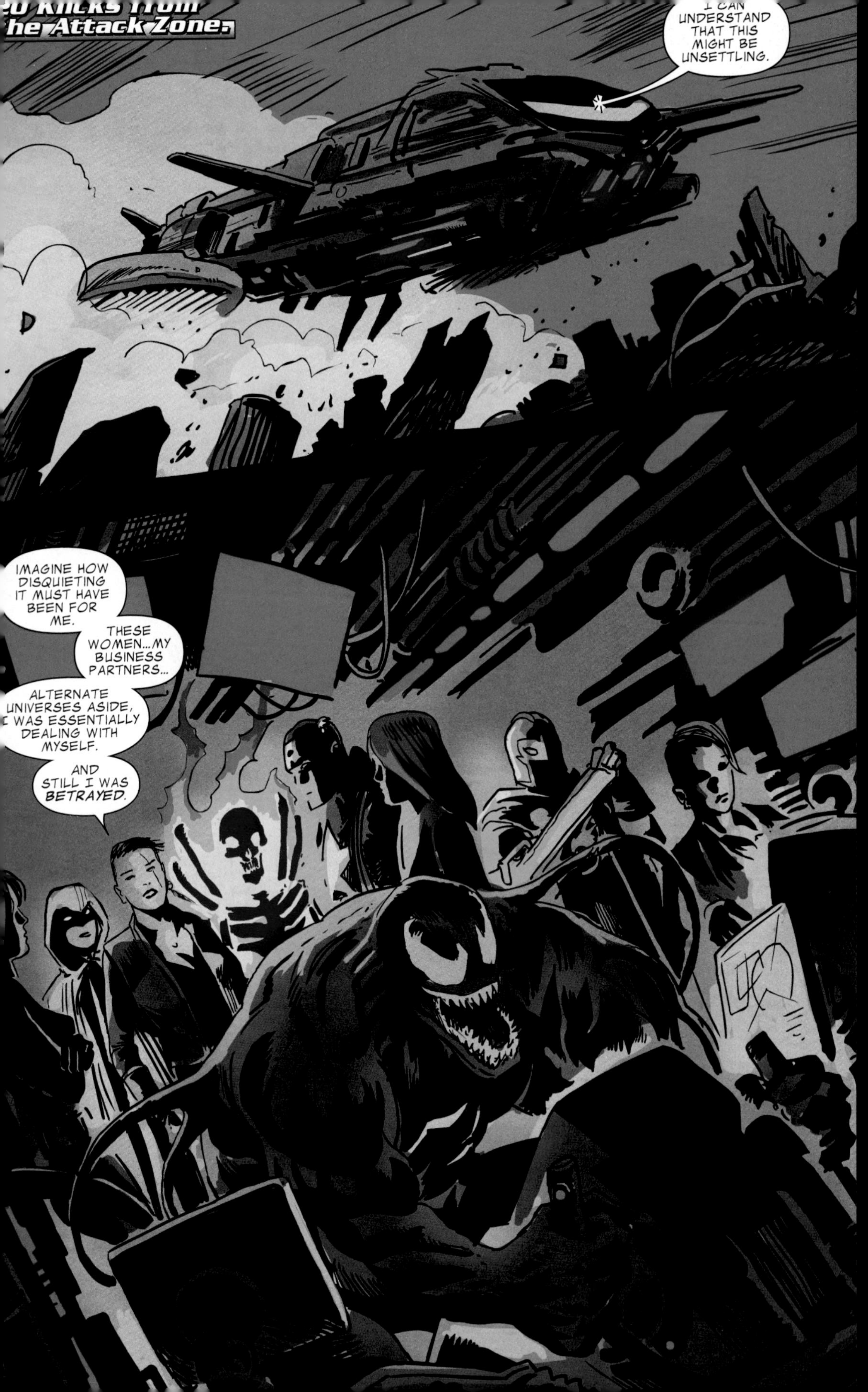
he Attack Zone.
I CAN UNDERSTAND THAT THIS MIGHT BE UNSETTLING.
IMAGINE HOW DISQUIETING IT MUST HAVE BEEN FOR ME.
THESE WOMEN...MY BUSINESS PARTNERS...
ALTERNATE UNIVERSES ASIDE, I WAS ESSENTIALLY DEALING WITH MYSELF.
AND STILL I WAS BETRAYED.

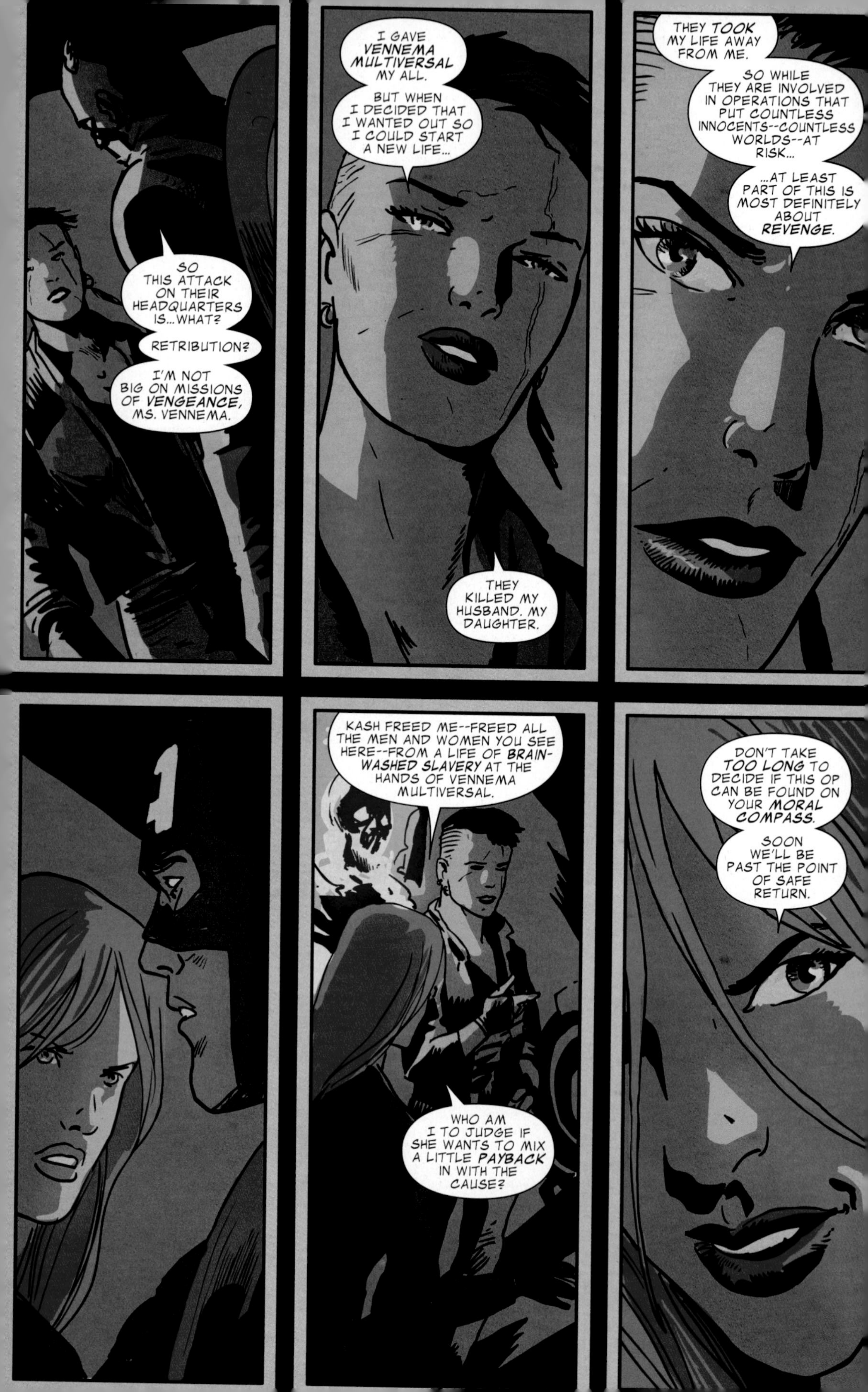
SO THIS ATTACK ON THEIR HEADQUARTERS IS...WHAT?
RETRIBUTION?
I'M NOT BIG ON MISSIONS OF VENGEANCE, MS. VENNEMA.
I GAVE VENNEMA MULTIVERSAL MY ALL.
BUT WHEN I DECIDED THAT I WANTED OUT SO I COULD START A NEW LIFE...
THEY KILLED MY HUSBAND. MY DAUGHTER.
THEY TOOK MY LIFE AWAY FROM ME.
SO WHILE THEY ARE INVOLVED IN OPERATIONS THAT PUT COUNTLESS INNOCENTS--COUNTLESS WORLDS--AT RISK...
...AT LEAST PART OF THIS IS MOST DEFINITELY ABOUT REVENGE.
KASH FREED ME--FREED ALL THE MEN AND WOMEN YOU SEE HERE--FROM A LIFE OF BRAIN-WASHED SLAVERY AT THE HANDS OF VENNEMA MULTIVERSAL.
WHO AM I TO JUDGE IF SHE WANTS TO MIX A LITTLE PAYBACK IN WITH THE CAUSE?
DON'T TAKE TOO LONG TO DECIDE IF THIS OP CAN BE FOUND ON YOUR MORAL COMPASS.
SOON WE'LL BE PAST THE POINT OF SAFE RETURN.

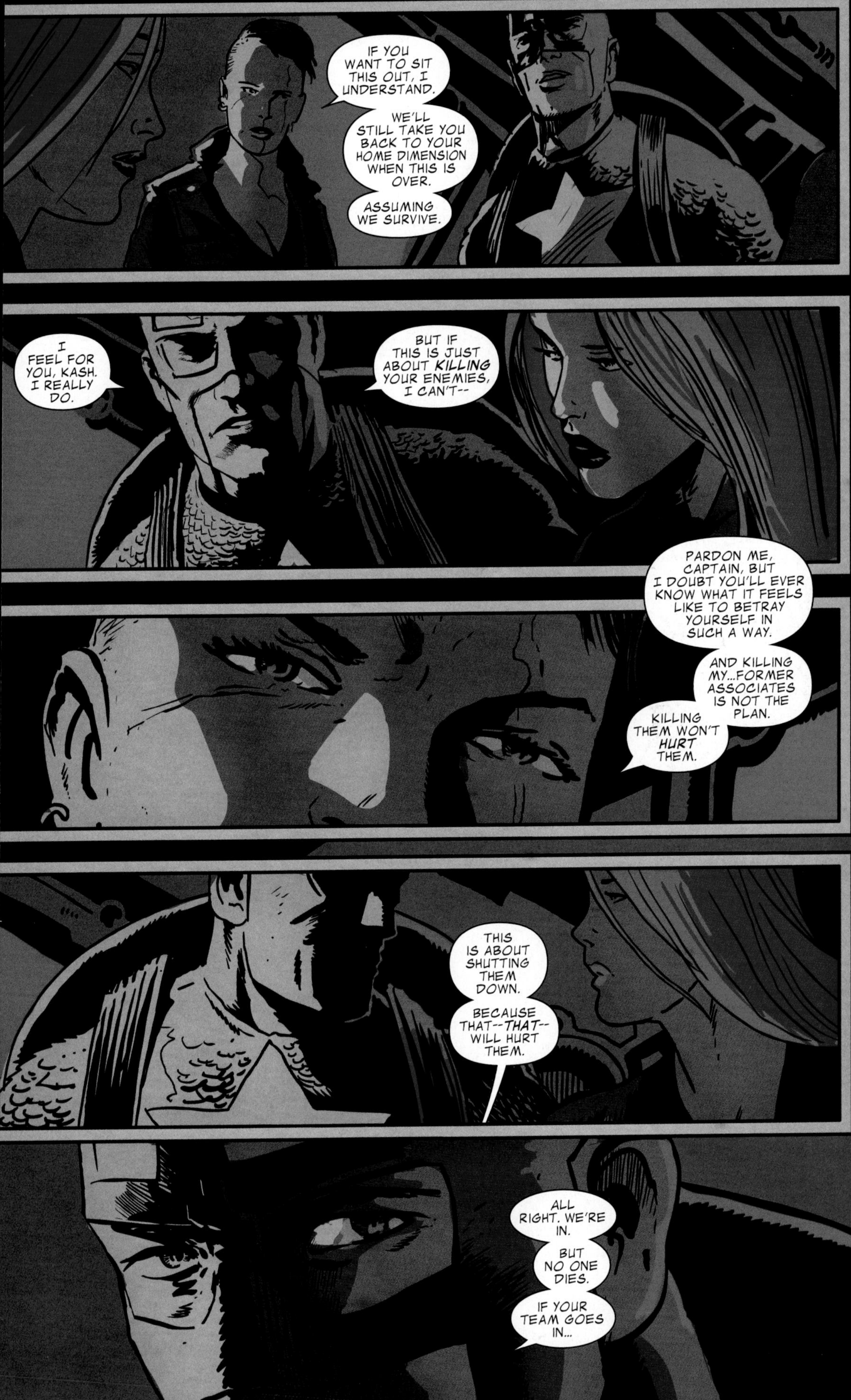
IF YOU WANT TO SIT THIS OUT, I UNDERSTAND.
WE'LL STILL TAKE YOU BACK TO YOUR HOME DIMENSION WHEN THIS IS OVER.
ASSUMING WE SURVIVE.
I FEEL FOR YOU, KASH. I REALLY DO.
BUT IF THIS IS JUST ABOUT KILLING YOUR ENEMIES, I CAN'T--
PARDON ME, CAPTAIN, BUT I DOUBT YOU'LL EVER KNOW WHAT IT FEELS LIKE TO BETRAY YOURSELF IN SUCH A WAY.
AND KILLING MY...FORMER ASSOCIATES IS NOT THE PLAN.
KILLING THEM WON'T HURT THEM.
THIS IS ABOUT SHUTTING THEM DOWN.
BECAUSE THAT--THAT--WILL HURT THEM.
ALL RIGHT. WE'RE IN.
BUT NO ONE DIES.
IF YOUR TEAM GOES IN...

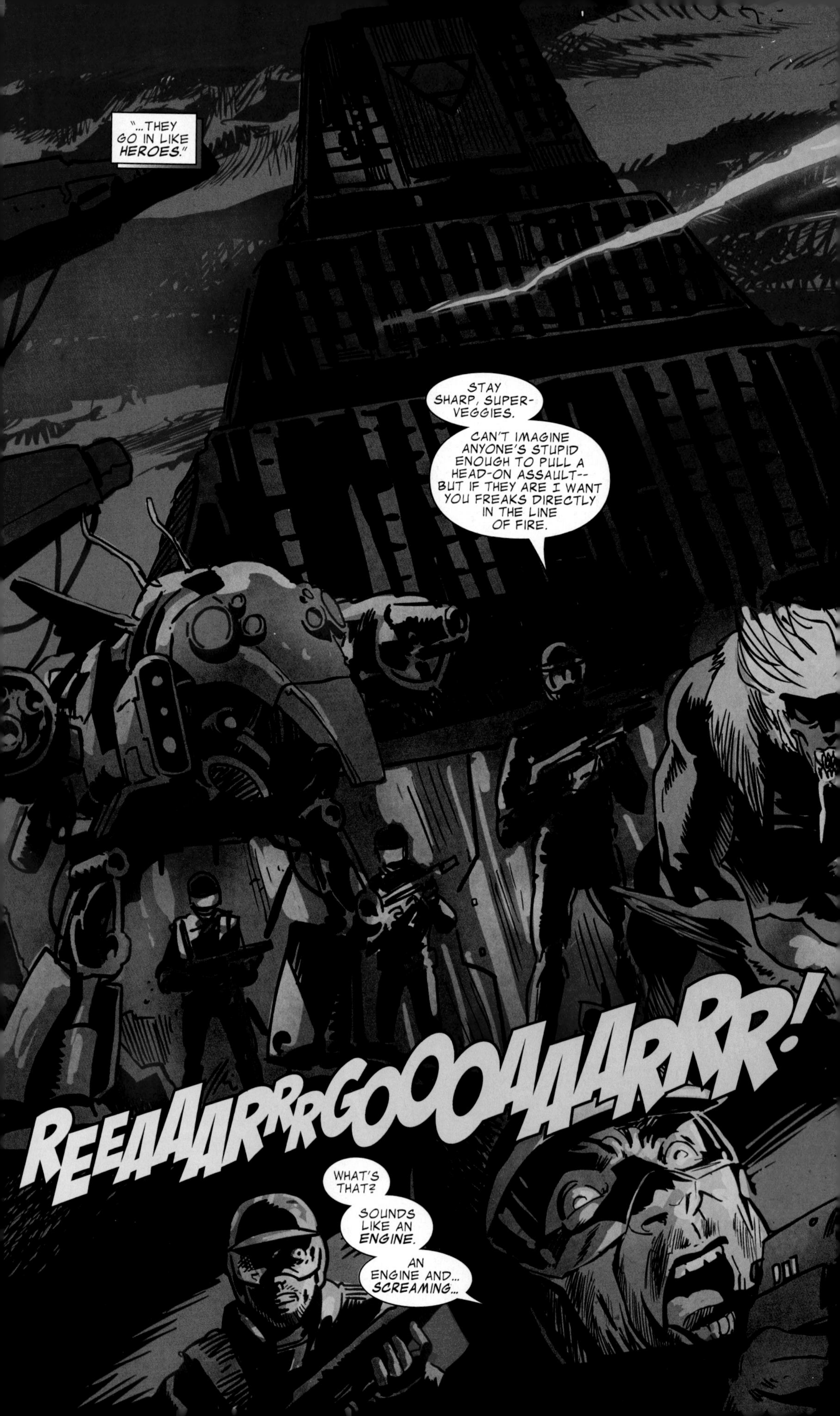
"...THEY GO IN LIKE HEROES."
STAY SHARP, SUPER-VEGGIES.
CAN'T IMAGINE ANYONE'S STUPID ENOUGH TO PULL A HEAD-ON ASSAULT-- BUT IF THEY ARE I WANT YOU FREAKS DIRECTLY IN THE LINE OF FIRE.
REEAAAARRRRGOOOAAARRR!
WHAT'S THAT?
SOUNDS LIKE AN ENGINE.
AN ENGINE AND... SCREAMING...

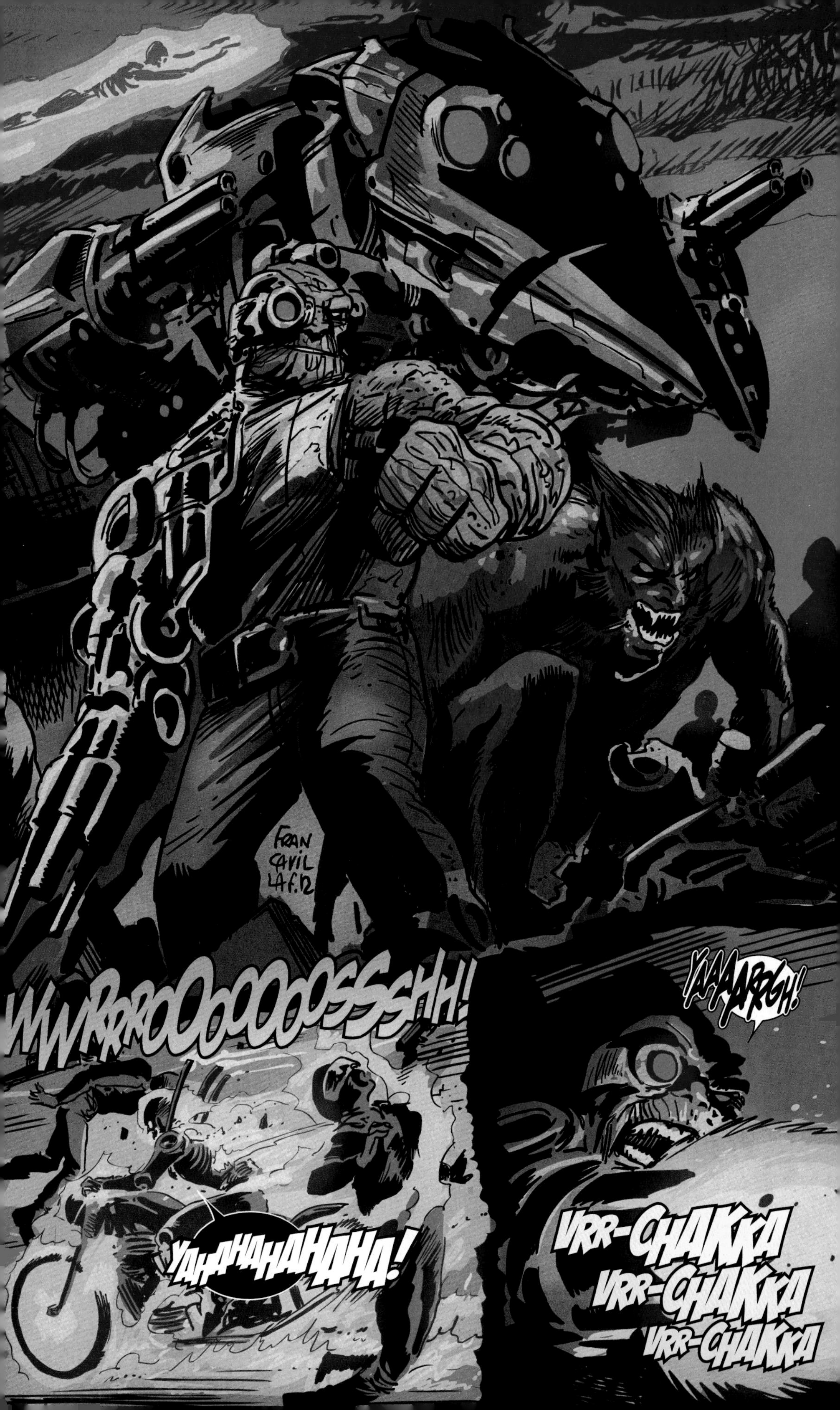

FRAN CAVIL 14 F. 12
WWRRROOOOOOOSSSHH!
YAAAARGH!
YAHAHAHAHAHAHA!
VRR-CHAKKA
VRR-CHAKKA
VRR-CHAKKA

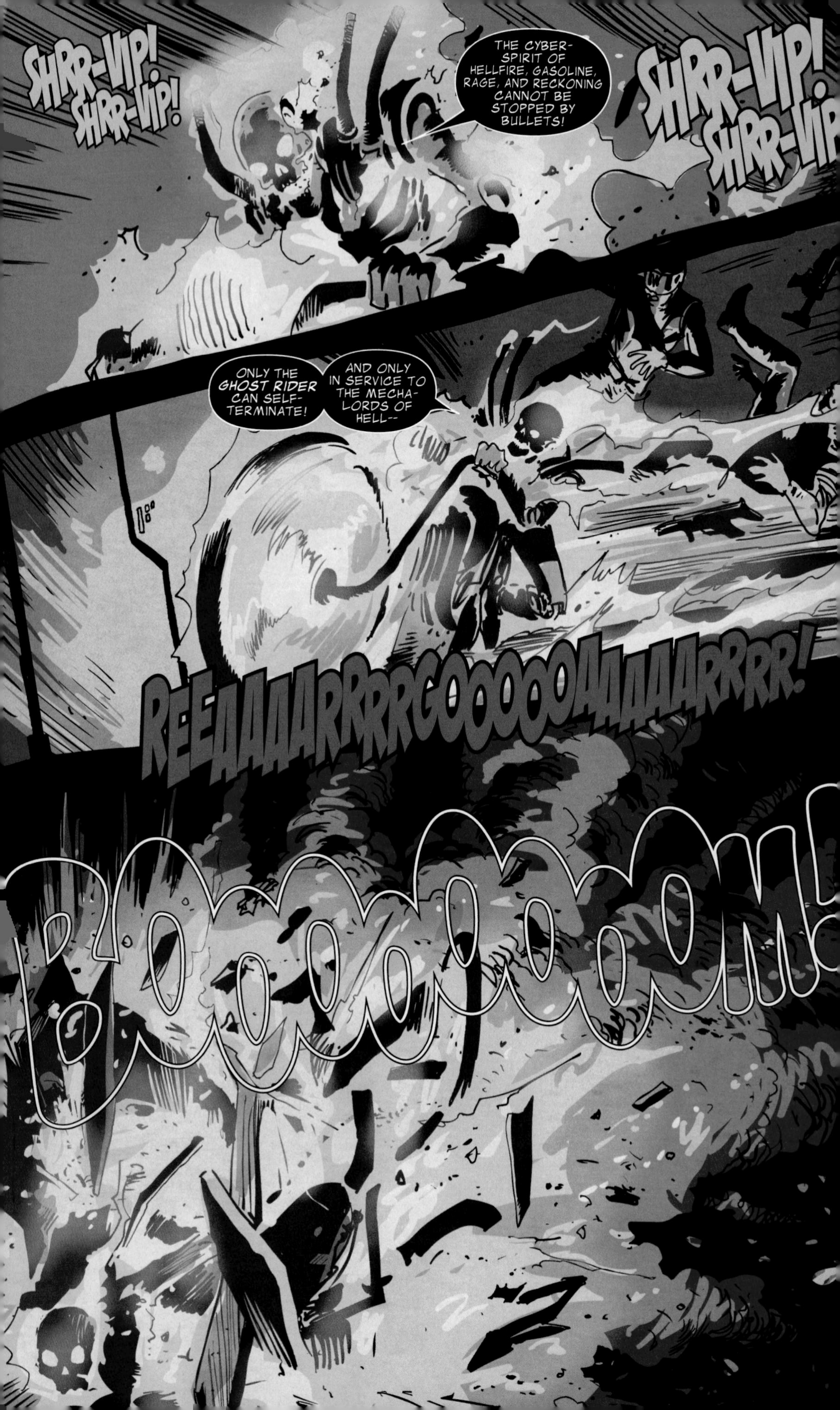
SHRR-VIP! SHRR-VIP!
THE CYBER-SPIRIT OF HELLFIRE, GASOLINE, RAGE, AND RECKONING CANNOT BE STOPPED BY BULLETS!
SHRR-VIP! SHRR-VIP!
ONLY THE GHOST RIDER CAN SELF-TERMINATE!
AND ONLY IN SERVICE TO THE MECHA-LORDS OF HELL--
REEAAAARRRRGOOOOOAAAAARRRR!
BOOOOOOOOOM!

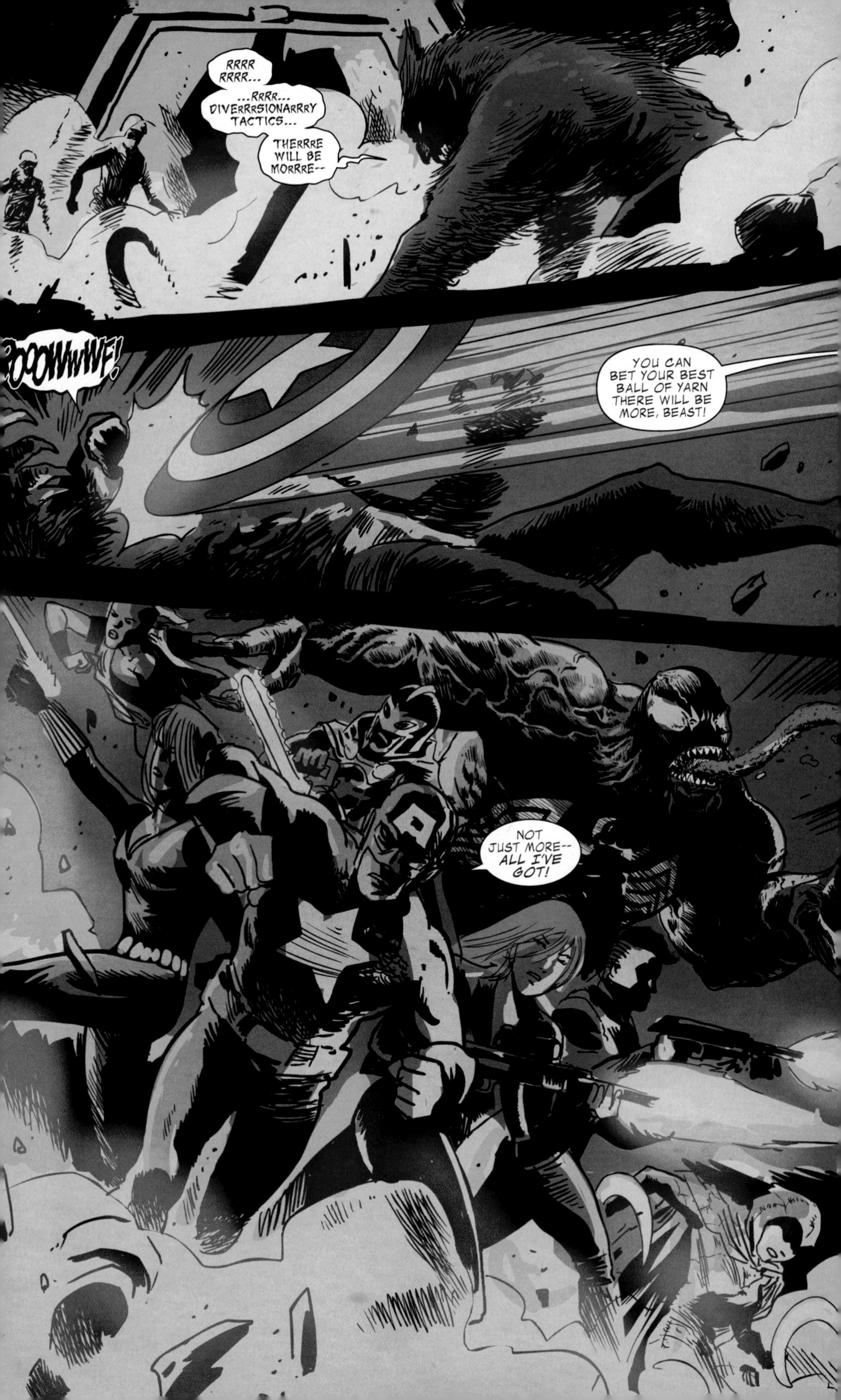

RRRR RRRR...
...RRRR... DIVERRRSIONARRRY TACTICS...
THERRRE WILL BE MORRRE--
FOOOMWWF!
YOU CAN BET YOUR BEST BALL OF YARN THERE WILL BE MORE, BEAST!
NOT JUST MORE-- ALL I'VE GOT!

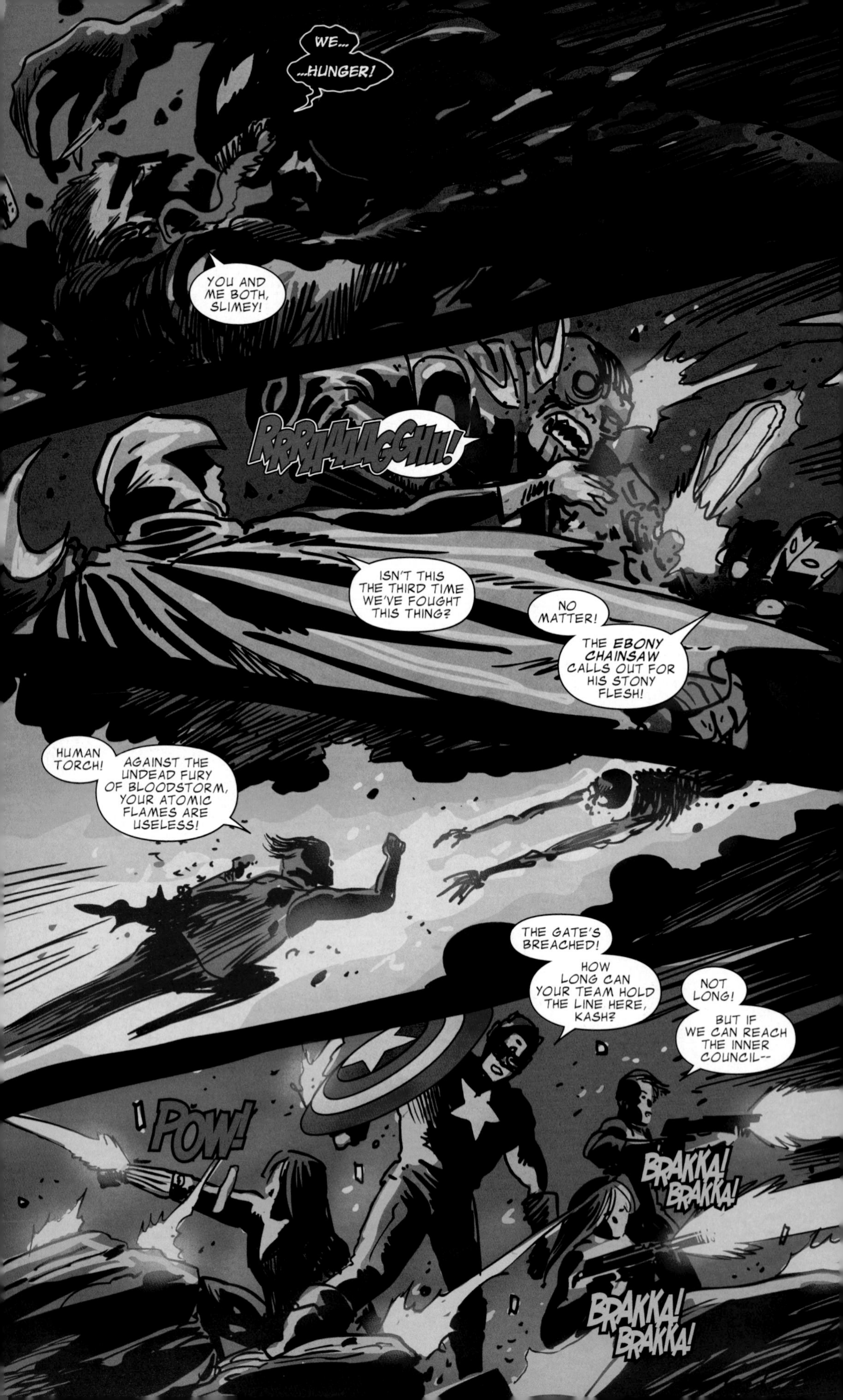
WE...
...HUNGER!
YOU AND ME BOTH, SLIMEY!
RRRAAAAGGHH!
ISN'T THIS THE THIRD TIME WE'VE FOUGHT THIS THING?
NO MATTER!
THE EBONY CHAINSAW CALLS OUT FOR HIS STONY FLESH!
HUMAN TORCH!
AGAINST THE UNDEAD FURY OF BLOODSTORM, YOUR ATOMIC FLAMES ARE USELESS!
THE GATE'S BREACHED!
HOW LONG CAN YOUR TEAM HOLD THE LINE HERE, KASH?
NOT LONG!
BUT IF WE CAN REACH THE INNER COUNCIL--
POW!
BRAKKA! BRAKKA!
BRAKKA! BRAKKA!

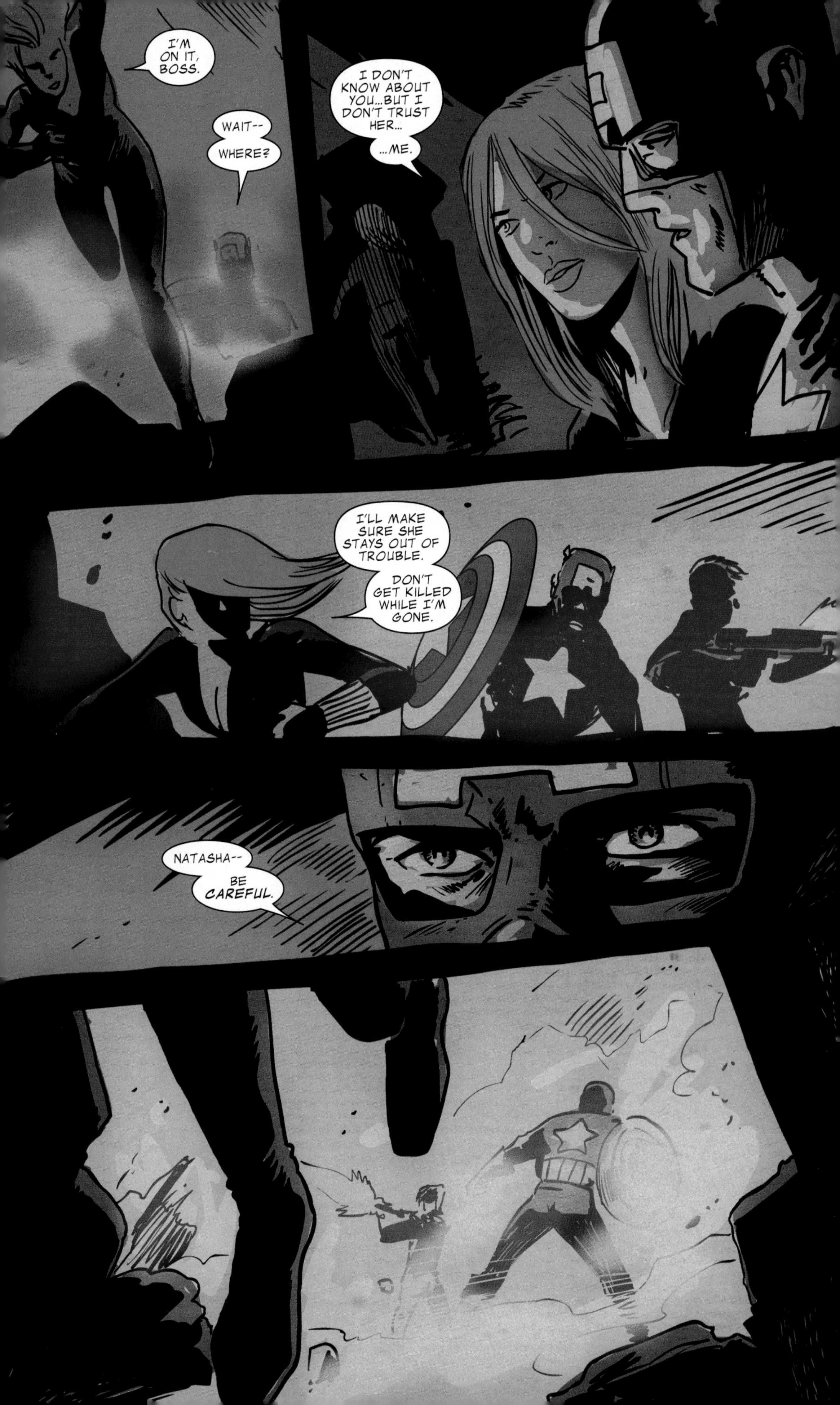
I'M ON IT, BOSS.
WAIT--
WHERE?
I DON'T KNOW ABOUT YOU...BUT I DON'T TRUST HER...
...ME.
I'LL MAKE SURE SHE STAYS OUT OF TROUBLE.
DON'T GET KILLED WHILE I'M GONE.
NATASHA--
BE CAREFUL.

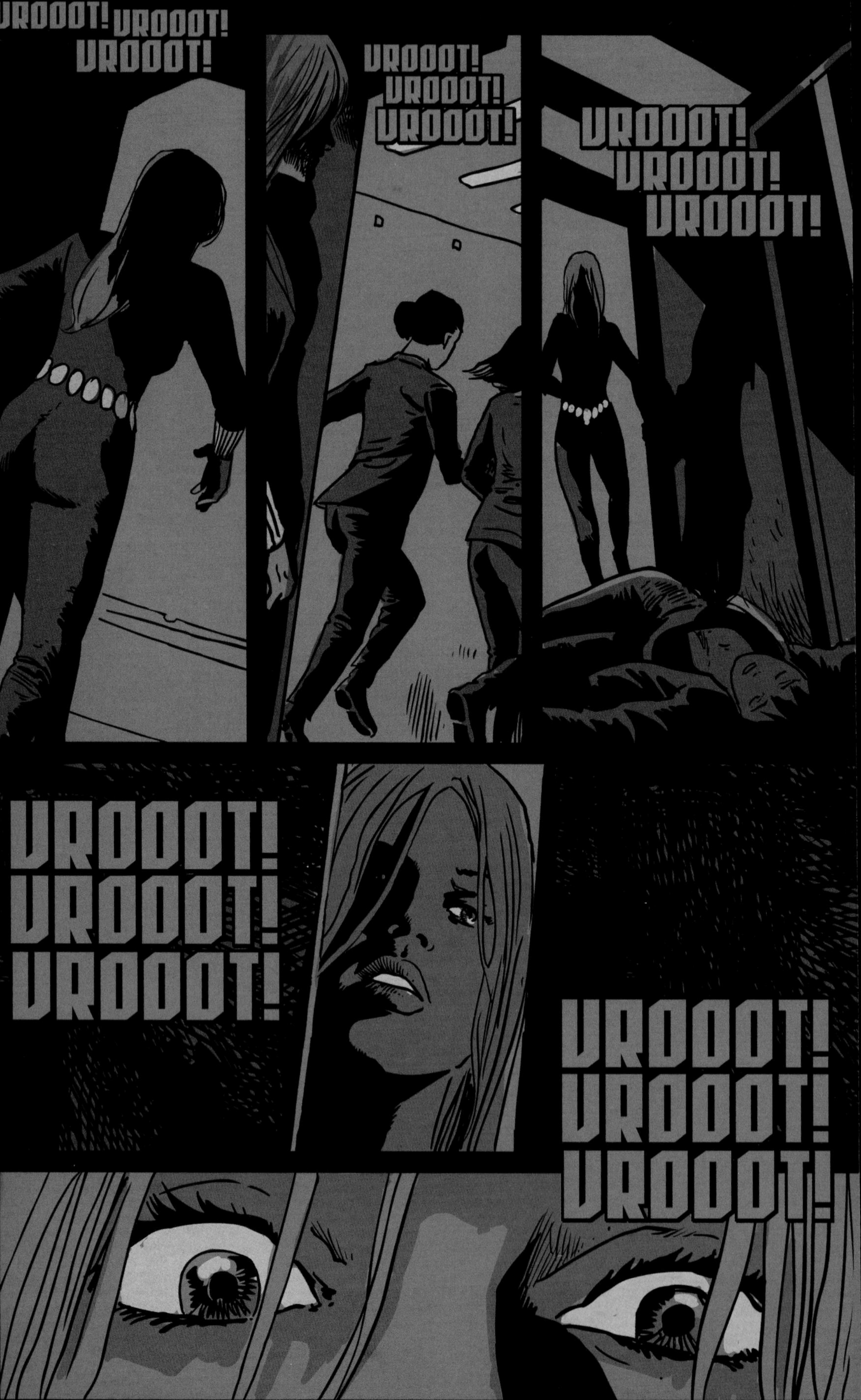
VROOOT! VROOOT!
VROOOT!
VROOOT!
VROOOT!
VROOOT!
VROOOT!
VROOOT!
VROOOT!
VROOOT!
VROOOT!
VROOOT!
VROOOT!
VROOOT!
VROOOT!

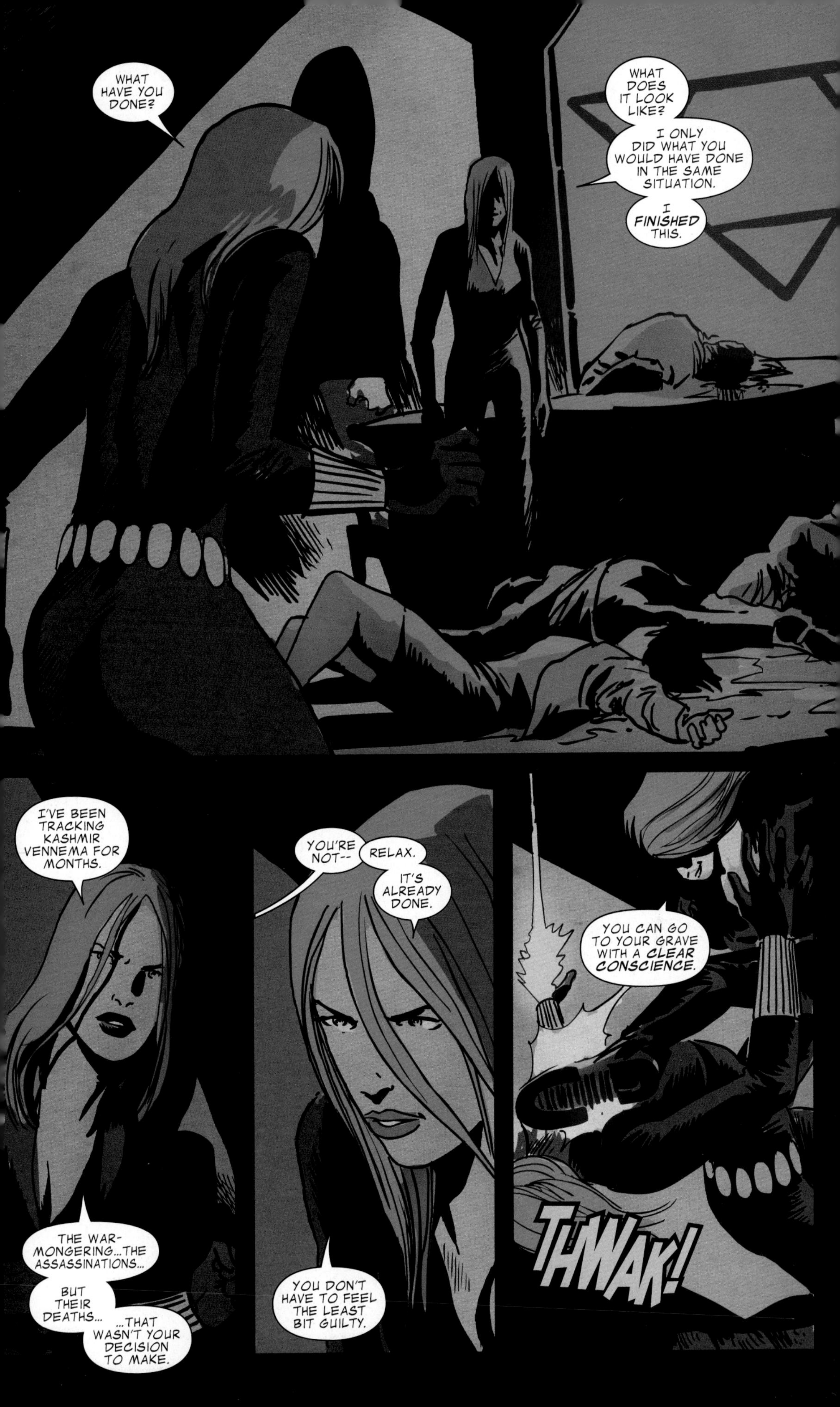
WHAT HAVE YOU DONE?
WHAT DOES IT LOOK LIKE?
I ONLY DID WHAT YOU WOULD HAVE DONE IN THE SAME SITUATION.
I *FINISHED* THIS.
I'VE BEEN TRACKING KASHMIR VENNEMA FOR MONTHS.
THE WAR-MONGERING...THE ASSASSINATIONS...
BUT THEIR DEATHS...
...THAT WASN'T YOUR DECISION TO MAKE.
YOU'RE NOT--
RELAX.
IT'S ALREADY DONE.
YOU DON'T HAVE TO FEEL THE LEAST BIT GUILTY.
YOU CAN GO TO YOUR GRAVE WITH A **CLEAR CONSCIENCE**.
THWAK!

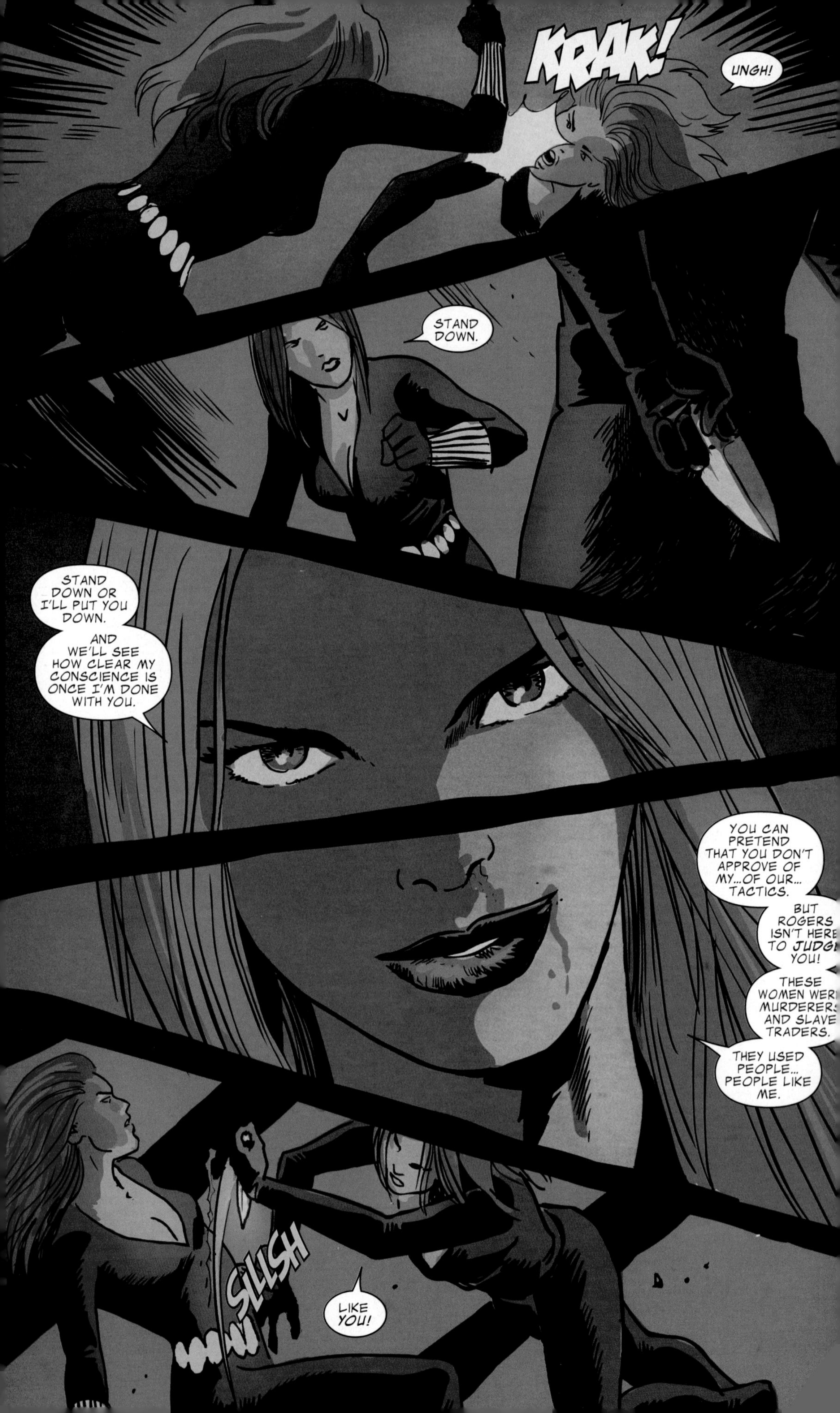
KRAK!
UNGH!
STAND DOWN.
STAND DOWN OR I'LL PUT YOU DOWN.
AND WE'LL SEE HOW CLEAR MY CONSCIENCE IS ONCE I'M DONE WITH YOU.
YOU CAN PRETEND THAT YOU DON'T APPROVE OF MY...OF OUR... TACTICS.
BUT ROGERS ISN'T HERE TO JUDGE YOU!
THESE WOMEN WERE MURDERERS AND SLAVE TRADERS.
THEY USED PEOPLE... PEOPLE LIKE ME.
SLISH
LIKE YOU!

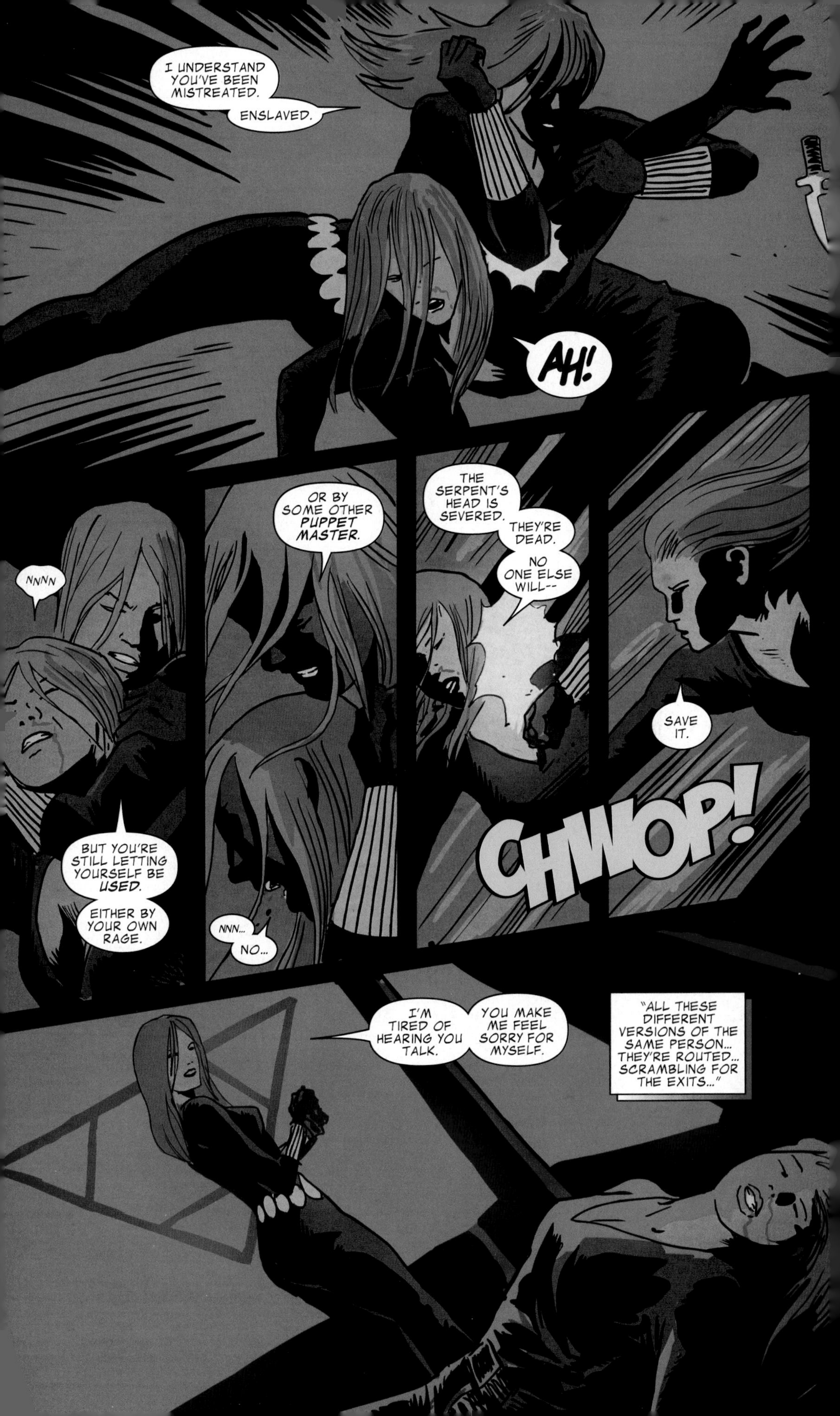
I UNDERSTAND YOU'VE BEEN MISTREATED.
ENSLAVED.
AH!
NNNN
BUT YOU'RE STILL LETTING YOURSELF BE *USED*.
EITHER BY YOUR OWN RAGE.
OR BY SOME OTHER *PUPPET MASTER*.
NNN... NO...
THE SERPENT'S HEAD IS SEVERED.
THEY'RE DEAD.
NO ONE ELSE WILL--
SAVE IT.
CHWOP!
I'M TIRED OF HEARING YOU TALK.
YOU MAKE ME FEEL SORRY FOR MYSELF.
"ALL THESE DIFFERENT VERSIONS OF THE SAME PERSON... THEY'RE ROUTED... SCRAMBLING FOR THE EXITS..."

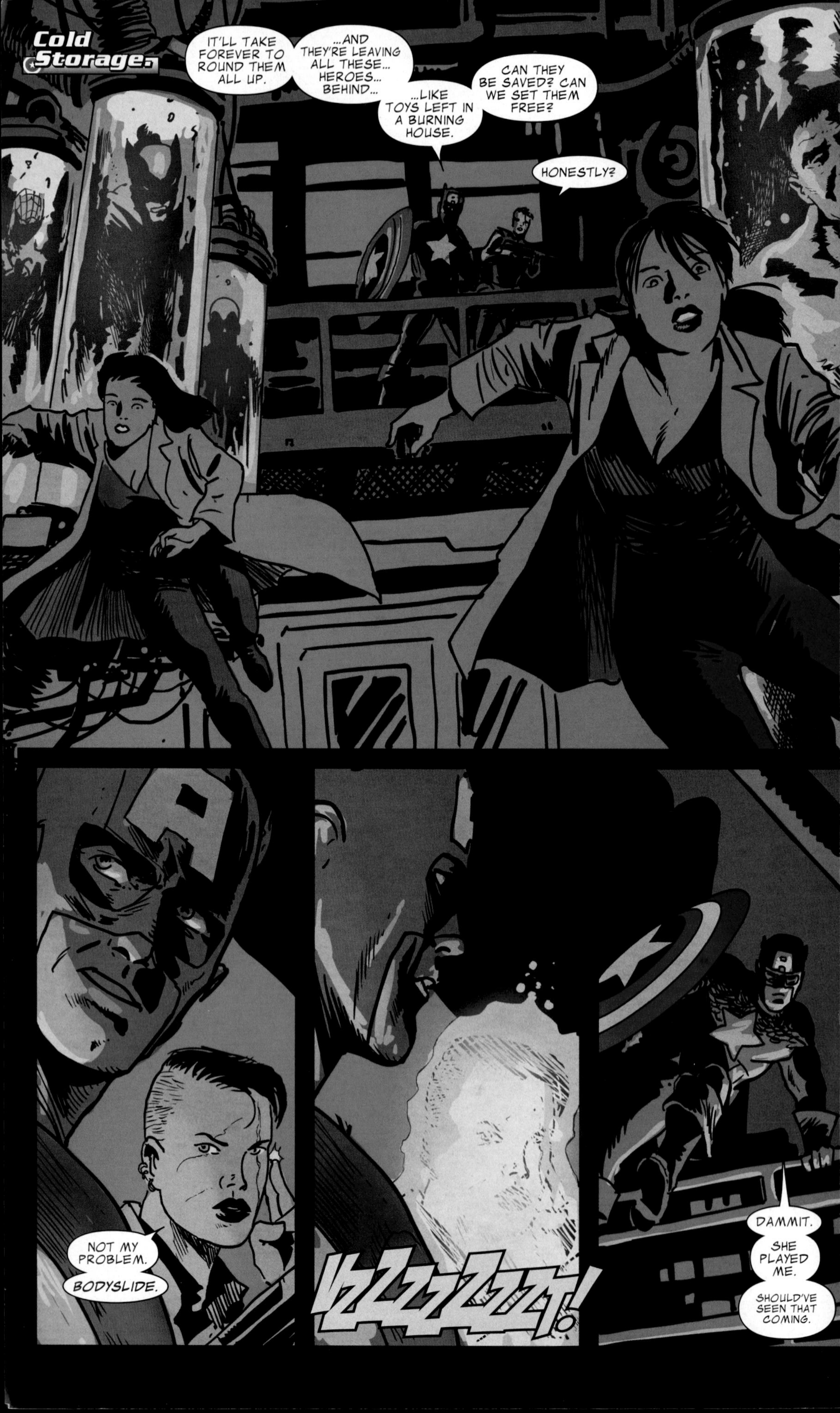
Cold Storage
IT'LL TAKE FOREVER TO ROUND THEM ALL UP.
...AND THEY'RE LEAVING ALL THESE... HEROES... BEHIND...
...LIKE TOYS LEFT IN A BURNING HOUSE.
CAN THEY BE SAVED? CAN WE SET THEM FREE?
HONESTLY?
NOT MY PROBLEM.
BODYSLIDE.
IZZZZZZZT!
DAMMIT.
SHE PLAYED ME.
SHOULD'VE SEEN THAT COMING.

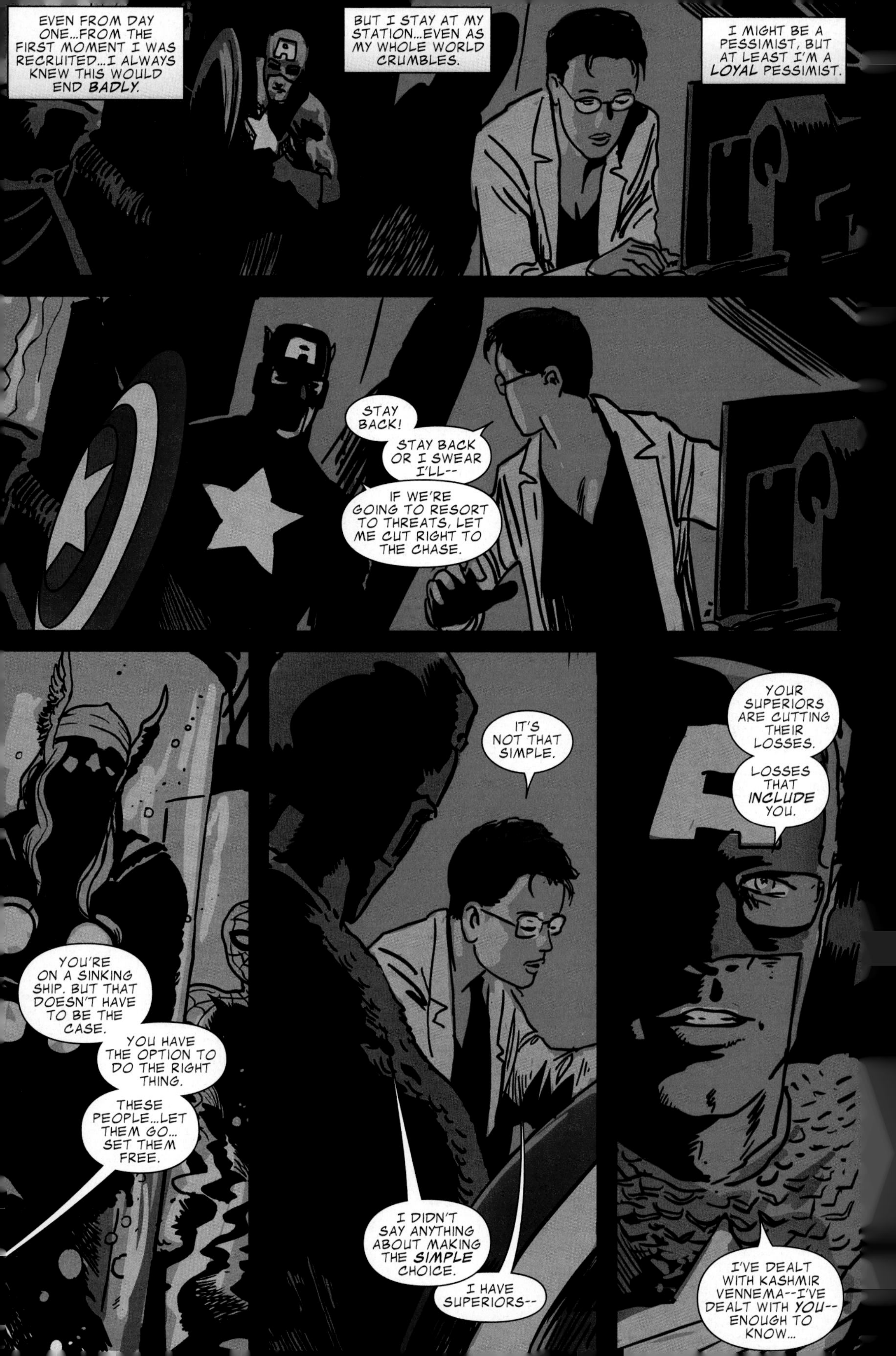
EVEN FROM DAY ONE...FROM THE FIRST MOMENT I WAS RECRUITED...I ALWAYS KNEW THIS WOULD END BADLY.
BUT I STAY AT MY STATION...EVEN AS MY WHOLE WORLD CRUMBLES.
I MIGHT BE A PESSIMIST, BUT AT LEAST I'M A LOYAL PESSIMIST.
STAY BACK!
STAY BACK OR I SWEAR I'LL--
IF WE'RE GOING TO RESORT TO THREATS, LET ME CUT RIGHT TO THE CHASE.
YOU'RE ON A SINKING SHIP. BUT THAT DOESN'T HAVE TO BE THE CASE.
YOU HAVE THE OPTION TO DO THE RIGHT THING.
THESE PEOPLE...LET THEM GO... SET THEM FREE.
IT'S NOT THAT SIMPLE.
I DIDN'T SAY ANYTHING ABOUT MAKING THE SIMPLE CHOICE.
I HAVE SUPERIORS--
YOUR SUPERIORS ARE CUTTING THEIR LOSSES.
LOSSES THAT INCLUDE YOU.
I'VE DEALT WITH KASHMIR VENNEMA--I'VE DEALT WITH YOU--ENOUGH TO KNOW...

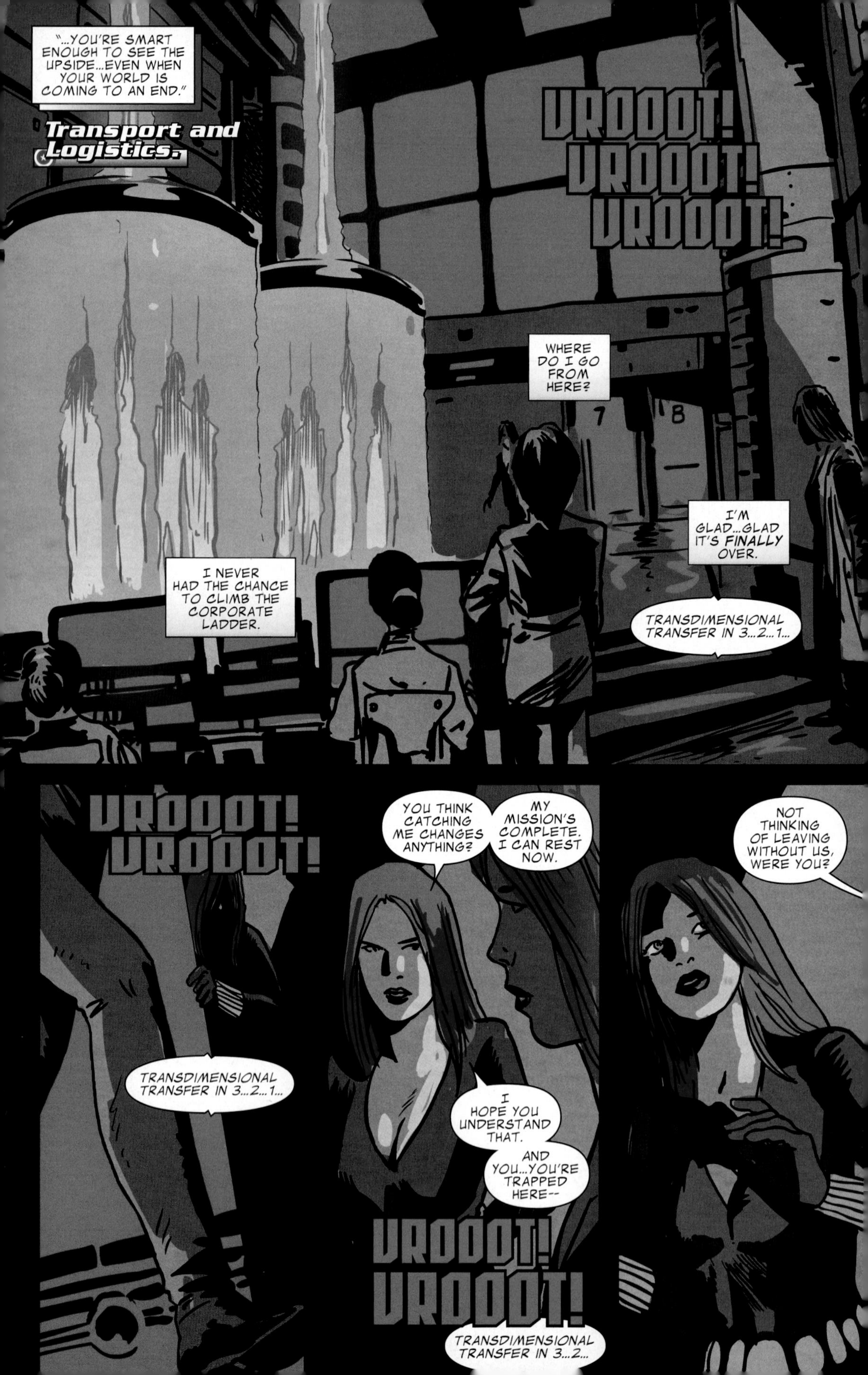
"...YOU'RE SMART ENOUGH TO SEE THE UPSIDE...EVEN WHEN YOUR WORLD IS COMING TO AN END."
Transport and Logistics.
VROOOT! VROOOT! VROOOT!
WHERE DO I GO FROM HERE?
I'M GLAD...GLAD IT'S FINALLY OVER.
I NEVER HAD THE CHANCE TO CLIMB THE CORPORATE LADDER.
TRANSDIMENSIONAL TRANSFER IN 3...2...1...
VROOOT! VROOOT!
TRANSDIMENSIONAL TRANSFER IN 3...2...1...
YOU THINK CATCHING ME CHANGES ANYTHING?
MY MISSION'S COMPLETE. I CAN REST NOW.
I HOPE YOU UNDERSTAND THAT.
AND YOU...YOU'RE TRAPPED HERE--
VROOOT! VROOOT!
TRANSDIMENSIONAL TRANSFER IN 3...2...
NOT THINKING OF LEAVING WITHOUT US, WERE YOU?

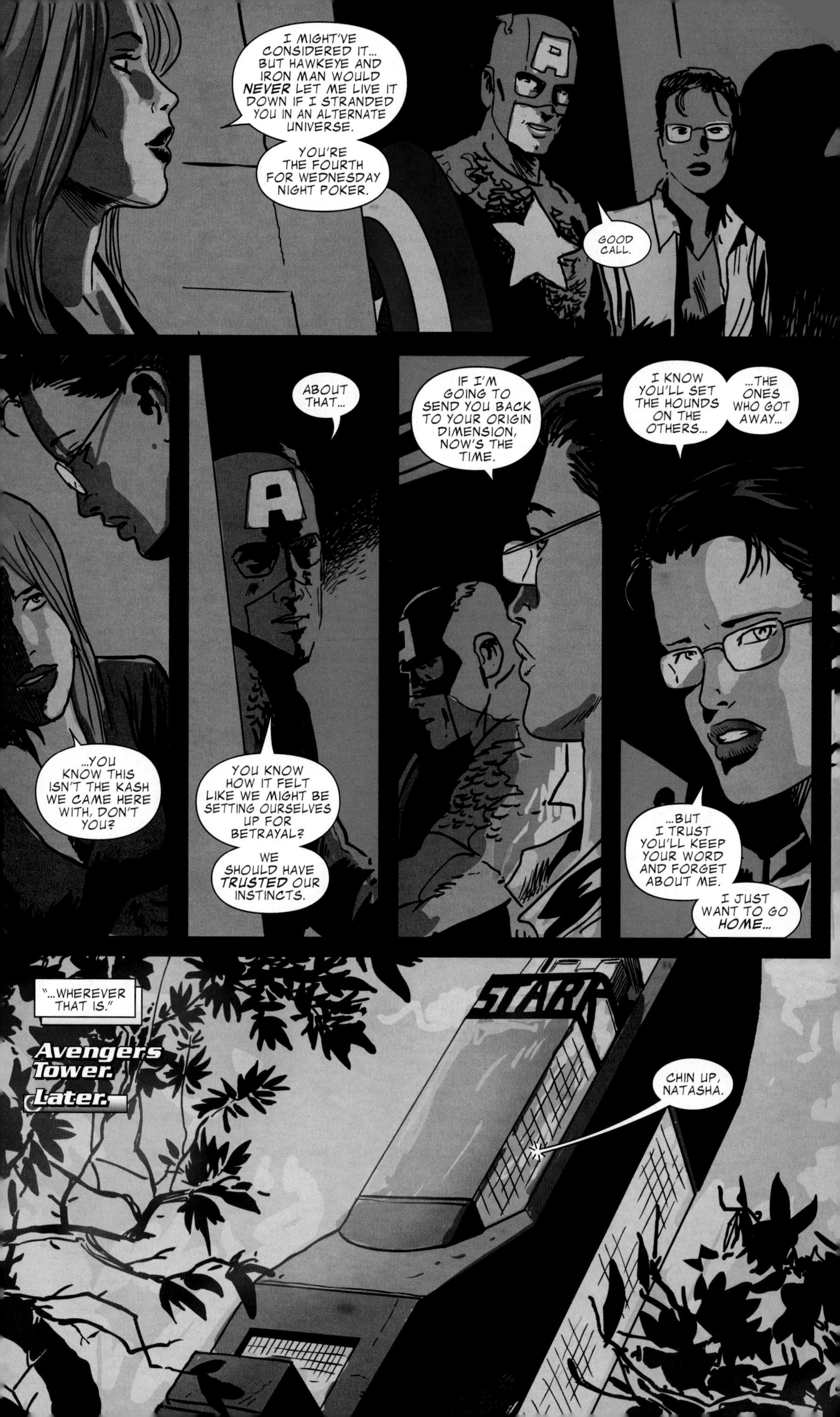
I MIGHT'VE CONSIDERED IT... BUT HAWKEYE AND IRON MAN WOULD NEVER LET ME LIVE IT DOWN IF I STRANDED YOU IN AN ALTERNATE UNIVERSE.
YOU'RE THE FOURTH FOR WEDNESDAY NIGHT POKER.
GOOD CALL.
...YOU KNOW THIS ISN'T THE KASH WE CAME HERE WITH, DON'T YOU?
ABOUT THAT...
YOU KNOW HOW IT FELT LIKE WE MIGHT BE SETTING OURSELVES UP FOR BETRAYAL?
WE SHOULD HAVE TRUSTED OUR INSTINCTS.
IF I'M GOING TO SEND YOU BACK TO YOUR ORIGIN DIMENSION, NOW'S THE TIME.
I KNOW YOU'LL SET THE HOUNDS ON THE OTHERS...
...THE ONES WHO GOT AWAY...
...BUT I TRUST YOU'LL KEEP YOUR WORD AND FORGET ABOUT ME.
I JUST WANT TO GO HOME...
"...WHEREVER THAT IS."
Avengers Tower.
Later.
STARK
CHIN UP, NATASHA.

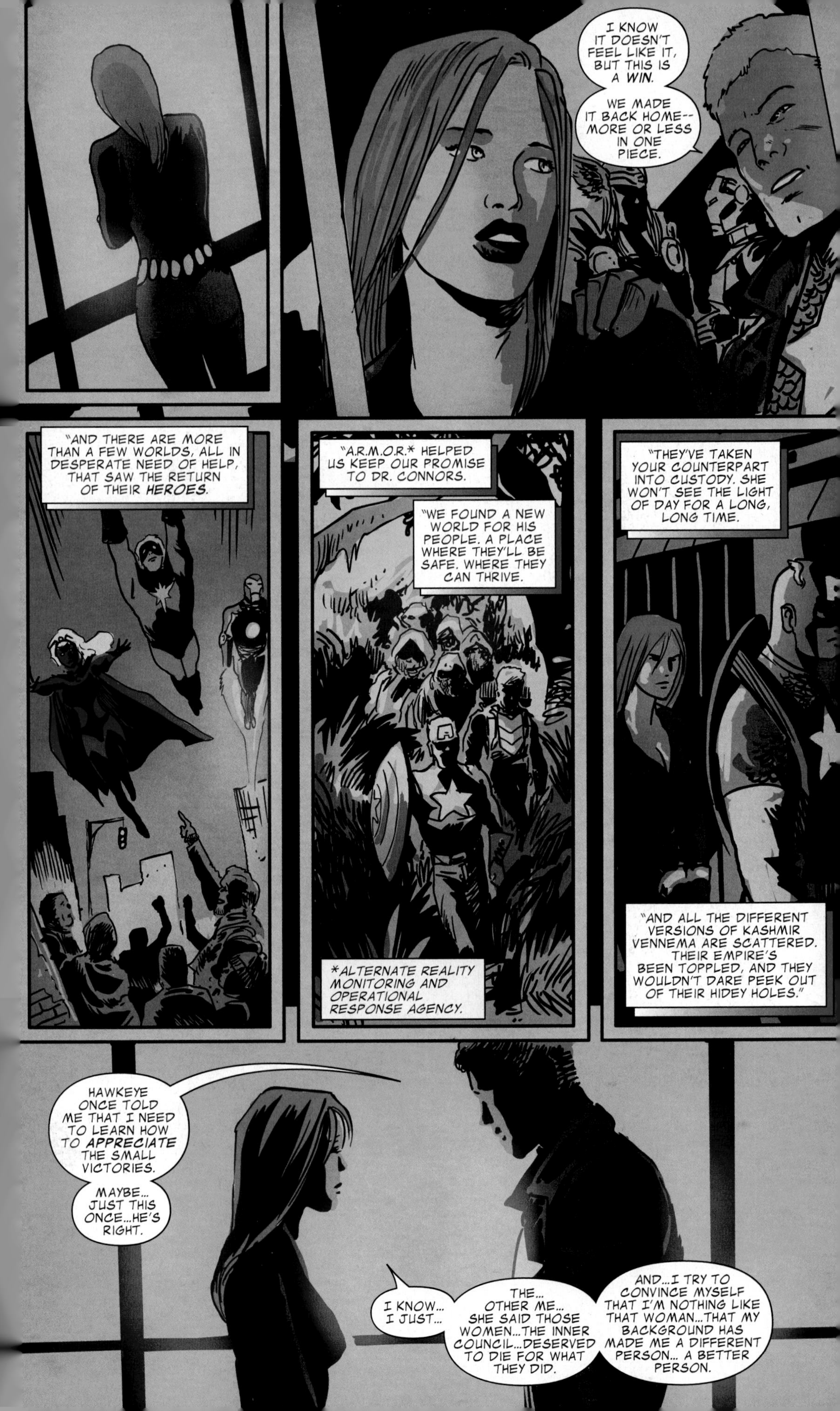

I KNOW IT DOESN'T FEEL LIKE IT, BUT THIS IS A *WIN*.
WE MADE IT BACK HOME--MORE OR LESS IN ONE PIECE.
"AND THERE ARE MORE THAN A FEW WORLDS, ALL IN DESPERATE NEED OF HELP, THAT SAW THE RETURN OF THEIR *HEROES*.
"A.R.M.O.R.* HELPED US KEEP OUR PROMISE TO DR. CONNORS.
"WE FOUND A NEW WORLD FOR HIS PEOPLE. A PLACE WHERE THEY'LL BE SAFE. WHERE THEY CAN THRIVE.
*ALTERNATE REALITY MONITORING AND OPERATIONAL RESPONSE AGENCY.
"THEY'VE TAKEN YOUR COUNTERPART INTO CUSTODY. SHE WON'T SEE THE LIGHT OF DAY FOR A LONG, LONG TIME.
"AND ALL THE DIFFERENT VERSIONS OF KASHMIR VENNEMA ARE SCATTERED. THEIR EMPIRE'S BEEN TOPPLED, AND THEY WOULDN'T DARE PEEK OUT OF THEIR HIDEY HOLES."
HAWKEYE ONCE TOLD ME THAT I NEED TO LEARN HOW TO *APPRECIATE* THE SMALL VICTORIES.
MAYBE... JUST THIS ONCE...HE'S RIGHT.
I KNOW... I JUST...
THE... OTHER ME... SHE SAID THOSE WOMEN...THE INNER COUNCIL...DESERVED TO DIE FOR WHAT THEY DID.
AND...I TRY TO CONVINCE MYSELF THAT I'M NOTHING LIKE THAT WOMAN...THAT MY BACKGROUND HAS MADE ME A DIFFERENT PERSON... A BETTER PERSON.

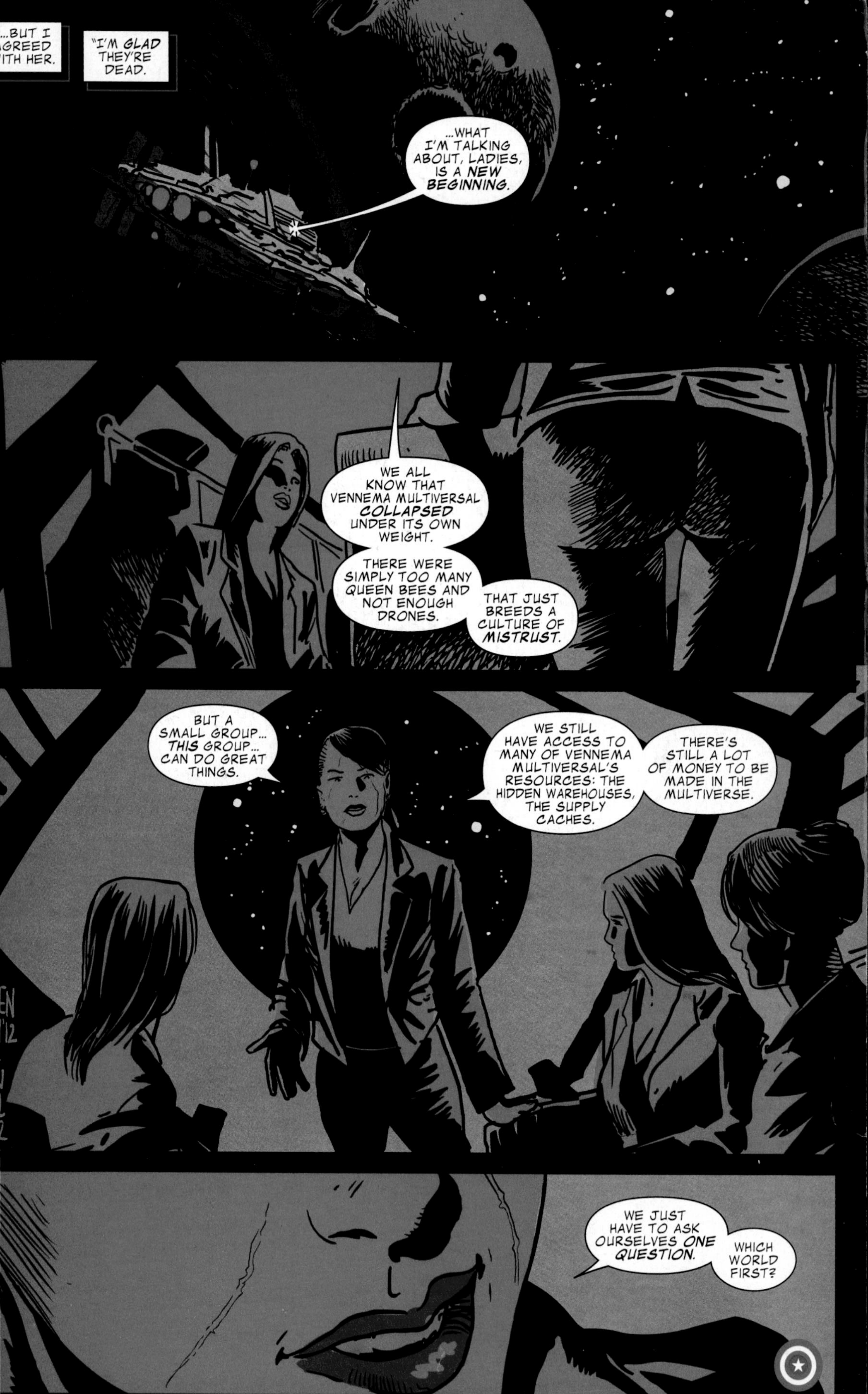

...BUT I AGREED WITH HER.
"I'M GLAD THEY'RE DEAD.
...WHAT I'M TALKING ABOUT, LADIES, IS A NEW BEGINNING.
WE ALL KNOW THAT VENNEMA MULTIVERSAL COLLAPSED UNDER ITS OWN WEIGHT.
THERE WERE SIMPLY TOO MANY QUEEN BEES AND NOT ENOUGH DRONES.
THAT JUST BREEDS A CULTURE OF MISTRUST.
BUT A SMALL GROUP... THIS GROUP... CAN DO GREAT THINGS.
WE STILL HAVE ACCESS TO MANY OF VENNEMA MULTIVERSAL'S RESOURCES: THE HIDDEN WAREHOUSES, THE SUPPLY CACHES.
THERE'S STILL A LOT OF MONEY TO BE MADE IN THE MULTIVERSE.
WE JUST HAVE TO ASK OURSELVES ONE QUESTION.
WHICH WORLD FIRST?

SOMEWHERE IN THE DISORGANIZED MESS THAT IS MY FILING SYSTEM, THERE'S A PIECE OF PAPER THAT SERVES AS A LITANY OF WHAT MIGHT HAVE BEEN.

I HAD THAT SHEET OF PAPER IN FRONT OF ME WHEN I HAD MY FIRST CONVERSATION WITH THE UBER-TALENTED (AND FELLOW '80s ACTION MOVIE FAN) LAUREN SANKOVITCH ABOUT THE POSSIBILITY OF DOING A CAPTAIN AMERICA TEAM-UP BOOK. IN ADDITION TO A FEW EXCITEDLY SCRAWLED NOTES, I STARTED A LIST OF CHARACTERS I WANTED TO SEE CAP JOIN ON A SERIES OF WILD ADVENTURES.

HAWKEYE, BLACK WIDOW, IRON MAN, NAMOR, HOWARD THE DUCK, VALKYRIE, THOR, HULK, U.S.ACE (ALONG WITH A MONKEY DRESSED IN A BUCKY COSTUME), THE ENIGMA FORCE, UNION JACK, DR. STRANGE... THE LIST GOES ON AND ON, BUT I REMEMBER THOSE NAMES AT LEAST. IT WOULD HAVE BEEN AWESOME TO TELL THOSE STORIES, BUT — ALAS — WE'VE REACHED THE END.

IN THE FIRST ARC OF THIS SERIES, HAWKEYE TELLS CAP "WE DID A GOOD THING HERE TODAY, STEVE. JUST BE HAPPY WITH IT." AND THOSE WORDS FROM THE JEREMY RENNER LOOKALIKE IN PURPLE APPLY TO THIS BOOK. WHILE I HAVE OTHER STORIES TO TELL, I WAS ABLE TO WRITE 13 ISSUES OF WILD CAPTAIN AMERICA ADVENTURES... AND I HAD A LOT OF FUN DOING IT. I INTRODUCED SOME NEW CHARACTERS... AND I HAVE IT ON GOOD AUTHORITY THAT YOU'LL BE SEEING KASHMIR "JUST CALL ME KASH" VENNEMA (WHO APPEARED IN ALMOST EVERY ISSUE OF THIS SERIES) AND THE COVENANT (WHO APPEARED IN THE NAMOR ISSUE) AGAIN.

I'D LIKE TO THANK LAUREN SANKOVITCH, JAKE THOMAS, JOHN DENNING, FRANCESCO FRANCAVILLA, ALESSANDRO VITTI, MATTEO BUFFAGNI, JAY LEISTEN, BARRY KITSON, WILL CONRAD, JAVIER TARTAGLIA, STUART IMMONEN, WADE VON GRAWBARGER, MATTHEW WILSON, GABRIELE DELL'OTTO, KALMAN ANDRASOFSKY, PATCH ZIRCHER, MATT HOLLINGSWORTH, CRIS PETER, JOE CARAMAGNA (WHO LETTERED THIS ISSUE; SO WHO KNOWS IF I REALLY THANKED HIM OR NOT), AND ALL THE OTHER FOLKS WHO HELPED BRING THIS SERIES TO LIFE. I'M SURE I MISSED SOMEONE IN THAT LIST, BUT I'M GRATEFUL TO ALL OF YOU FOR "TEAMING UP" WITH ME TO WORK ON THIS SERIES.

MOST OF ALL, THANKS TO YOU GUYS FOR READING THE BOOK! I HOPE YOU HAD AS MUCH FUN READING IT AS I HAD WRITING IT!

-CULLEN BUNN